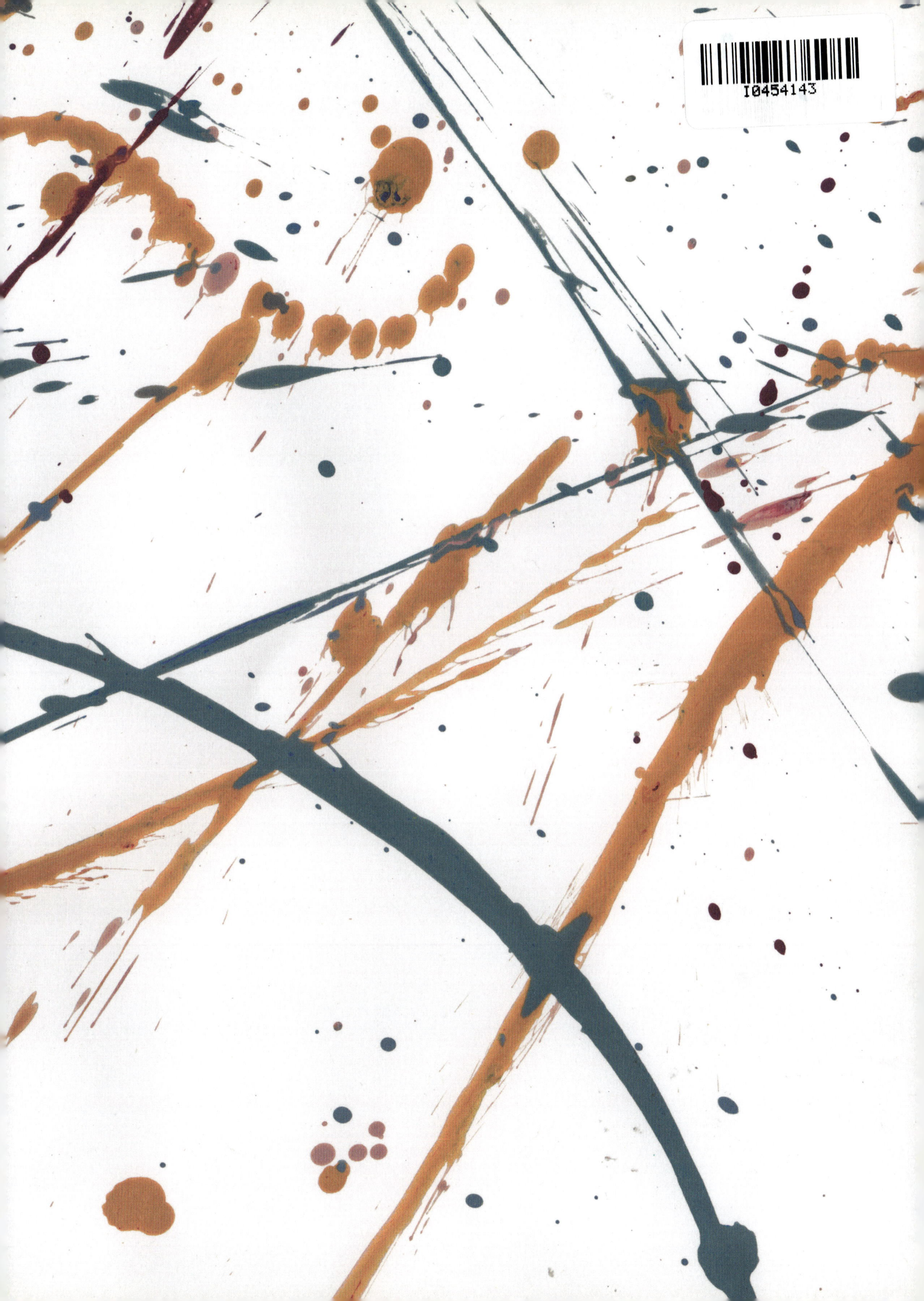

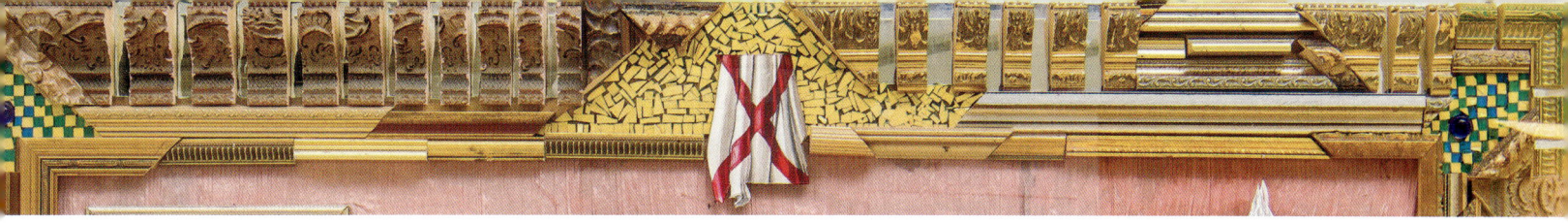

NALL
AT
TROY

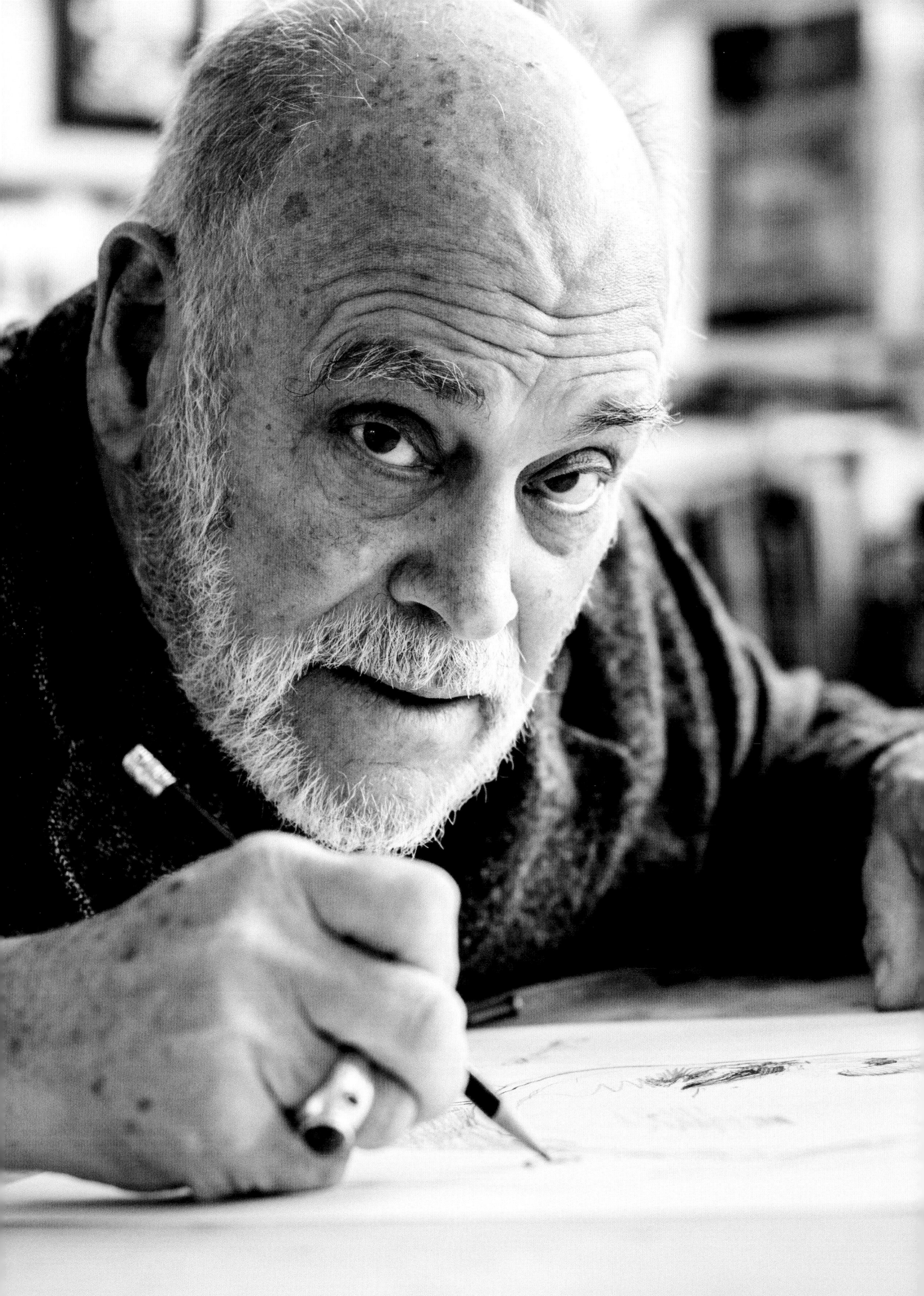

NALL
AT
TROY

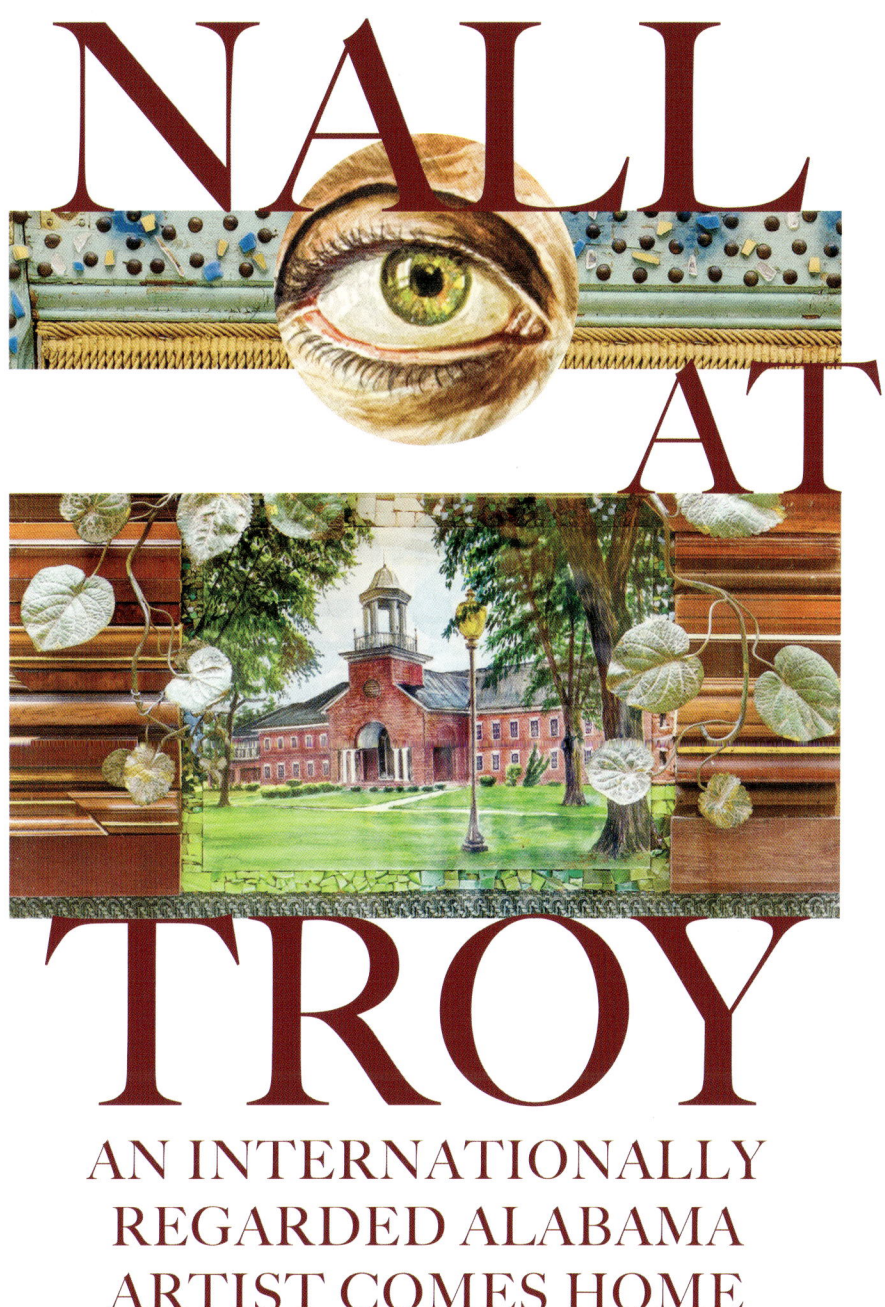

AN INTERNATIONALLY
REGARDED ALABAMA
ARTIST COMES HOME

Artist's Statement by Nall Hollis
Foreword by Janice Hawkins
Artist Profile by Al Head
Afterword by Jack Hawkins Jr.

Published by NewSouth Books
in collaboration with

TROY UNIVERSITY™

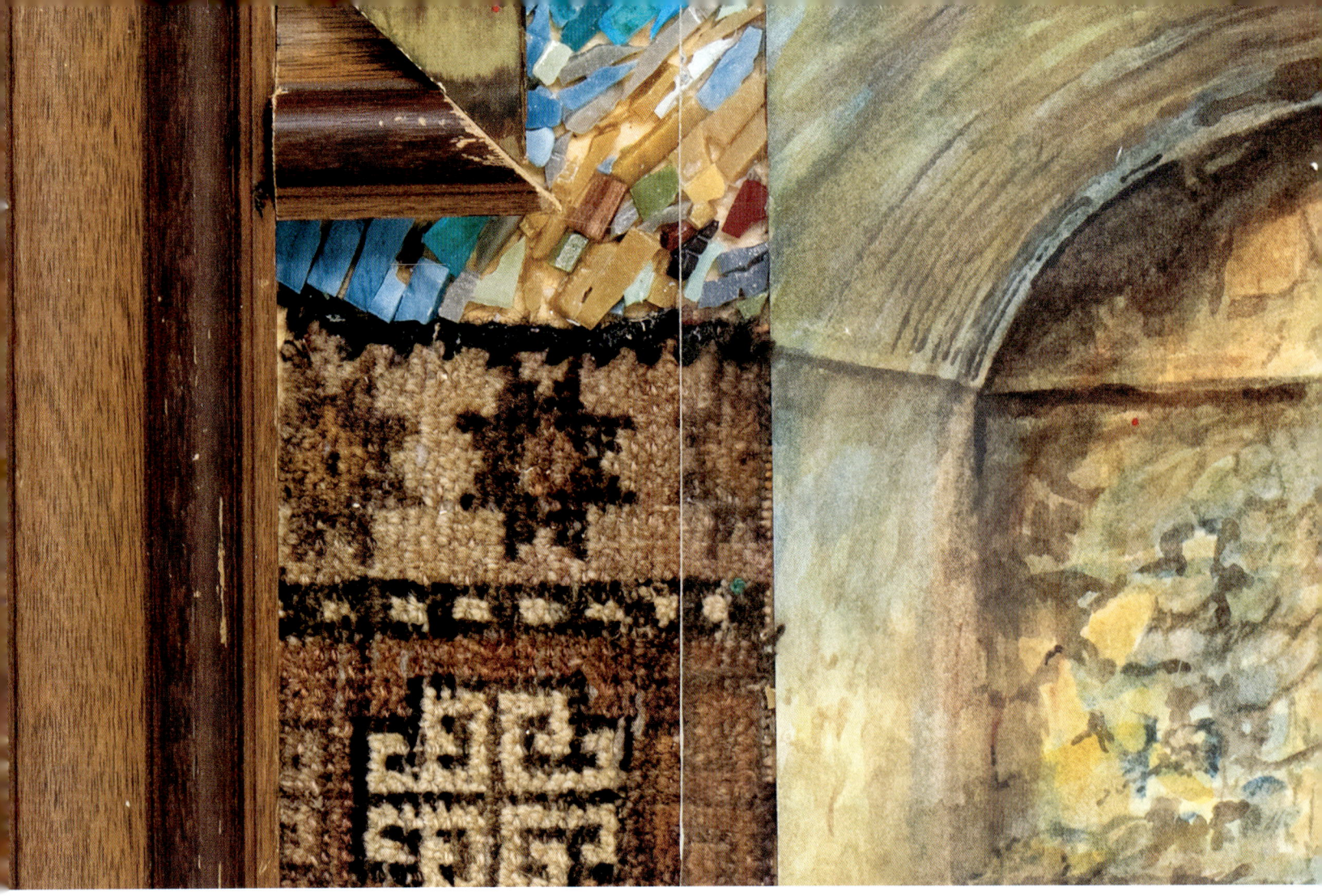

POMPEII—DETAIL
MIXED MEDIA
23.5" X 19.5"
2011—2018

NewSouth Books

105 S. Court Street, Montgomery, AL 36104

Publisher's Cataloging-in-Publication Data

Names: Hollis, Fred Nall, artist. | Head, Al, author.

Description: Montgomery: NewSouth Books [2021].

Identifiers: LCCN 2020948953 | ISBN 9781588384386 (hardcover).

Subjects: Hollis, Fred Nall, 1948–. | Troy University—Alabama. | Artists—Alabama. |
Artists—Biography. | Mixed Media—Art. | Artists' Books—Individual Artists—Art. I. Title.

Design by Edward M. Noriega
Photography by Mark Moseley
First Printing
Printed in South Korea

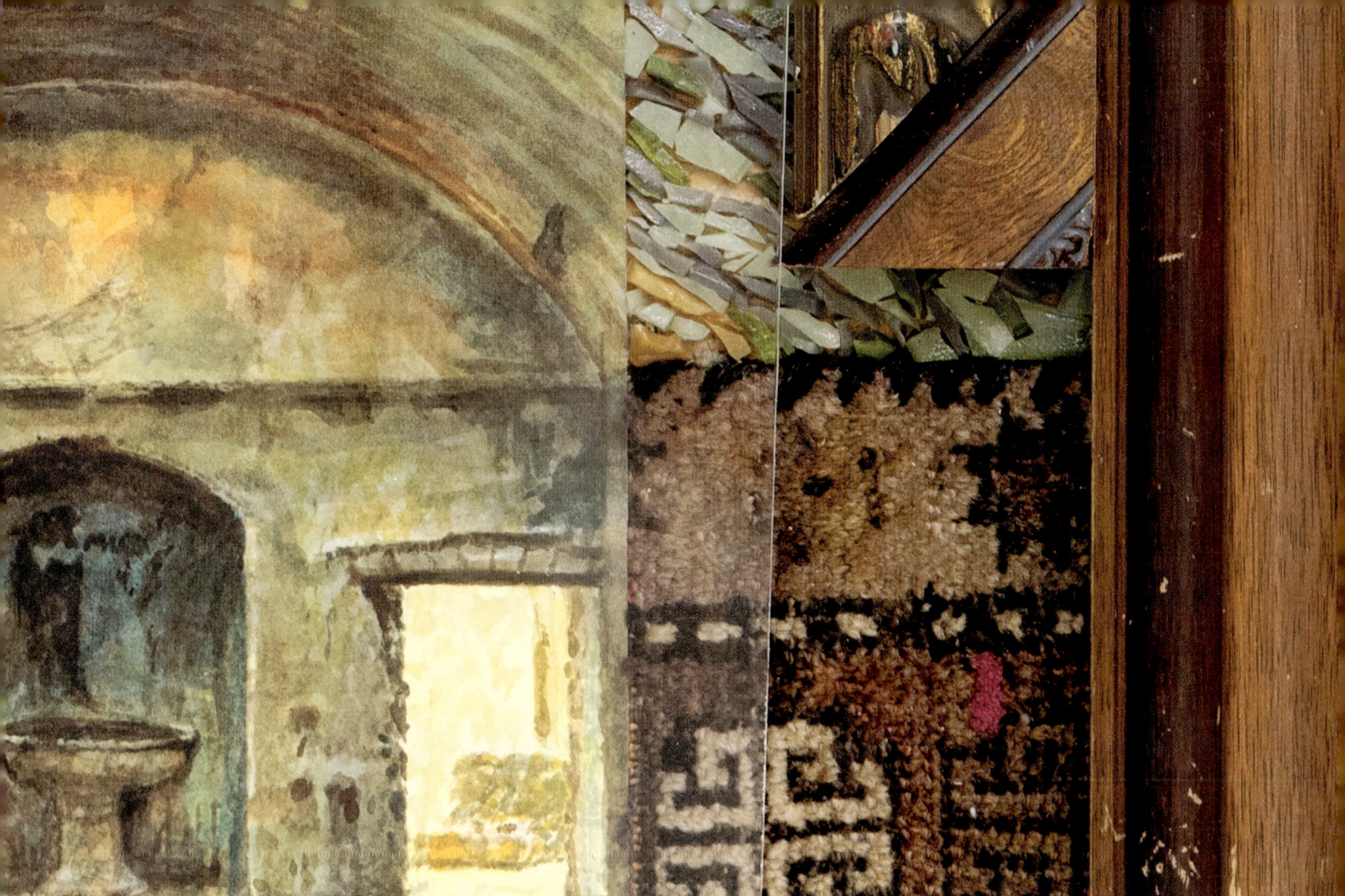

Contents

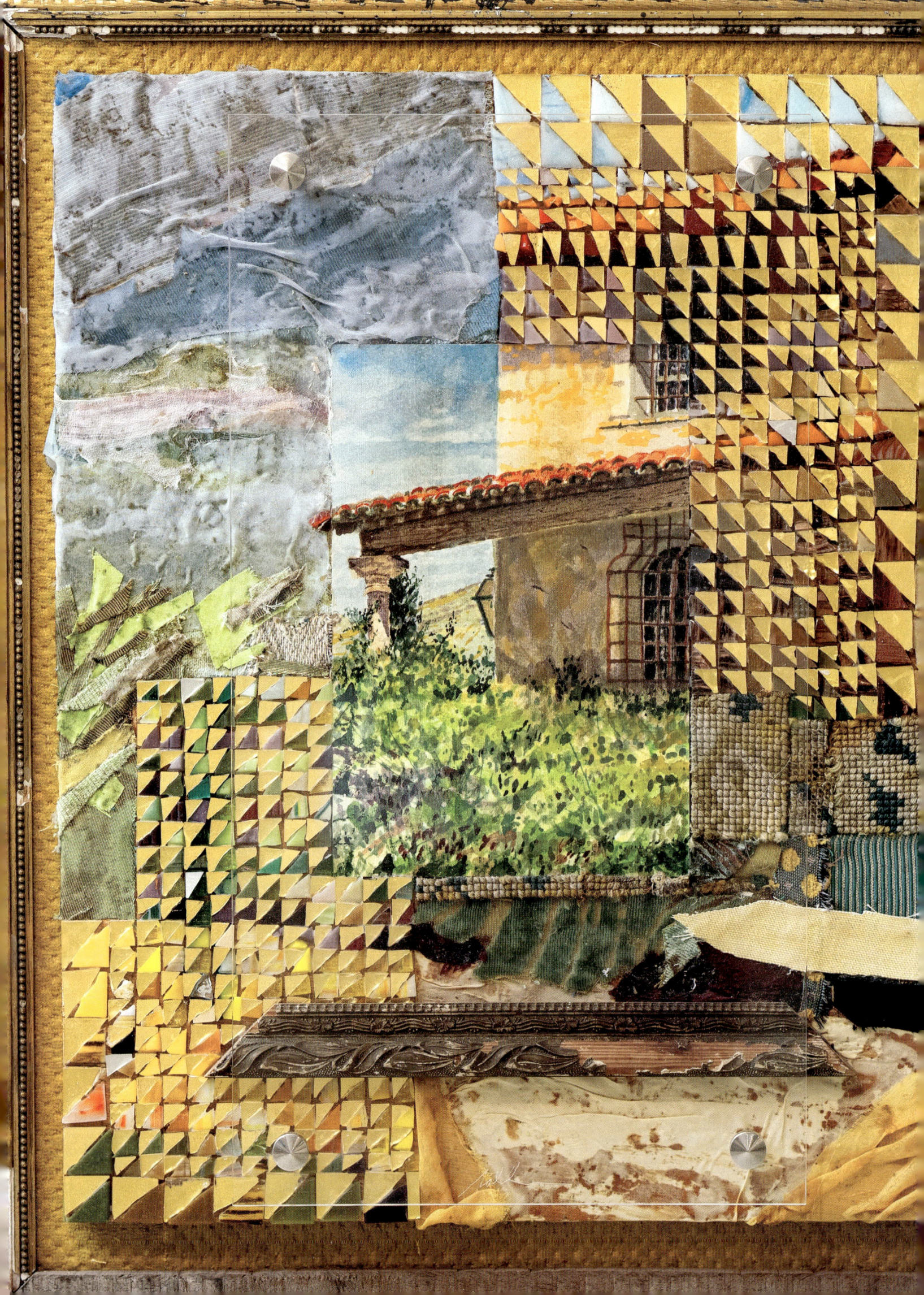

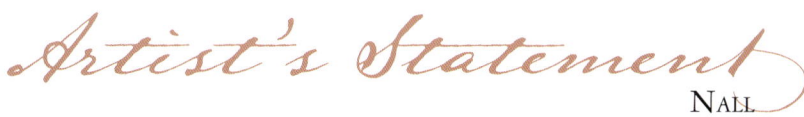

Artist's Statement

NALL

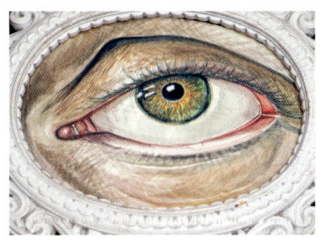

FIRST AND FOREMOST, I want to thank Troy University and especially Chancellor Jack Hawkins Jr. and his wife, Janice, for their support of me and my work over many, many years. From my being asked to serve as an artist-in-residence, to being presented with an honorary doctorate, to being honored with the establishment of the Nall Museum, their generosity, respect, guidance, and, yes, love are gifts I will always cherish.

As I gave great thought to my legacy and a special home for the extensive collection of my artwork, it became increasingly clear that what I was looking for was in Alabama at Troy University. Over six decades of making art, many of my favorite and best pieces were never offered for sale. I always thought these special pieces should be permanently located where the general public, young and old, black and white, rich and poor, would be able to see and appreciate the work. The Nall Museum at the International Arts Center on the Troy University campus proved to be that perfect spot.

It was always my hope that part of the collection that included the work of other Alabama artists would be made available to tour other museums in cities large and small, in Alabama and beyond. It was also my hope that a book sharing my story would be published to provide context for art reflecting my Alabama roots and my time working in Europe and different parts of the world. It pleases me that this publication accomplishes my desire to make my work accessible to a broad and diverse audience. The book also creates greater awareness of Troy University's commitment to international outreach, exhibiting art of the highest quality, and enhancing the education of thousands of students.

I realize that this book has been made possible through the work and support of many individuals, and I extend my sincere thanks to all those involved in the ambitious endeavor. The Nall Museum, the International Arts Center, and the Janice Hawkins Cultural Arts Park are all part of a shared dream and part of my coming home to Troy, Alabama.

VIEUX MAS
WATERCOLOR
26" X 21.5"
ca. 1990

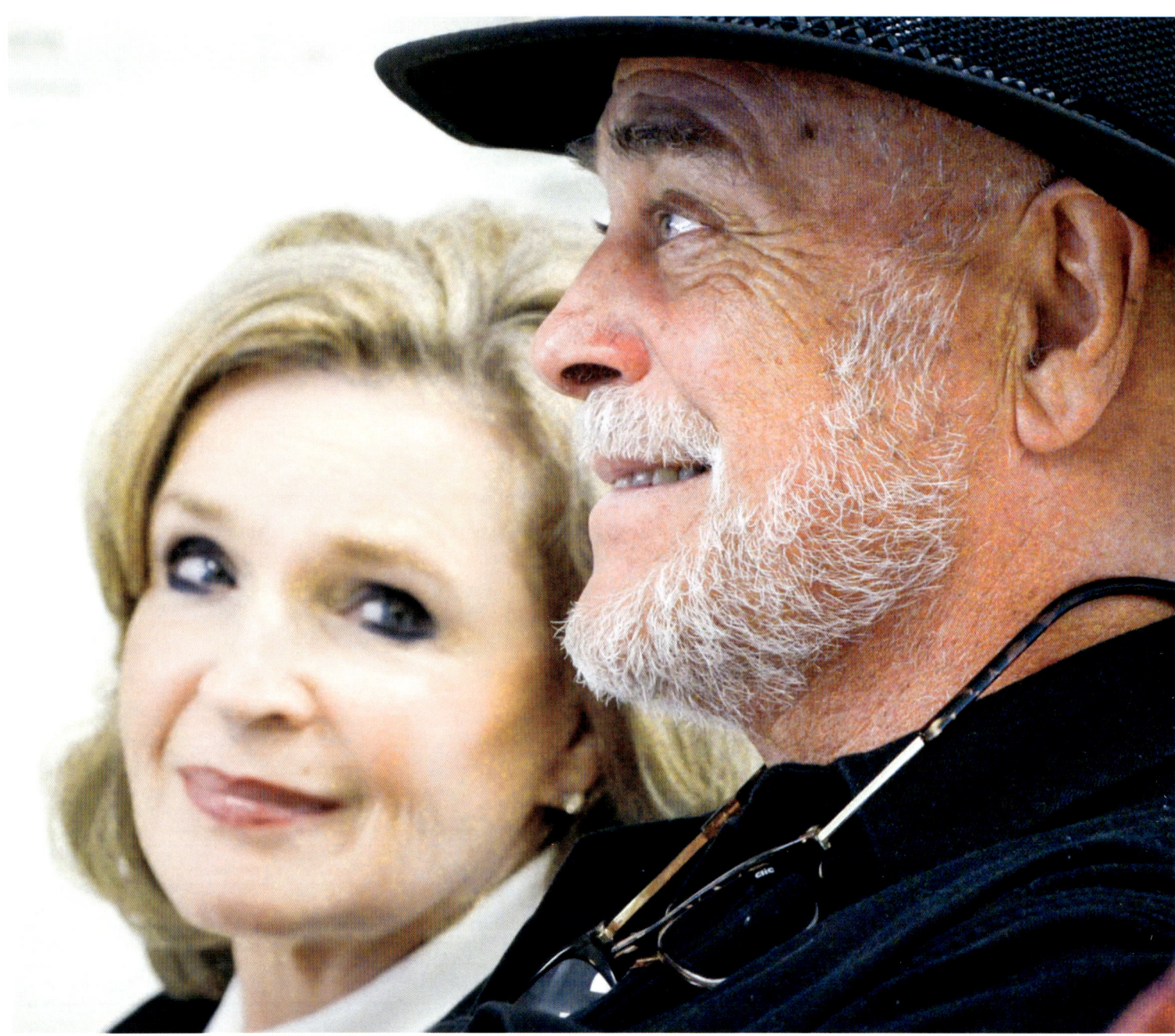

Janice Hawkins and Nall

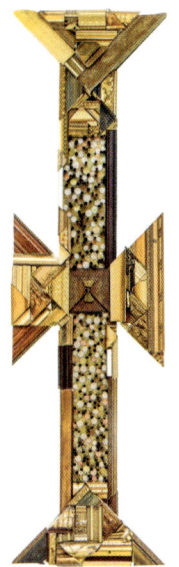

Foreword

JANICE HAWKINS

IMAGINE MEETING SOMEONE who not only impacts your life but changes your life forever. That is how I would describe my initial meeting with Nall!

First, how many people have you known who go through life with one name and get away with it? Jack and I first met Nall during the 1990s. He let us know he was coming "back to his roots" in Troy, and wanted to meet the Hawkins. Of course, he and his entourage were invited to the Chancellor's Home for dinner. From the moment of his arrival, Nall's presence was impactive, impressive, and BIG! I remember it was difficult to get an accurate first impression of him, because one just knew he was presenting only one of the many faces of Nall! We were asked to join the NALL Foundation as board members that evening, and so began a friendship that has exceeded two decades.

Some of the highlights of this friendship include a trip to France and Monaco for the European opening of Nall's Alabama Art, along with many of the thirteen original artists of the Alabama Art exhibit, including Kathryn Tucker Windham, Charlie Lucas, and Mose Tolliver, to name a few. We experienced dancing alongside Prince Rainier at the Red Cross Ball, touring the palace and the Jacques Cousteau Museum, as well as

meeting many wonderful people who love the artist Nall.

The next major memory includes Nall's invitation to be artist-in-residence at Troy University in 2000 and 2001. And in his fashion, Nall filled the place with his presence.

One of the first things he did was to throw a "baby shower" for the new dog given to his cousin, "Brother" Chapman. Of course, the dog's name was Small Nall! Many friends from the town and University were invited to attend and bring their dogs to his classroom/studio in Malone Hall. There was a cake, balloons galore, and loud music. So many attended, we filled the studio and flowed into the courtyard!

The main event occurred the next day when Nall and his students were listening to the music that played constantly in his classroom and studio. The song "Is There a Heaven for Balloons?" came on, and Nall said to his students, "Let's release these balloons to see if they can find heaven!" They did, and the balloons found their way to the transformer that serves all the University and half the town, and, yes, all electricity was lost for the rest of the day and night.

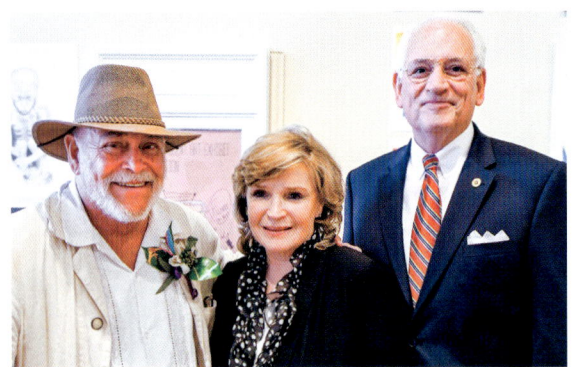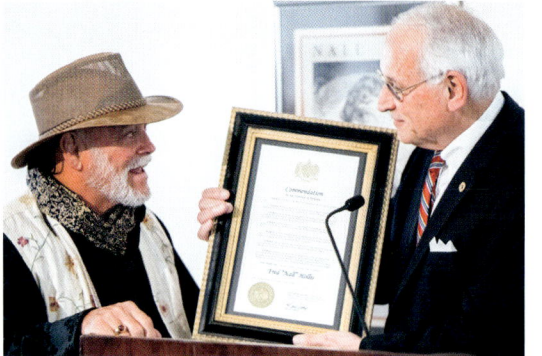

Before the dust had settled from that debacle, Nall and Tuscia decided after fifteen years of marriage to renew their vows. Sounds normal, but it was to be anything but. Nall was convinced he was part Native American and African American in addition to his Southern roots, so we had two ceremonies with a full complement of bridesmaids, groomsmen, and singers in the form and dress of canaries. Of course, all friends and acquaintances participated, including the mayor, the governor's wife, the chancellor, Miss Troy State University, Kathryn Tucker Windham, and many others. Melba (Alex and Jane Whaley's ancient lab) was a bridesmaid! Of course, we were all in costume.

Probably the best contribution to the NALL Foundation made by the Hawkins was to introduce Nall to Dr. David Bronner, chief executive officer of the Retirement Systems of Alabama (RSA). David believes in displaying only Alabama artists throughout RSA properties such as office buildings and hotels.

It began with Nall placing his works in the Grand Hotel on Alabama's Gulf Coast and morphed into finding talent in the state to provide artwork for future properties. Today, you will see each hotel and clubhouse along the Robert Trent Jones Golf Trail filled with Alabama's wonderfully talented artists' work.

Dr. Bronner also had an Alabama Art show at 55 Water Street in New York City, an RSA property. He purchased the "Big Apple" painting Nall did as a result of the tragic events of September 11, 2001, and it hangs today in that building.

In a 2002 story in the *Troy Messenger*, Dr. Bronner was quoted: "Like all great artists, you either love them or hate them. While some of Nall's work might be considered, by you and me, to be controversial, there are those who think it's the greatest in the world. Art is like beauty. It's in the eye of the beholder. You might not like what he does at one end of the spectrum, but fall in love with what he does at the other end."

Nall has a huge following of admirers of his artwork in Europe, and, as readers of this book will learn, he has achieved many significant accomplishments around the world. I believe it was Dr. Bronner opening those doors that finally allowed Nall to be recognized in Alabama for the genius he is.

Nall has contributed much more to Troy University than his art. He has sent us many talented students in the fine arts, and he has supported them both financially and personally. On May 11, 2001, we presented Nall with the University's highest honor, the Honorary Doctor of Fine Arts. Dr. Nall Hollis and Troy University will be forever intertwined!

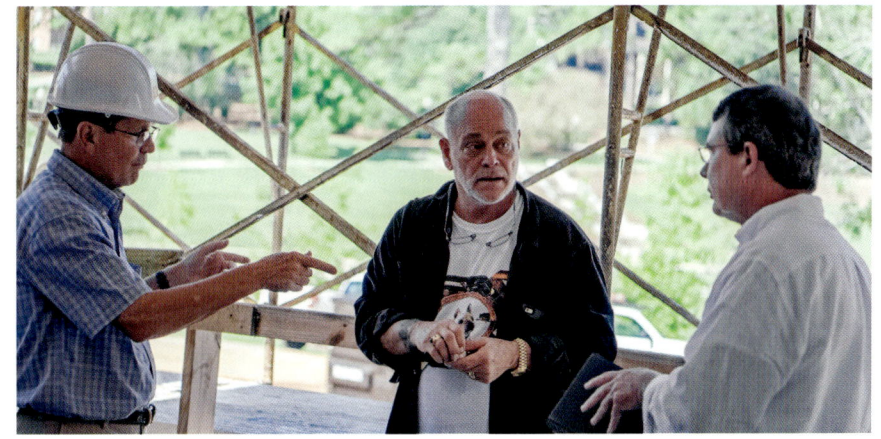

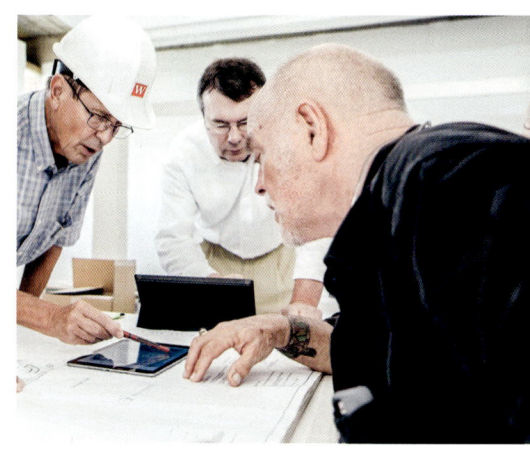

Nall's most important and significant contribution came in 2016 when we opened the International Arts Center (IAC) and the Janice Hawkins Cultural Arts Park. We built the galleries in the IAC and hoped the collections would come. Nall helped in so many ways, but mostly he filled the permanent gallery with the most eclectic collection of his works: painting, sculpture, china, hand-blown crystal, silver flatware, and Nall books. He also donated his original 13 Alabama artists' portraits and two of each of their works. All of this Nall gave to Troy University, and in turn we christened the Fred Nall Hollis Gallery. He has since added greatly to this collection.

Nall's gallery in the IAC complements the works of another great friend of Troy, an internationally renowned artist in his own right, the late Dr. Huo Bao Zhu. We met Huo in 2000 on one of our first trips to China. Huo changed the landscape of all four of our campuses with his sculptures of Terracotta Warriors and the *Thinker* and *Trojan Warrior* statues.

Nall and Huo held each other in high professional regard. Both had made their marks internationally, both have galleries named for them in the International Arts Center, and both were awarded the honorary Doctor of Fine Arts from Troy. I was asked to entertain Dr. Huo on one of his trips to the University, so I showed him the work we were doing to convert an old dining hall into the International Arts Center.

While we were touring, Dr. Huo asked the question, "Where does East meet West?" Huo's bronze statue of the famed Terracotta Warrior had been placed on University

ABOVE:
Nall working with Mr. Alex Whaley Sr. (right) of Whaley Construction and Mr. Walter McKee (left) of McKee & Associates.

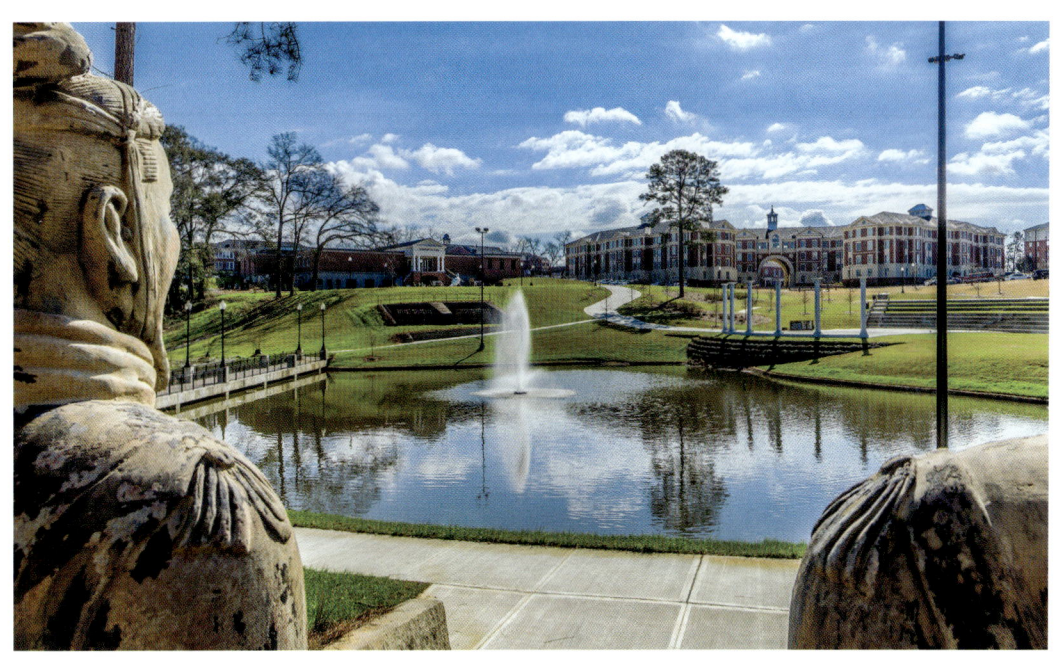

Janice Hawkins Cultural Arts Park

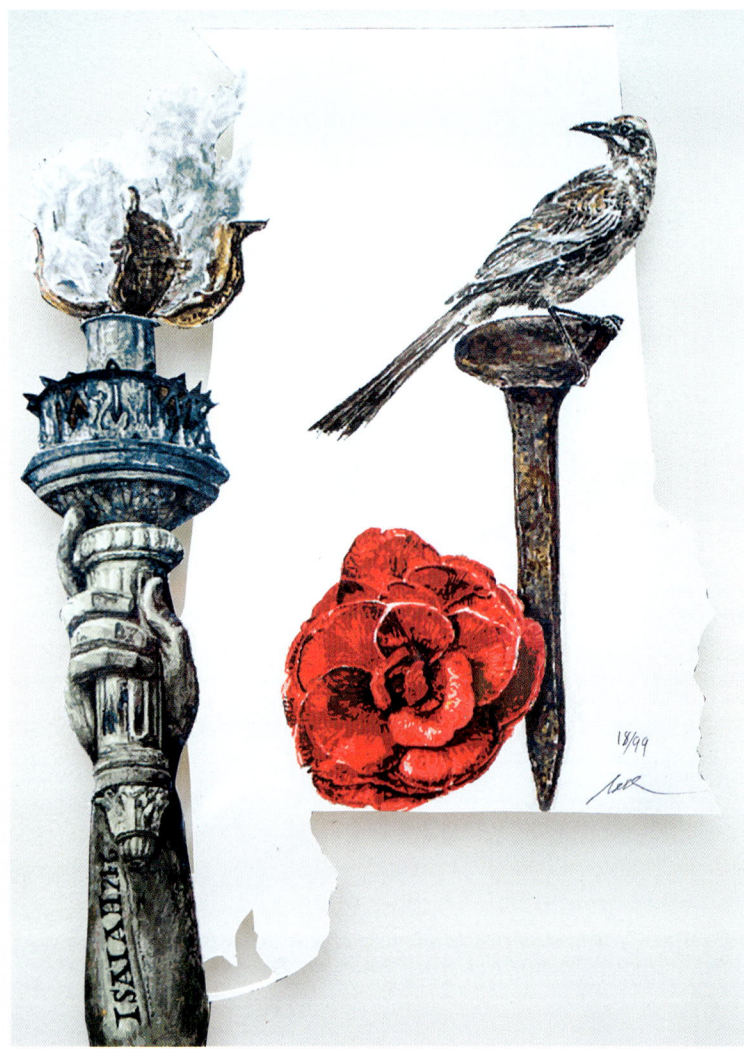

GO SET A WATCHMAN
MIXED MEDIA
39" X 31"
1960

This piece was transferred to limited-edition giclee prints for use on the cover of Harper Lee's high-profile novel that is the prequel to the 1960 Pulitzer Prize-winning literary epic, *To Kill a Mockingbird. Go Set a Watchman* was published the year before Lee's 2016 death following unprecedented publicity. Nall's imagery of the mockingbird, railroad spike, "watchtower" torch, and red camellia visually bridges the primary themes of the two famous novels.

Avenue facing the park. I took Dr. Huo to see Nall's *Violata Pax Dove*—or *"Peace Dove"*—which we planned to place in the plaza behind the IAC and situated on the opposite end of the park from Dr. Huo's sculpture. Huo saw the statue while it was still crated and was immediately impressed. He said, "It's magnificent! This is where East meets West!" The next day, Huo committed his donation of one hundred Terracotta Warriors to stand guard over the International Arts Center and the Cultural Arts Park.

Huo and Nall met over lunch in 2016 to discuss their respective galleries prior to the dedication of the park and the arts center on November 4. Perhaps nothing embodied Huo's vision of the theme of "East meets West" more than this meeting of two great Trojans, one born in Troy with a following across Europe, the other from Xi'an, China, whose art is displayed across Asia and the United States.

I have often stated that I believe Nall to be one of the most generous people I have ever known. I am so grateful to call Nall my dear friend and a loyal Trojan. I am also pleased that those who read this book will learn more about this fascinating Alabama artist and his strong, meaningful connection to Troy University.

JANICE HAWKINS is the
First Lady of Troy University

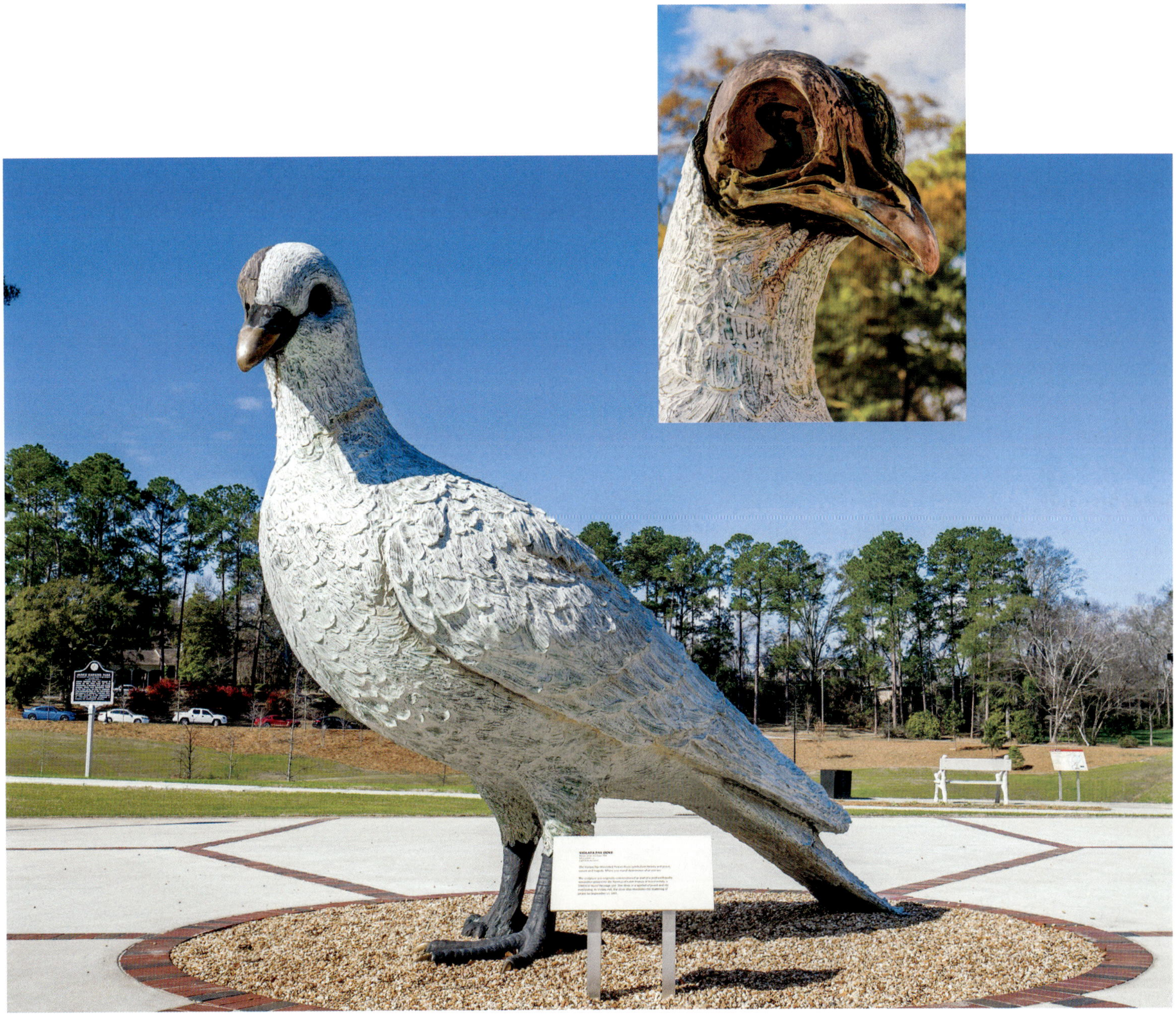

Peace Dove
Bronze
116" x 119" x 60"
2000
Daniel Foundation Plaza,
Janice Hawkins Cultural Arts Park

VIDEO

The image of a wounded dove as a symbol of peace maimed by violence and strife was inspired by my encounter with a one-legged pigeon while sitting outside of a café in France. I quickly sketched this little bird with a wounded foot, and the drawing later inspired the creation of this statue, which was made in 2006 at a foundry in Pietrasanta, Italy. In its original installation, the statue was positioned so that its wounded face looked out at visitors as they entered the St. Francis cathedral, a reminder of their own need for restoration and healing. As they exited the cathedral, visitors made whole through prayer would then encounter the dove, restored and made whole as well.

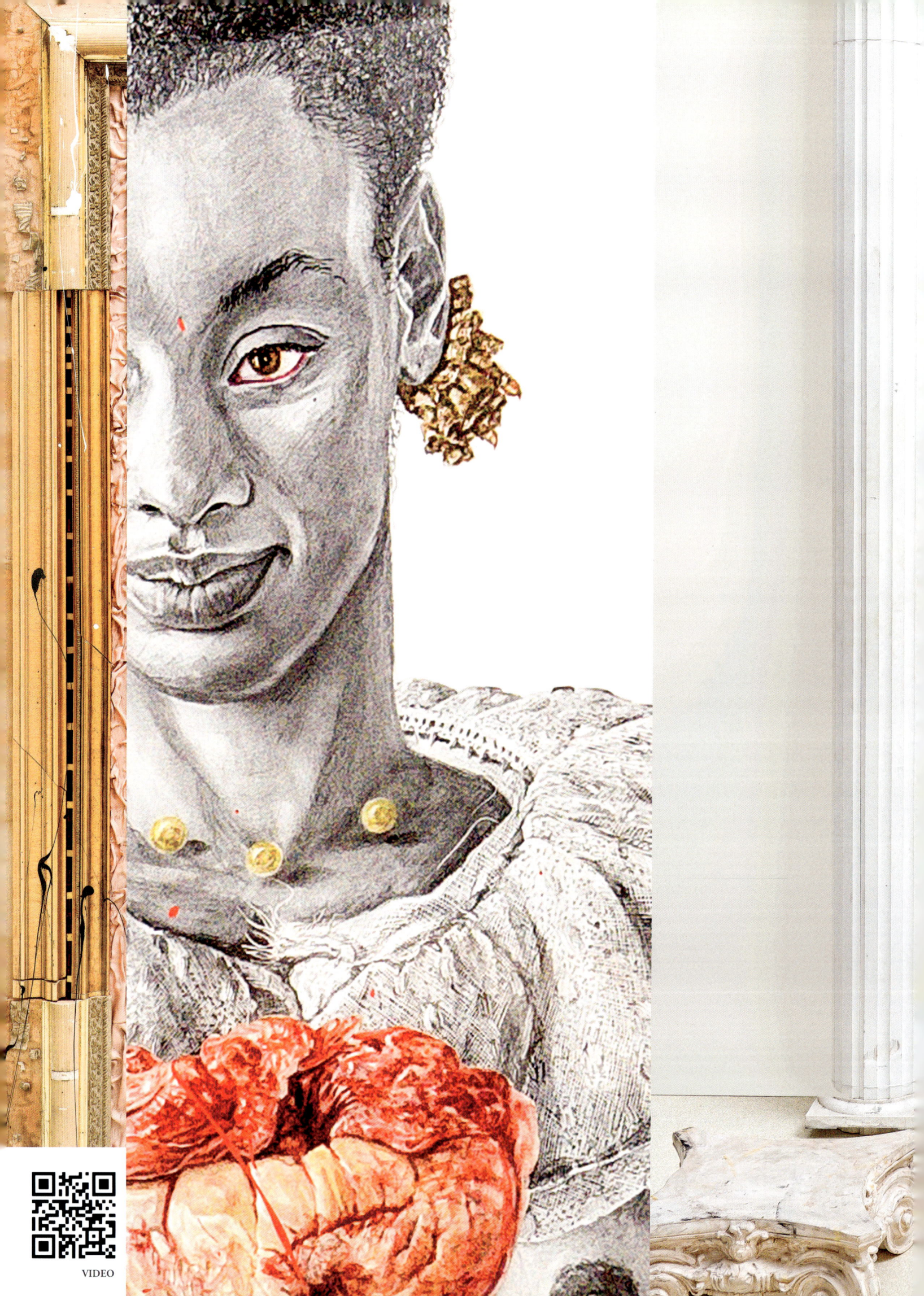

VIDEO

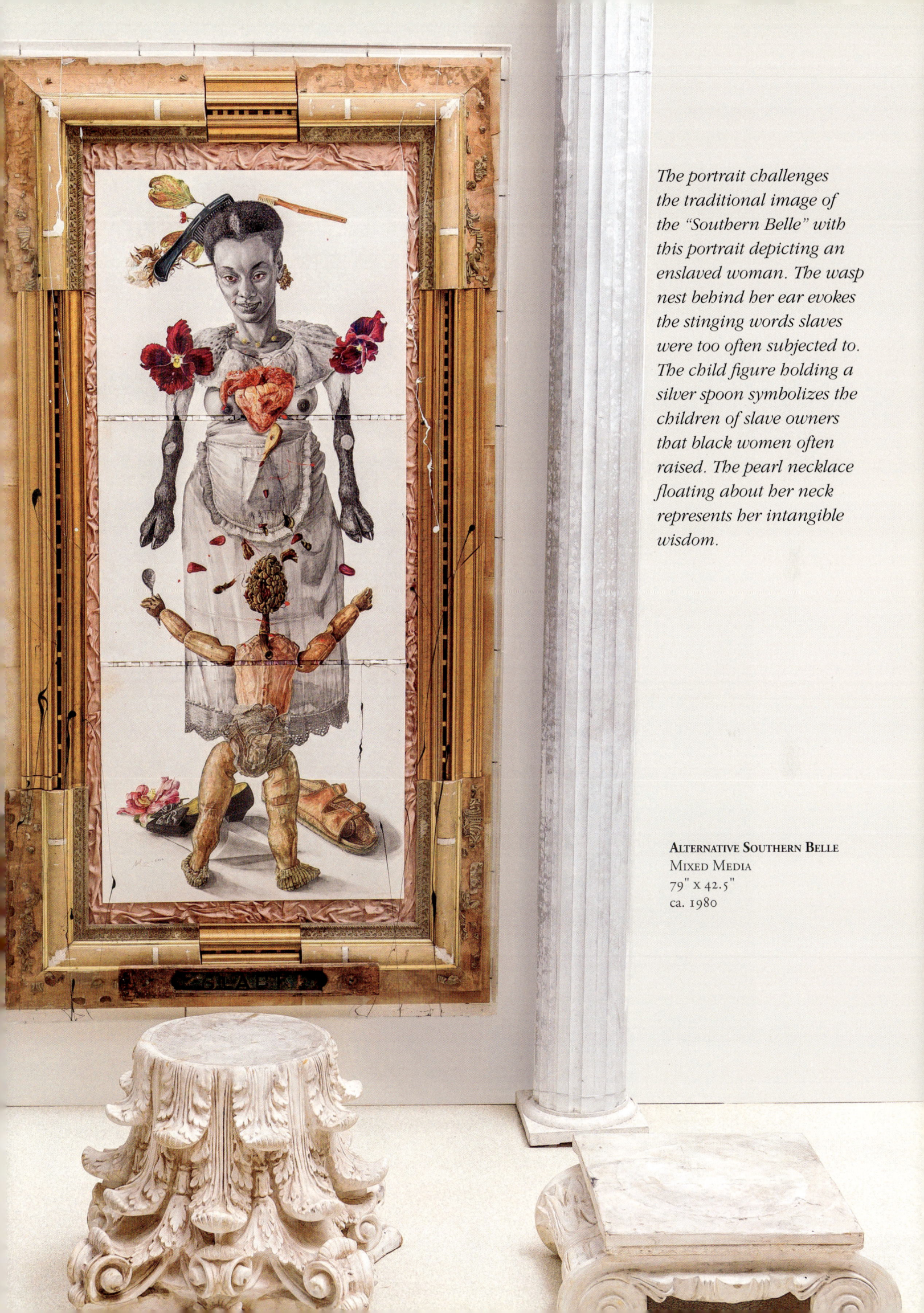

The portrait challenges the traditional image of the "Southern Belle" with this portrait depicting an enslaved woman. The wasp nest behind her ear evokes the stinging words slaves were too often subjected to. The child figure holding a silver spoon symbolizes the children of slave owners that black women often raised. The pearl necklace floating about her neck represents her intangible wisdom.

ALTERNATIVE SOUTHERN BELLE
MIXED MEDIA
79" X 42.5"
ca. 1980

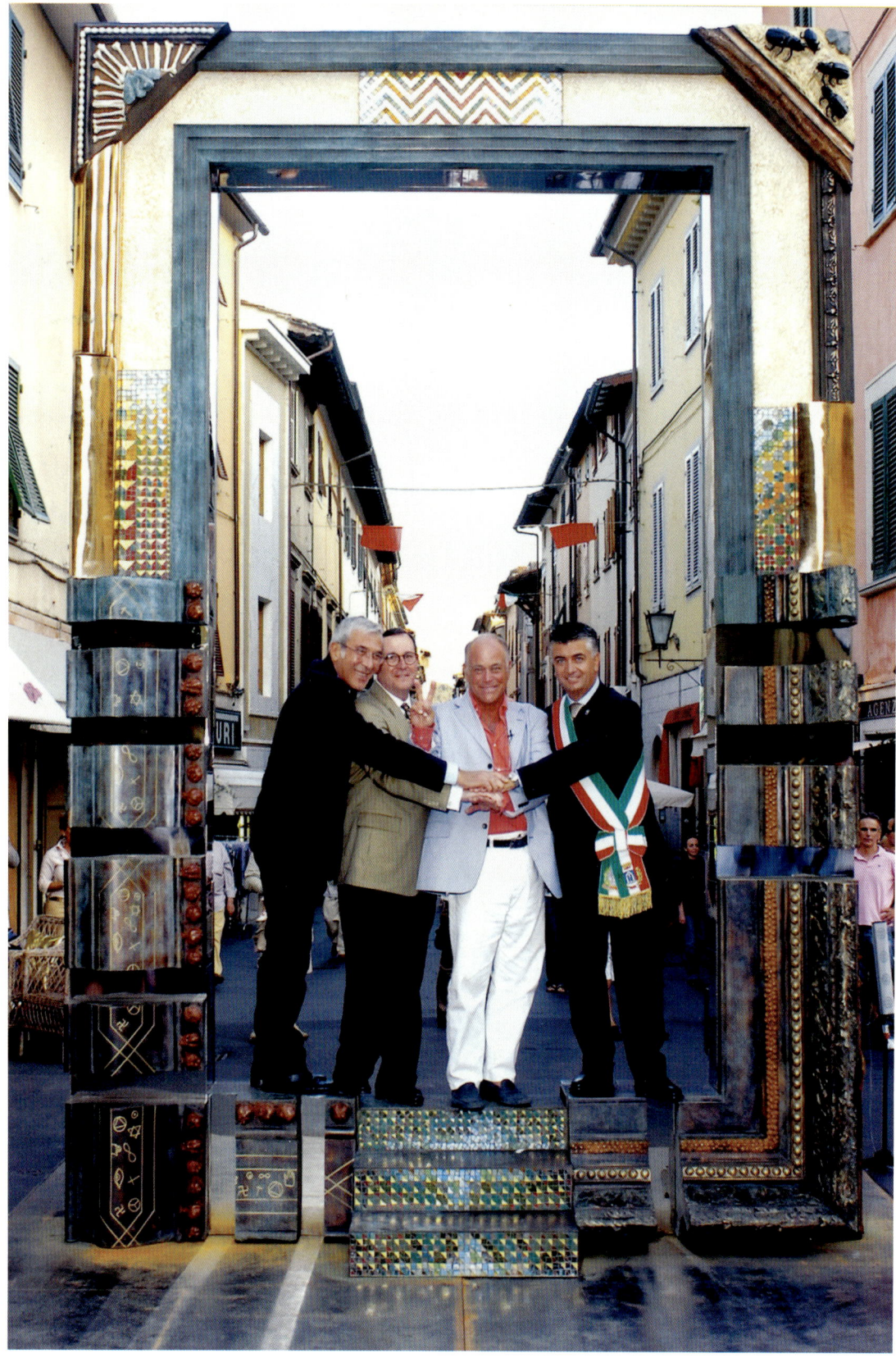

Peace Frame Dedication:
Pietrasanta, Italy
2005
From Left: Dr. Daniele Spina, Pietrasanta
Commissioner of Culture; Al Head, executive
director, Alabama Council on the Arts; Nall,
Peace Frame Artist; Massimo Mallegni,
Pietrasanta Mayor

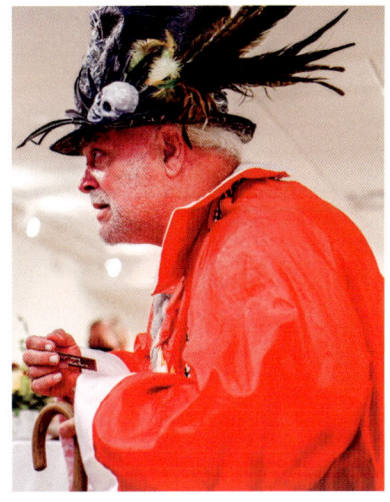

The Alchemist: Creation and Transformation

Al Head

THE REMARKABLE STORY OF NALL has many more chapters than the pages of any book can accommodate. The focus of this particular account is on his early years in Troy, Alabama, his journey to international fame, and his path back to his hometown. Nall's "coming home" was an essential part of his desire not only to share a vast body of work with kindred spirits but also to spotlight the work of outstanding contemporary Alabama artists. His chosen vehicle turned out to be a special partnership with Troy University.

For a more comprehensive study of Nall, there have been five major publications, in several languages, plus numerous exhibit catalogs. What readers will find in this particular book is an abbreviated sketch of Nall's amazing career and life in the arts, a profile of his important body of work, and an artist who has had a major impact on other artists, students, and a global audience. That impact has shaped the cultural landscape of Alabama, the United States, and a rapidly changing world.

A general description of Nall as a homegrown Alabama artist—immersed in red clay, a "Sweet Home Alabama" artist—is at the least an interesting paradox. That is to say, we find paradoxical elements in Nall's artistic style, his cultural orientation, his visual communication, and his creative points of reference. All of these elements—those steeped in "Old South" traditions and those molded by a much broader universe of ideology—reflect a rich cultural stew. Put yet another way, Nall is from Alabama but for the most part does not fit any common Alabama mold in his art, personality, lifestyle, or worldview. To the extent this analysis is true, one must understand where Nall's artistic journey and amazing life story began.

TROY FROM ITS FORMATIVE years could be described as a traditional, stereotypical Southern town, located in the region of Alabama known as the "Wiregrass." However, this somewhat unassuming community over its 164-year history has produced notable businessmen, politicians including an Alabama governor, educators, athletes, doctors, and artists. Of all these high-profile individuals from every walk of life, it would be accurate to say the city has produced only one Fred Nall Hollis, a rare artist with a body of work incomparable in Alabama history.

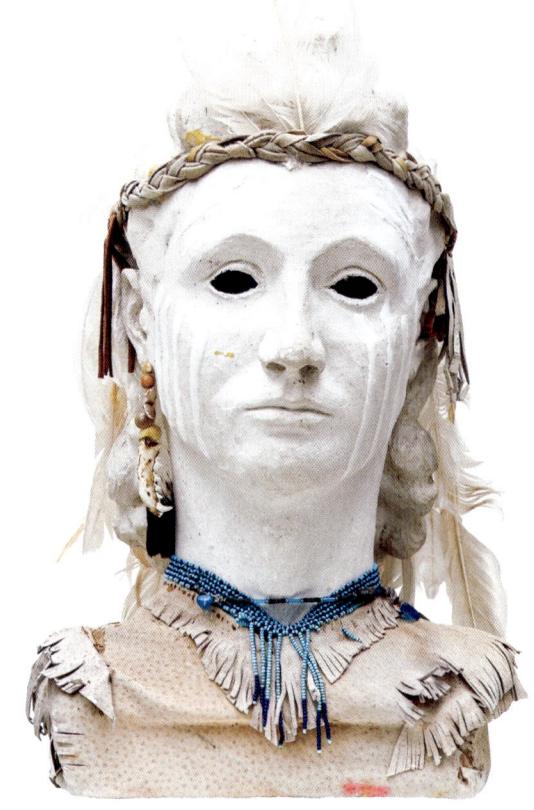

The three busts display Native American scalps, symbolizing the brutality shown by European settlers towards the native tribes. The "savagery" of the setters is depicted in the "war paint" applied to the vintage European and American portrait paintings.

The incredible story of an internationally famous artist and Troy native begins on April 21, 1948, when Fred Nall (later to be known simply as Nall) was born the only son of Joe Frost Hollis and Mary Winifred Nall Hollis. By date of birth, Nall is a "Baby Boomer," along with millions born in the U.S. in the decade after World War II. Of all of the characteristics generally associated with the Southern demographic of this group, Nall fits few. With the exception of being a free spirit from an early age, Nall was different, especially in comparison to his young male peers in Troy. It became clear that hunting, fishing, and sports, favorite activities of the guy culture, would not be compatible with Nall's interests and creative spirit.

Joe Hollis was a conservative banker and a rather hard to please father, who neither appreciated nor encouraged Nall's early interest and talent in the arts. Ironically, Joe was inclined to occasional drawing and would pronounce that young Nall could never achieve his expertise, a challenge that haunted the younger Hollis for years. Joe's financial background contributed to Nall's broader knowledge, but the son remained committed to a future in the arts. Later in his career, Nall discovered that his father's self-proclaimed drawing skill was more of a talent for tracing other artists' work. The revelation of the artistic hoax by his boastful father was liberating and a competitive burden was lifted.

Nall's mother, Mary Winifred Hollis, was the typical Southern lady—refined, proper, raised conforming to tradition, and devoted to family. She supported her son's passion for the arts and connected him to other family members who had similar interests. Pronouncing later in life that "Nall was born with a pencil in his hand," Miss Mary became increasingly proud of her son even though she admitted not understanding all of his artistic inclinations that produced drawings throughout the house. When asked why he had such confidence of being successful as an artist, Nall said, "My mother always told me I could do anything I wanted and be anything I wanted. I went through life believing that."

Of family influences regarding

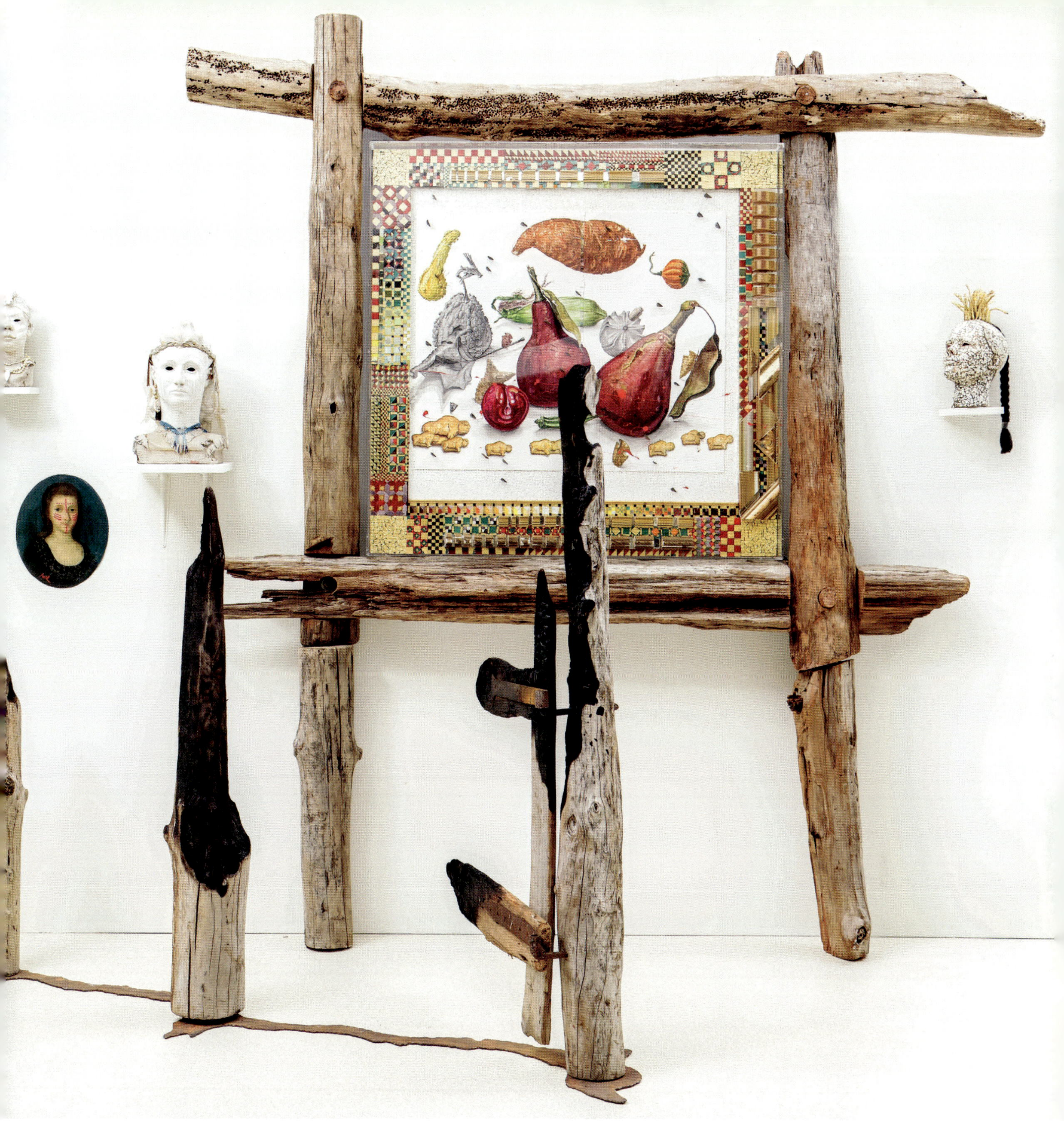

THANKSGIVING RSVP
NALL WITH
BRUCE LARSEN
MIXED MEDIA
96" x 96"
2007

Having Creek Indian heritage, in this piece I explore the plight of Native Americans, who lost their homes and lives at the hands of European settlers. The painting depicts the loss of the Native Americans' food supply as they were forced from their land. The wood surrounding the piece evokes the frame of a European settler's home, built from wood taken from Native American land.

The burned fence in front symbolizes that though the settlers may have tried to suppress the Native American culture, it could not be contained.

VIDEO

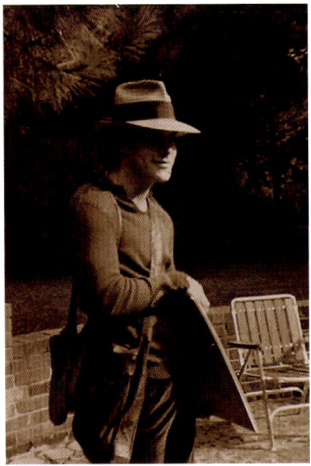
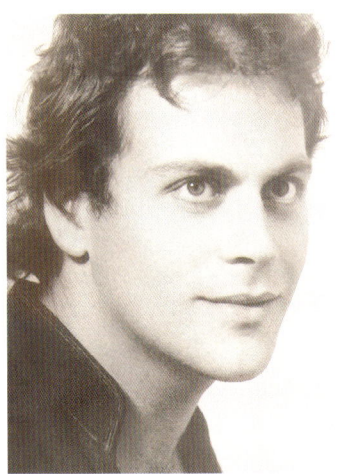
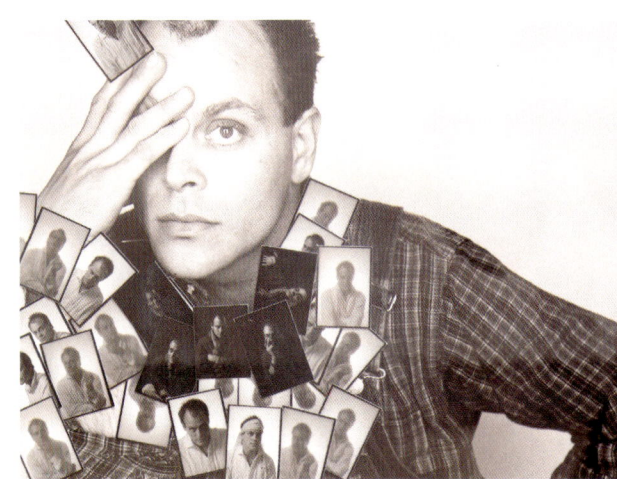

Early portraits of Nall

Nall's early interest in the arts, primary credit has to be given to his grandmother Lucy Nall, the family matriarch and Troy "godmother." This is the Miss Lucy who would ask the police to park her car when she came shopping with friends in Montgomery. Miss Lucy lived across the street from Murphree Park which housed an arts and crafts hut that resulted in Nall's first formal lessons in painting and drawing. It was here his exceptional talent blossomed and became recognized around town.

Nall's Troy family included both maternal and paternal grandparents living in close proximity to his College Street/Murphree Street neighborhood. His early stomping grounds were in the more affluent part of town. Family ancestral lines and roots in Pike County are expansive. On his mother's family tree, Nall's cousins were branches of the exceptionally large Henderson family. Eli Henderson, one of the early settlers of Pike County, had thirteen children including Jeremiah Augustus Henderson, who was the father of Charles, a prominent Troy businessman and Alabama governor. Nall's great-grandmother, Susan, was

Jeremiah's younger sister. It is still true that being related within the Eli Henderson family translates to being related to half of the Troy population.

Nall's teenage years were spent in Birmingham and the little town of Arab, where Joe Hollis had accepted different bank presidencies. Nall's artistic interest and skill continued to grow and set him apart from fellow students. Functioning in a conservative, Southern male environment obsessed with hunting, fishing, football, and pickup trucks proved to be an ongoing frustration. Skills in the arts were not nurtured by his community or peers.

After graduation from high school in 1966, Nall enrolled at the University of Alabama in Tuscaloosa. There he was immersed in fraternity life, Bear Bryant football, and the social expectations that go with a party university in the 1960s. The decade for the "Boomer" generation for the most part meant sex, drugs, and rock and roll. Nall did his best to carry that banner.

Meanwhile, his passion for the arts continued but his professors concentrated most of their instruction on commercial and abstract art, the

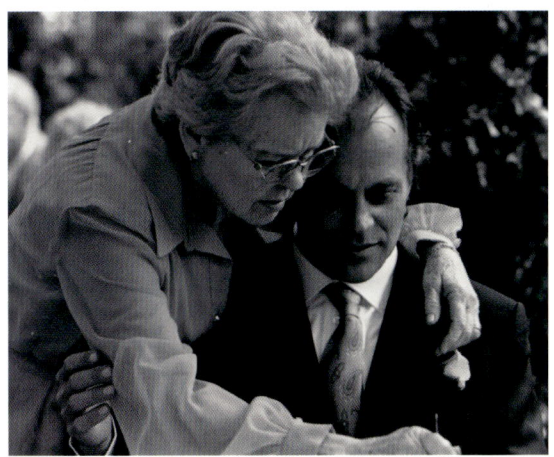

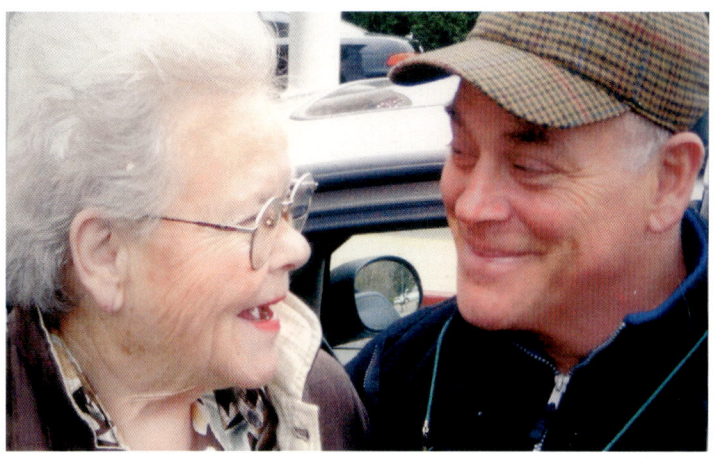

Mrs. Mary Nall Hollis, Nall's mother

academic preference of the time. Drawn to another creative path, Nall craved more exposure to drawing, watercolors, and classical forms of making art. Seeking stimulation and inspiration from a variety of sources, Nall ventured into a world of alcohol and drugs. While clearly not a personal high point in his life, this period was an important soul-searching passage in his finding a creative focus that would profoundly shape his art in the years to come. During the 1960s, Nall was trying to find both a personal identity and a place in the arts world. His struggle was heightened during a time of social unrest involving war protests, assassinations of iconic leaders, sexual revolution, and challenges to long-standing institutions such as law enforcement, politics, family, higher education, and, yes, "Jim Crow" racism. Nall's progressive and conflicted mind faced many questions about his artistic direction and future. The complexity of his life as the decade came to a close is revealed as he later described himself as a "hippie with a Mercedes"—yet another paradox of his tug of war identity.

After leaving college life and Tuscaloosa, Nall felt a desire and need to explore the New York art scene. As invigorating and stimulating as the big city was known to be, it did not inspire the young artist as he anticipated. While the artistic climate in New York was alive with Kandinsky, Warhol, and Pollock, Nall was more interested in the work of Norman Rockwell, Andrew Wyeth, and Vargas, given his passion for drawing and highly detailed realism. Feeling that New York was more oriented to commercialism, superficial modernism, and pop culture, Nall concluded its art scene was "terribly boring." He realized that he must leave America and cross the pond to the traditional art meccas of the old world. And what a turning point decision this turned out to be.

TO DESCRIBE THE EXPERIENCES and maturation process of the young Alabama artist in Europe, our narrative must compress Nall's story with summarized highlights of his career. The people, places, and adventures of Nall over a five-decade period are somewhat hard to comprehend given the road that had to be traveled to reach a lofty position of international prominence. It is important to understand that the first three decades abroad, 1970–2000, exploring diverse cultures and following the call of different muses, laid the groundwork for Nall's permanent return to Alabama and new chapters in his life.

Picturing the world in 1971, one sees that Richard Nixon is president, the Vietnam War is at its height, the Space Race and Cold War with Russia are ongoing, Walt Disney World in Orlando opens, the Kennedy Center for the Performing Arts is dedicated, the South Tower of the World Trade Center is the second tallest building in the world, and Charles Manson is found guilty of multiple murders in Los Angeles.

Also in 1971, Nall travels to Paris and is accepted to study at the

École des Beaux-Arts. His absorption with the City of Light's creative environment leads to relationships with other artists and important people in the arts world. He still admits that "Paris is my mistress." At this time Nall's work is being influenced by Hieronymus Bosch, Gustav Mossa, and Salvador Dali. He later became Dali's friend and apprentice, and it was Dali who urged the young artist to continue drawing from life and to pursue beauty through his artwork. A well-known Dali quote was "Begin by learning to draw and paint like the Old Masters. After that you can do as you like; everyone will respect you." These words no doubt resonated with the aspiring young artist, and Nall's emphasis on and skill in drawing grew to a level that gained him

GUARDIA, ALGERIA ST. & MOSQUE
WATERCOLOR
12" x 8.75"
1982

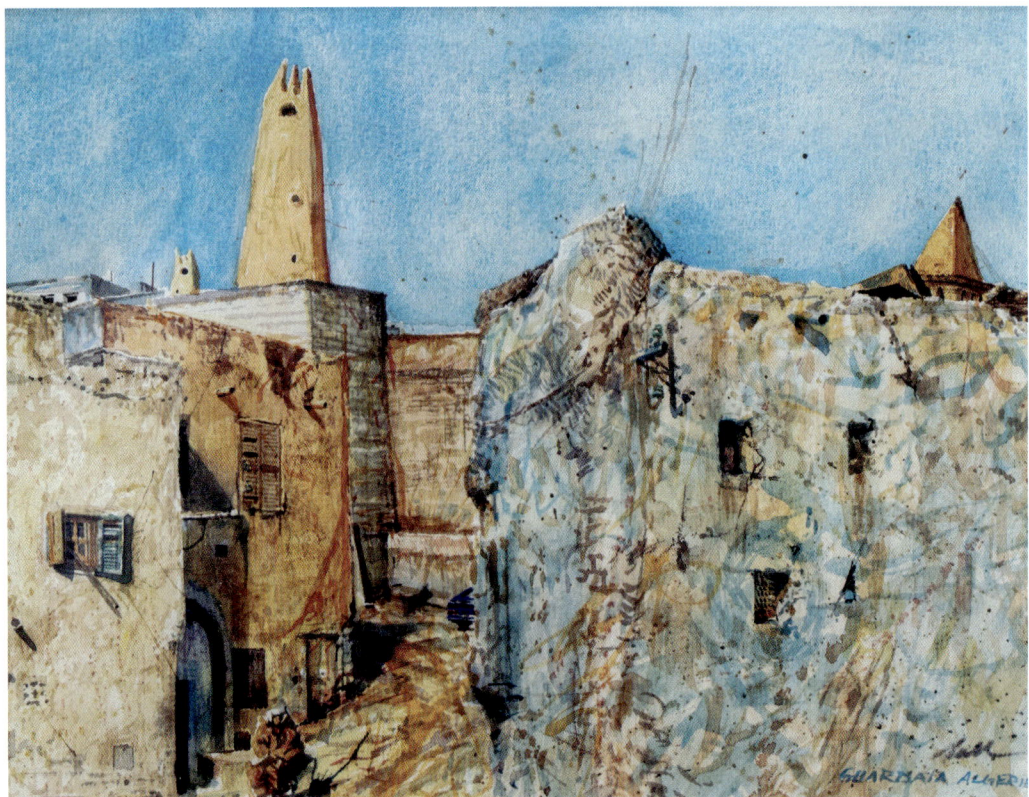

considerable recognition in Europe. While the fame of and relationship to Dali was clearly a career boost for the young Alabamian, when asked who had the greatest influence on his work, Nall states without hesitation: "Gustav Adolph Mossa" (1883–1971). The French artist's symbolist work in the early twentieth century sparked Nall's fascination with the human body, fantasy, landscapes, and undogmatic pointillism. The work of the two artists would be shown together in an exhibition, "Nall-dialogues-Mossa," in 1997 in Nice, France.

Fascinated with travel, Nall spent time in the Middle East, North Africa, India, and Mexico. Many of his drawings and etchings focused on ancient architecture, reflecting his time in different countries and environments. In 1975, Nall took a turn in subject matter with the provocative pencil drawing "The Last Supper." The piece, while somewhat controversial due to haunting imagery and the inclusion of human hair, received high critical acclaim and was considered a major new work by a young artist on the rise. In the late 1970s, Nall completed a series of drawings and etchings entitled "Alice in Wonderland." These thirty-two fantasized interpretations of Lewis Carroll's famous book reflected a surreal and unsettling body of work. The pieces also proved to be a window into Nall's struggle to understand his inner self and a world in turmoil. The series is now considered among the best of his vast portfolio.

NALL'S STUNNING IMAGES AND his engaging personality produced an

BOTTOM LEFT:
LE CAGNES
WATERCOLOR
8" x 6"
1980

BOTTOM RIGHT:
BEACH STAIRS AT NISHAT
WATERCOLOR
10.25" x 6.25"
1980

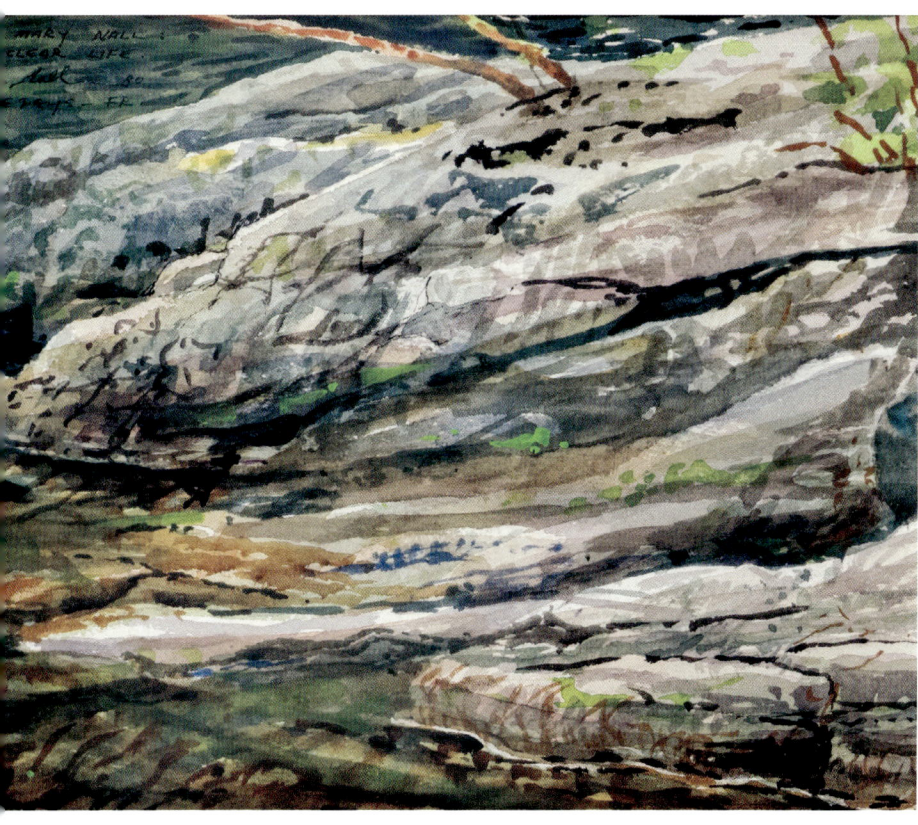

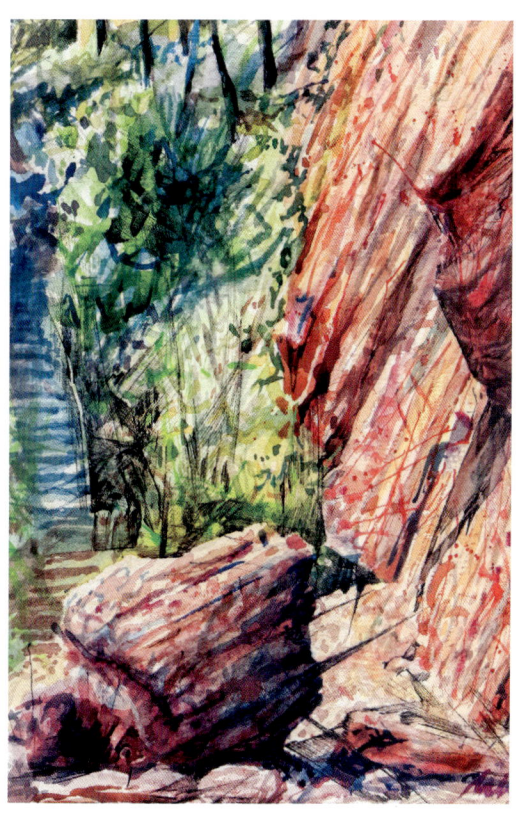

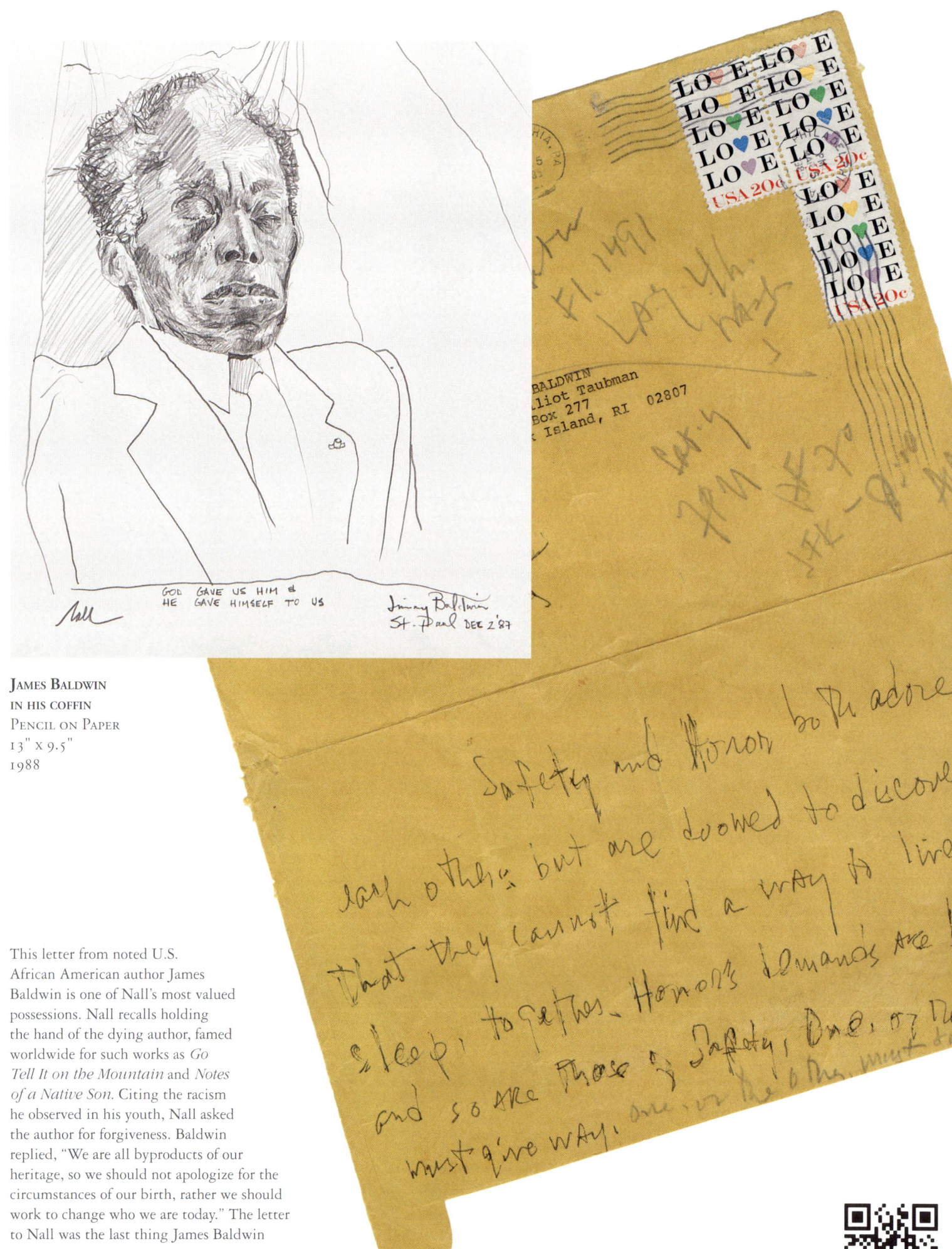

GOD GAVE US HIM &
HE GAVE HIMSELF TO US

Jimmy Baldwin
St. Paul DEC 2 '87

James Baldwin
IN HIS COFFIN
PENCIL ON PAPER
13" X 9.5"
1988

This letter from noted U.S. African American author James Baldwin is one of Nall's most valued possessions. Nall recalls holding the hand of the dying author, famed worldwide for such works as *Go Tell It on the Mountain* and *Notes of a Native Son*. Citing the racism he observed in his youth, Nall asked the author for forgiveness. Baldwin replied, "We are all byproducts of our heritage, so we should not apologize for the circumstances of our birth, rather we should work to change who we are today." The letter to Nall was the last thing James Baldwin wrote.

VIDEO

abundance of exhibitions, museum purchases, commissions, and friends in high places. These friendships led to portraits of celebrities such as Prince Albert of Monaco, Catherine Deneuve, and Ringo Starr and wife Barbara Bach. Portraiture became an important part of Nall's work. In these early portraits and others that followed, Nall stayed true to Dali's advice, "Draw from life." All of Nall's portraits consisted of great detail and were reflections of his subjects' personalities and objects that related to their interests, professions, achievements, beloved pets, or relationships to the artist.

A wide range of other commissioned work began coming Nall's way, in part due to his growing celebrity but primarily due to recognition of his unique and rare talent. His friend Prince Albert commissioned Nall to create two major pieces of public art for the Performing Arts Center in Monaco. This project resulted in a pair of massive five-by-five-meter ceramic wall hangings. Prince Albert said, "His two monumental Sunrise and Sunset mosaics welcome visitors to Monaco's Grimaldi Forum, and have been tremendously admired … he has been such a fine cultural ambassador for his native land of Alabama." Nall's other public art and site-specific exhibitions included the Pisa Airport, Monaco Cathedral, the Monastery of St. Francis of Assisi, Pietrasanta, Italy, and Menton, France.

Nall's notoriety, prolific output of provocative work, and love for human interaction led to important and lasting relationships. One of the most significant of these was with the famous American author James Baldwin, who had made his home in Paris in the twilight of his life. Nall and Baldwin, longtime friends, valued sharing stories of home, racism in the South and beyond, and the need for artists to reflect universal truths and address issues of social relevance. Nall provided bedside care for the declining Baldwin and was present at his death. His portrait of Baldwin from that period is particularly poignant.

As Nall's career was reaching new heights in Europe in the 1990s, ironically the scope and breadth of his growing fame was known only to a small circle of arts professionals, arts patrons, and fellow artists in his home state. Just a handful of friends, relatives, and Troy artists knew of Nall's global success and notoriety. Nall had made trips home to visit his mother, grandparents, and cousins, but the vast amount of his time for twenty years had been spent in Europe and international travel. As part of his creative maturation, Nall progressively came to appreciate his Alabama roots and the impact his Southern background was having on his work. The trips home allowed Nall to establish relationships with Alabama artists and to gain respect for their personal visions of a shared cultural landscape. He began to find various ways to support and showcase the work of these artists, including purchasing their art and adding it to his growing personal collection.

Nall was especially interested in the work of visionary, folk, and outsider artists who were speaking to him with images of his home state of Alabama that were raw and more aesthetically powerful than much of the contemporary work he saw in Europe. He was particularly drawn to the sculpture and paintings of Charlie Lucas, Mose Tolliver, Jimmy Lee Sudduth, and Frank Fleming and the quilts of Yvonne Wells. This list of artists would expand dramatically in the years to come.

The 1990s proved to be significant both at home and abroad. In 1991, Nall married Tuscia Cole, a lady of royal status and financial means, born in Italy and carrying the weight of great connections throughout Europe. She enthusiastically shared Nall's ambition for artistic greatness and recognition internationally. Also in 1991, of particular importance, the N.A.L.L. Art Association was established in Vence, France, on a nine-acre estate dating back to the eleventh and twelfth centuries. Being rewarded from his work, meditation, prayer, and cleaner living, Nall was now able to purchase the complex of buildings that had been Jean Dubuffet's studio. In addition to serving as a personal residence, it provided ample space for a studio, museum, and gathering spot for special guests. The Association also became a place for students, exhibitions, and various events, enhanced by a spectacular view of the Mediterranean Ocean. Nall spent several years designing spaces that included Matisse tiles and windows from a cathedral in Algiers; the result reflected the mission of the Association and the excellent taste of a multi-talented artist. This beautiful site would become Nall's place of hospitality for many Alabama artists, arts patrons, state dignitaries, and celebrities coming to take part in elaborate celebrations for the arts.

IN THE LATE 1990s, Nall's more frequent trips back to his home state gave him the idea to mount a major exhibition of exceptional Alabama artists. The project would include representative pieces by twelve artists, plus original new portraits of each by Nall. The concept included a book with text by significant Alabama authors, museum directors, and state officials, along with stunning color images of the artwork in the exhibit. While Nall was the inspiration of and project director for the "Alabama Art" exhibition, implementation of the idea became a collaborative effort with the Alabama State Council on the Arts, the Montgomery Museum of Fine Arts, and various museum professionals.

The 2000 premiere of "Alabama Art," attended by thousands, took place at the Montgomery Museum of Fine Arts and the gallery of the Alabama State Council on the Arts. The final component of the multifaceted endeavor was a tour

NALL SELF-PORTRAIT
JUGGLING ALABAMA ARTISTS
MIXED MEDIA
57" X 46"
2000

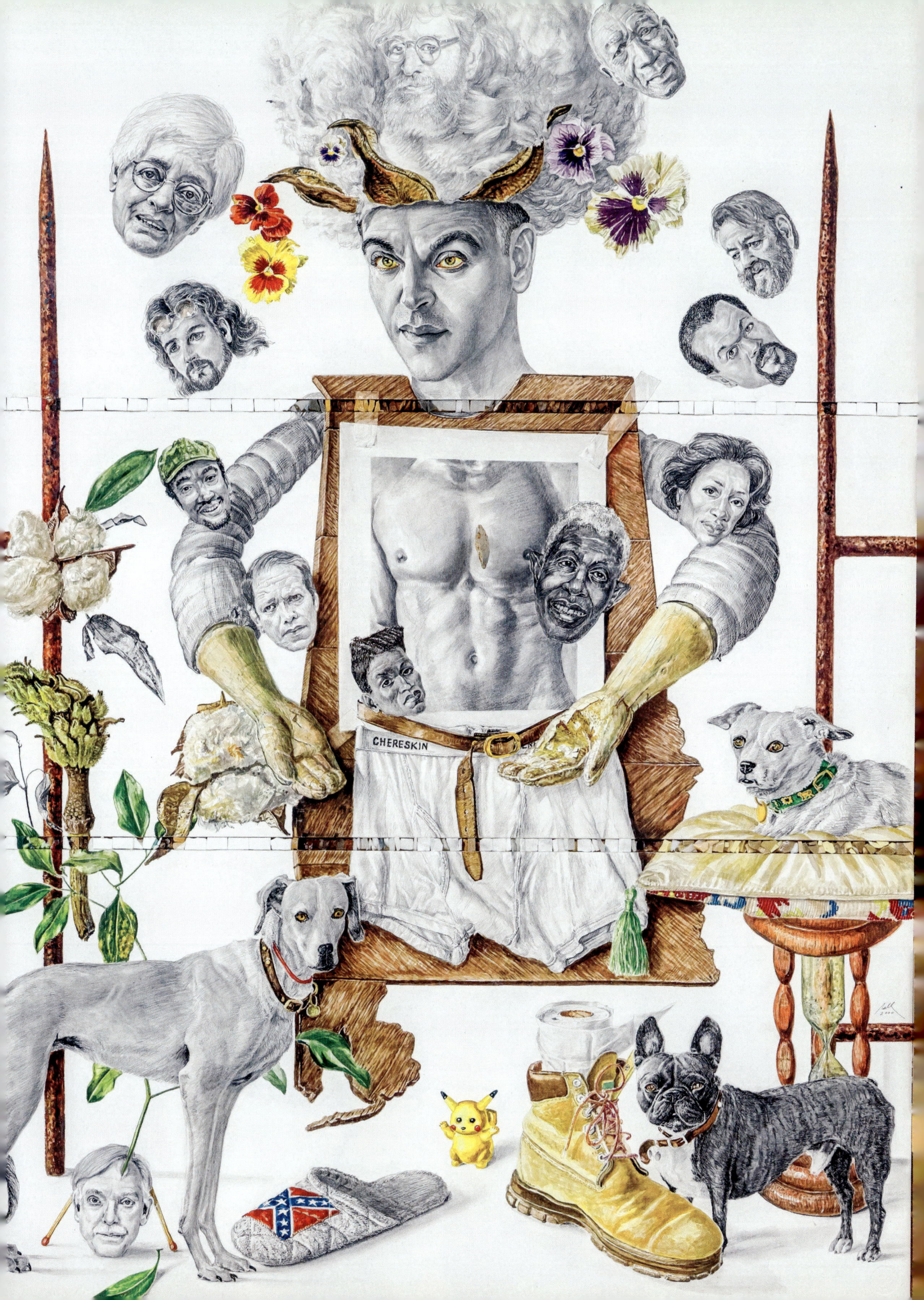

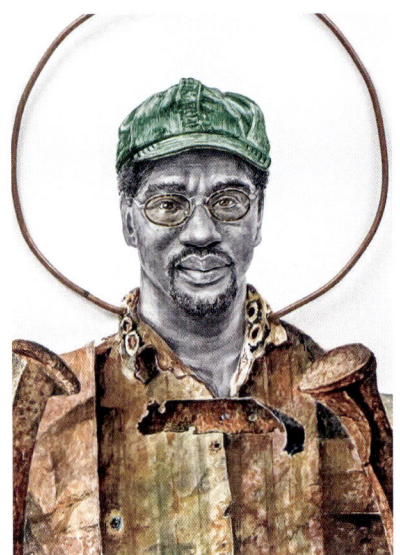

CHARLIE LUCAS (TIN MAN)

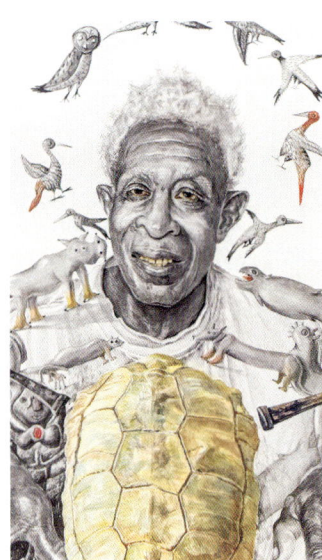

MOSE T

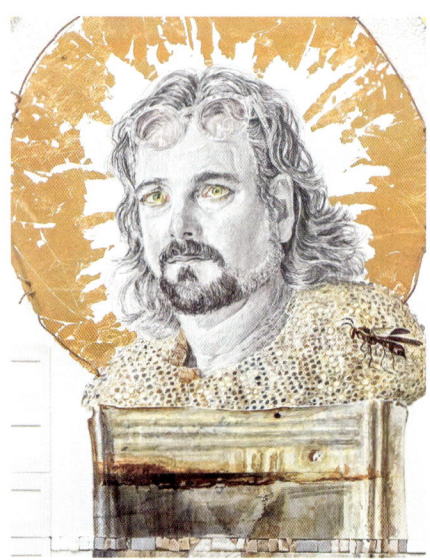

CHIP COOPER

in the south of France of the same exhibit that had been mounted in Alabama. Nall's idea was to show off the incredible work of his fellow Alabama artists and his own work. Of Nall and the Alabama exhibition, Prince Albert of Monaco (now King Albert) declared,

The Principality of Monaco and the United States have for many years entertained a bond of affection. I am therefore delighted to see that Nall is presenting in the south of France the works of thirteen artists from Alabama. With his natural enthusiasm, Nall, whose second homes are Monaco and Vence, has created a grand show allowing us to discover through the works of painters, photographers, and sculptors the heart and soul of "his Alabama." At the dawn of the new millennium, Nall, whose only desire is to promote and sponsor the arts, has set the stage for us to enjoy this unique event.

The views of French visitors to the exhibit, from dignitaries to the man on the street, were extremely positive. Reactions like "we have never seen anything like this" were common. The *Alabama Art* book accompanying the exhibit included Nall's personal quotes about each artist.

Sculptor Charlie Lucas: "Charlie Lucas's sculptures are like kudzu, they remold the silhouette of an object, casting it in a new light. His subjects are the African mask, the slave, chains from the past and industrial future."

Photographer Chip Cooper: "As a European aristocrat clings to his past, Chip Cooper's color photographs speak clearly of his own heritage, through rusted tin roofs, and crumbling Doric columns."

Photographer Kathryn Tucker Windham: "The photographs and stories of Kathryn Tucker Windham set the stage in the 1950s as far back as I can remember. They are profound and simple and touch me in their poetry, mystery, and anguish of childhood."

Painter Mose Tolliver: "In 1984 I became a friend and collector of

Mose T for many years, I gave him a poster of my work entitled *Southern Belle* which he had thumbtacked to the head of his bed. Mose T has only been influenced by his soul, a genetic memory, and a turbulent past."

Draftsman Steve Skidmore: "God rest his soul, has tied knots and drawn circles around Piranesi, and then torched the whole thing. Skidmore's Renaissance style of perspective, in his small architectural monuments as well as the larger masterpieces, is ever refined by the tightness of his line by sheer quantity and quality."

Painter Jimmy Lee Sudduth: "Mud in a ditch, mud on a painting. How natural authentic and brilliant. His images were raw and simple, like the familiar red clay of Alabama, and they touched my soul."

Photographer/painter William Christenberry: "Christenberry's photographs have brought to attention Alabama's *Arte Povera*, our everyday rust and ruins turned into art. Pioneer architectural structures parallel eighteenth-century Neapolitan nativity scenes or Chinese Houses of Spirits and remain monuments to our past."

Sculptor Clifton Pearson: "Pearson has revered his past and his passions through Southern stoneware. His glazes are red, white, and black, symbolic of the mixture of the 'American race.'"

Painter/sculptor Bill Nance: "Nance has taken his sculptor's hands, his artist's eyes, and enlarged his

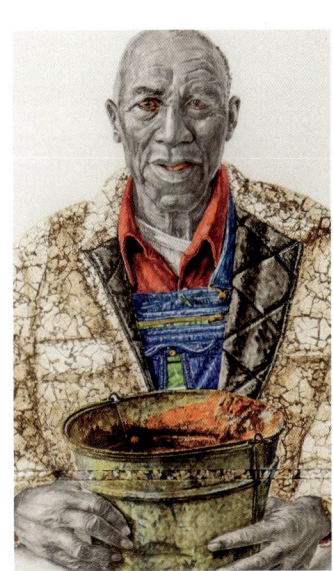

JIMMY LEE SUDDUTH

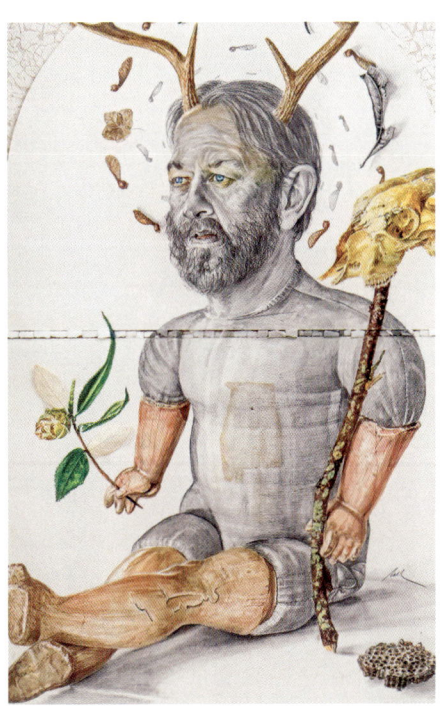

FRANK FLEMING

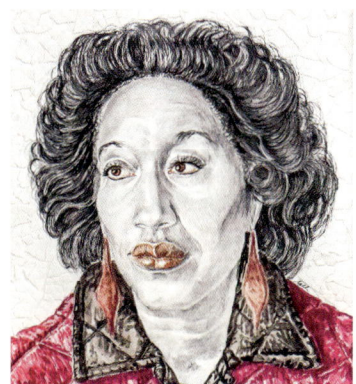

YVONNE WELLS

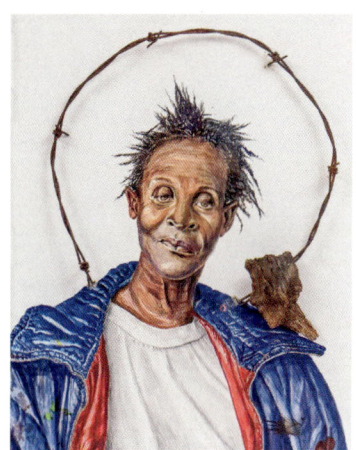

BETTY SUE MATTHEWS

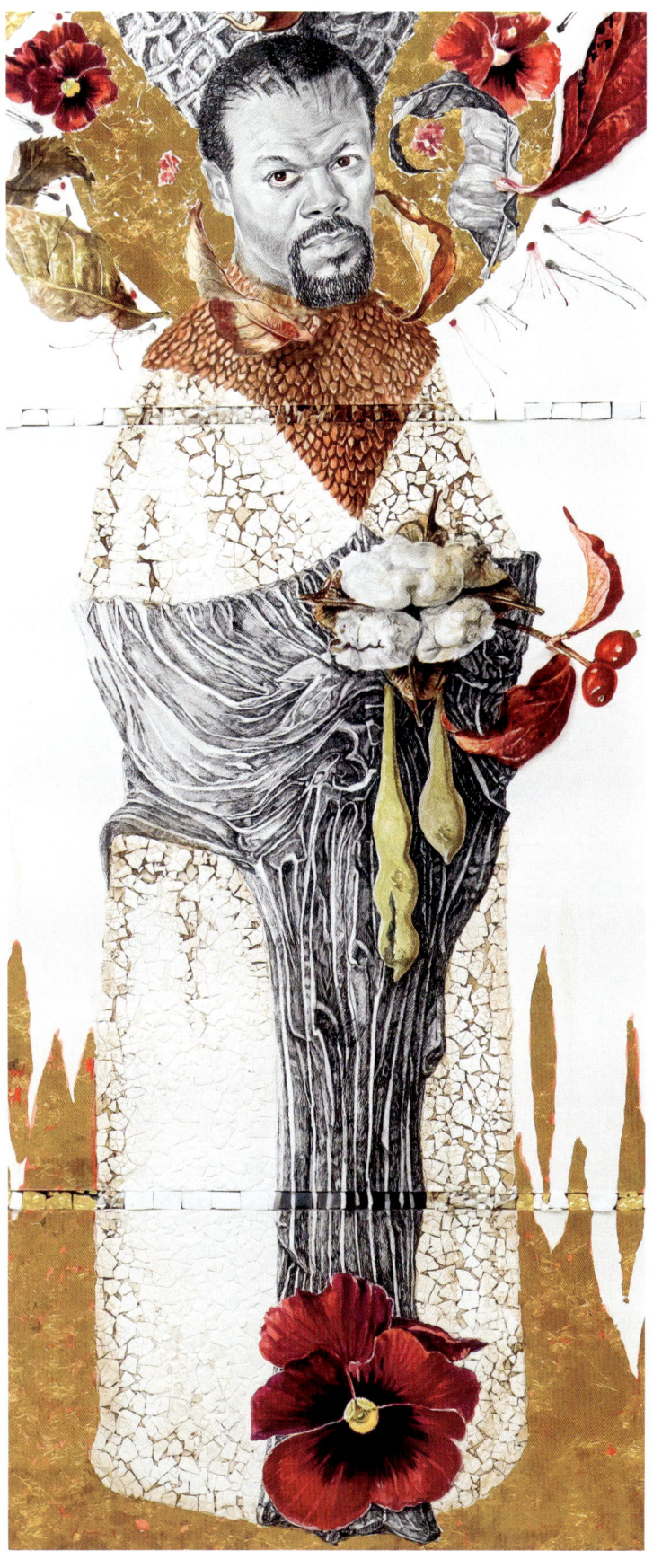

CLIFTON PEARSON

canvas to gardens. His exquisite palette of bushes and shrubs, ground covers, and lanes weave around and through his geometrically abstract foliage."

Quilter Yvonne Wells: "The patchwork quilt has long been synonymous with 'Southern heritage' or scraping together an artist bent, just to keep warm. Wells takes it miles further and defines the quilt as contemporary art … her artistic soul delivers the social punch of Angela Davis."

Photographer Flemming Tyler Wilson: "Wilson has focused on a liberated decadent South, and his work is honest to a fault. He sets up scenes for present-day icons which cavort and twist to massage his pain. For revenge he dresses the gods in contemporary clothes and hangs them out to dry."

Sculptor Frank Fleming: "We use the same symbols but instead of drawing in pencil, he molds in clay. His branches metamorphose into chairs. His animals are stacked or carry flowers, or intimidate the viewer by sitting on a corn cob. Frank's work is erotic and pure Alabama."

In describing the exhibition, Nall wrote,

In viewing "Alabama Art" the subject matter reveals a common thread consistent with Southern Gothic writers Tennessee Williams, Flannery O'Connor, Truman Capote, and William Faulkner, as well as Fannie Flagg, Rick Bragg, Winston Groom, Mark Childress, and Daniel Wallace. Although techniques vary from "outsider art" to more sophisticated schooled works and photography, the unifying message is alive and strong, not commercially diluted. It was born from a necessity of exorcising Alabama's racial past, her isolated peculiarities and rural morality. "Art from the Guts" would better describe "Alabama Art."

Another deeply personal and different perspective in the exhibition's book came from Rick Bragg, one of the state's great, common-man, story-telling authors:

Art was in the quilts of my grandmother sewed from scrap, turning other people's leavings into precious keepsakes. It was in the stories my uncle told on the front porch, their words painting as rich and vivid a portrait as any oils ever could. It was in the baskets and fishnets the old men and women wove, the patterns as delicate as spider webs, and in the cornices and lattices my uncles carved and hammered into place, hanging from ladders, nails between their teeth. No, we always had art in us. We may have had a secondhand sofa sitting on our front porch, but we had, by God, art.

The multifaceted project was a huge success on many levels, not the least of which was the high-profile media coverage in the United States, France, and many parts of Europe. CNN did several features on Nall and the exhibition. The showcase was concluded with a "Stars Falling" on Alabama dinner celebration, Southern-style, featuring famous Alabama chefs, musicians, and a host of Alabama dignitaries including the governor and first lady. A Nall portrait of Governor Don Siegelman and First Lady Lori was unveiled at the N.A.L.L. Art Association complex, the site for the festivities.

The evening event might have been best captured by yet another of Alabama's most recognized and beloved authors, Fannie Flagg, when she wrote:

How to explain the phenomenon that is Nall? In the 1830s there was a night where they say a million silver comets were falling; stars lit up the Alabama sky and

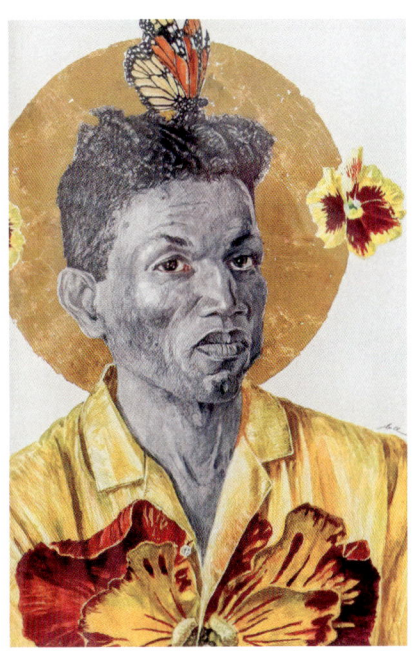

FLEMMING TYLER WILSON

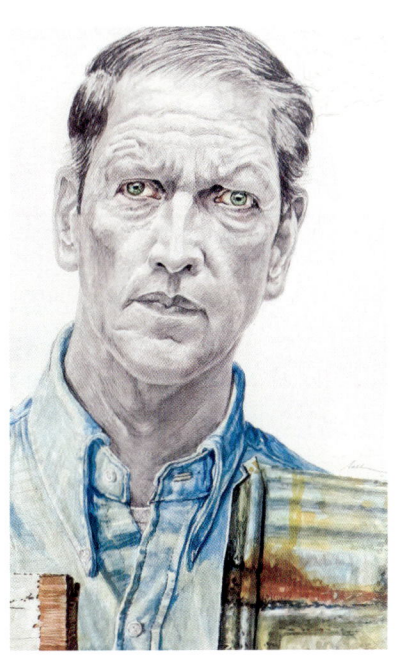

WILLIAM CHRISTENBERRY

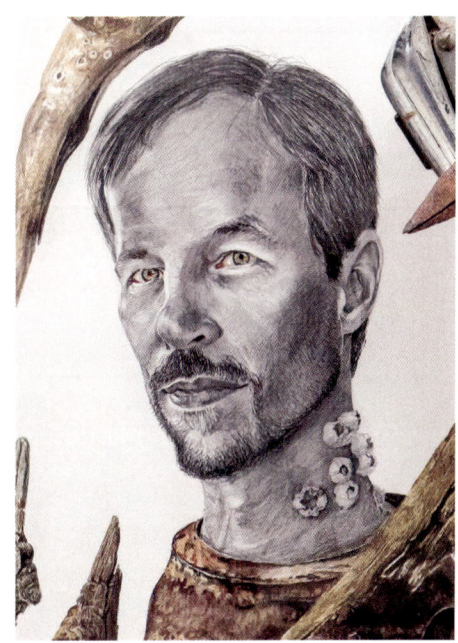

BRUCE LARSEN

turned the entire night as bright as day until morning. This was a night for Nall, just made for Nall.

So one might say the closing evening event of "Alabama Art" was the kick-off of Nall's coming home to Alabama, coming home to Troy, coming home to friends and kin, and coming home to the red clay and collard greens that gave him a strong passion for art and lust for life.

THE NEW MILLENNIUM found Nall and Tuscia establishing homes and roots both in Troy and Fairhope while still maintaining the N.A.L.L. Art Association in France. His European calendar included sculpting *Peace Frame*, cast in Pietrasanta, Italy, designing porcelain china patterns for Haviland, partnering with Christian Dior for an exhibition and a new line of fragrances, and the designing of sets and costumes for two major Puccini Opera Festival productions, *La Fanciulla del West* and *La Rondine*. Nall's life in the arts was incredibly busy.

In the United States, following "Alabama Art" a major exhibition of Nall's work along with that of fellow Alabama artist friends took place at 55 Water Street in New York City, in partnership with the Retirement Systems of Alabama, which owned the massive building. An eclectic crowd of more than nine hundred Alabama artists, state officials, a close family of arts friends, and New York art patrons attended the celebration. This event began a long relationship with RSA CEO David Bronner and the chain of

five Marriott resort hotels in Alabama. In each of these five hotels, thanks to Nall, the original work of Alabama artists was displayed. A publication featuring this work and the statewide project was compiled by Nall and made available to resort visitors. If one is fortunate enough to stay at the legendary Marriott Grand Hotel and Resort in Point Clear, Alabama, checking out the "Nall Suite" in the historic part of the hotel will enhance the visit.

For his artistic career, work with students, and humanitarian spirit he extended to fellow Alabama artists, Nall was awarded an honorary doctorate from Troy University. The honor turned out to be symbolic of a long and fruitful relationship with the chancellor, first lady, and the entire University family. In addition to outstanding work with students and generous contributions to the University, the Troy native brought attention and support to other arts activities in the community and region. Nall's arts profile in his hometown was now skyrocketing at the same pace as it had in the U.S. and Europe.

In 2005, after months of sculpting and casting in Pietrasanta, Italy, Nall donated *Peace Frame* to the City of Pietrasanta as a gesture of goodwill and the beginning of cultural exchange with the State of Alabama. The dedication and installation of this large bronze sculpture on the main street indeed became the starting point of a lasting cultural exchange between Pietrasanta, arguably the sculpture capital of the world, and

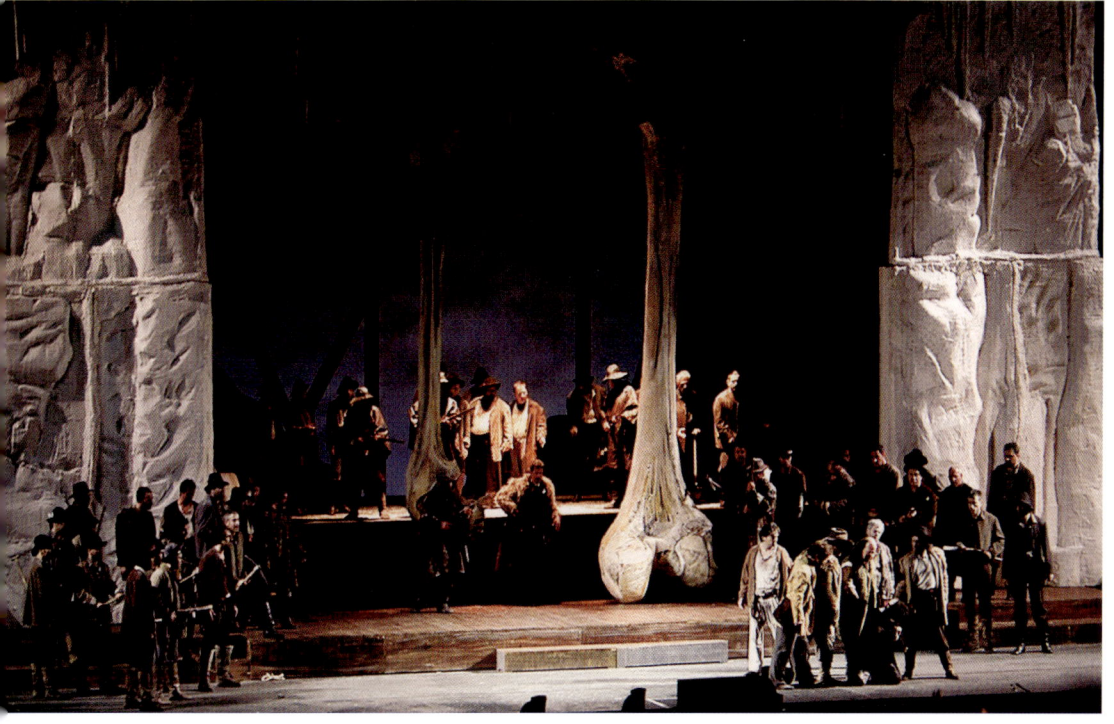

PUCCINI OPERA
Nall designed the sets and costumes for this production of Giacomo Puccini's 1910 opera "La Fanciulla del West," or "The Girl of the Golden West," which was featured at the 2005 Puccini Festival in Torre del Lago, Italy.

Alabama. The exchange also led to "sister city" resolutions between Pietrasanta, the city of Montgomery, and the city of Sylacauga. The latter is the home of major quarries of marble once commonly used for sculpting and national monuments.

Facilitated and funded by the Alabama State Council on the Arts, a group of Alabama sculptors, painters, musicians, writers, arts administrators, and public officials traveled to Pietrasanta for a week in 2008 for an inaugural festival celebrating the exchange. As part of the festivities and ceremonies, Nall was presented with an award from both the Alabama State Council on the Arts and the Commissioner of Culture for Pietrasanta for his role in making the exchange a reality. Exhibitions, concerts, literary readings, and Alabama films were showcased. Pietrasanta audiences were appreciative and enthusiastic; thousands gathered in the piazza to

hear the Birmingham Sunlights, a legendary gospel group, after a full day of viewing multiple exhibitions of Alabama art. Nall enjoyed observing the fruits of his labors in bringing the two cultures together.

In 2009, Italian artists and city officials including the mayor, commissioner of culture, and commissioner of tourism traveled to Montgomery, Sylacauga, Birmingham, and Monroeville as part of activities illustrating the spirit of exchange between Alabama and Pietrasanta. Nall's initial contributions can't be overstated. The exchange continues today and has led to Troy University, with First Lady Janice Hawkins as the primary advocate and emissary, establishing a study-abroad program in Pietrasanta, Pisa, and the region of Tuscany. Students of dance, music, theater, and related disciplines spend summers in Pietrasanta broadening their skill as well as their understanding and appreciation for

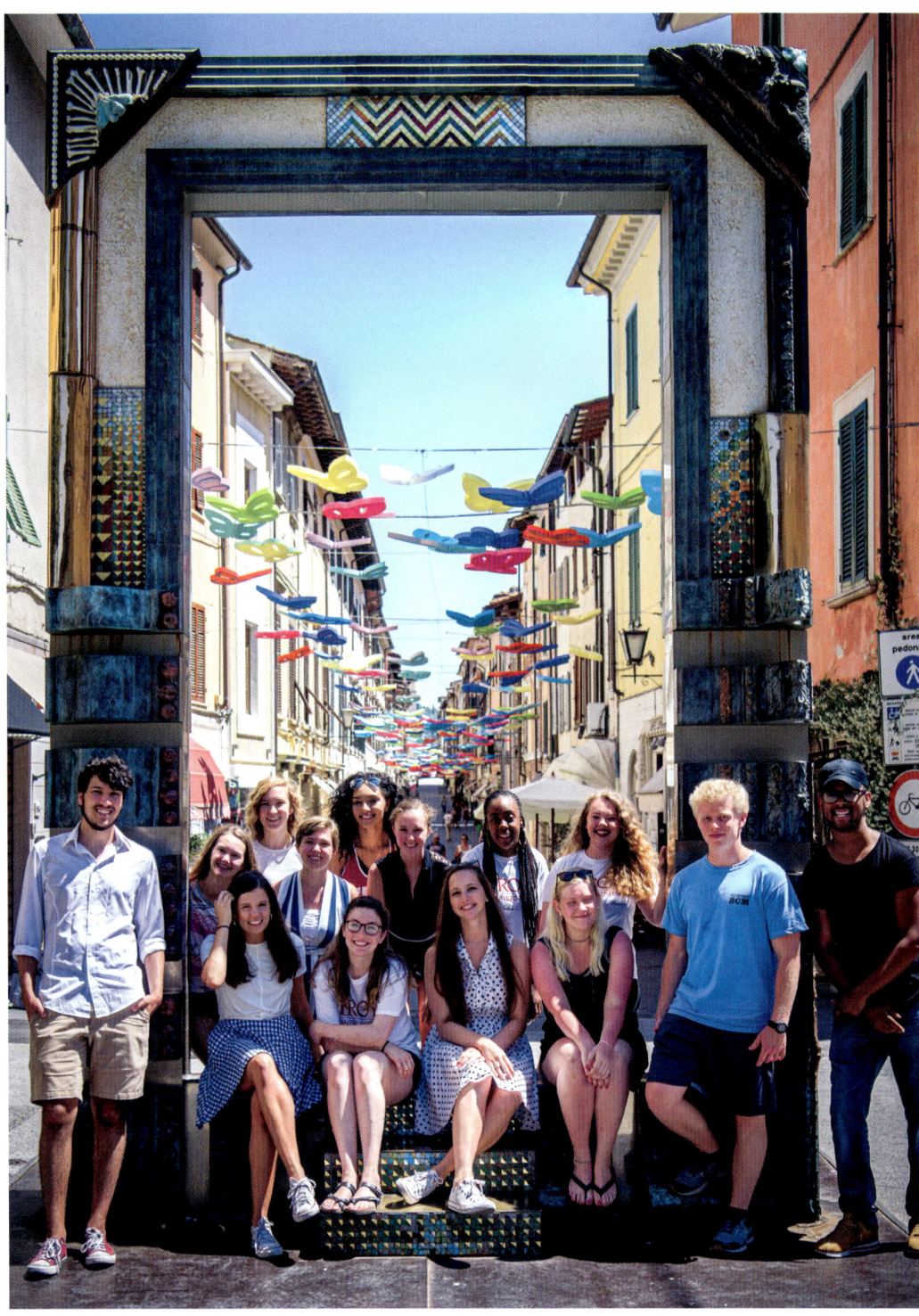

Troy University students visiting Nall's *Peace Frame* in Pietrasanta, Italy 2018.

one of the great classic art regions of the world. Education of students was one of the initial priorities of the exchange, and with the involvement of Troy University that goal has become a reality.

The breadth of Nall's creative energy might be reflected best by the exceedingly ambitious project in 2018 that would become known as Violata Pax. Here we find the artist at age fifty-eight stretching to meet a major

challenge in the form of "Stations of the Cross of Humanity"—A Journey by Nall. In this monumental project, a global audience is confronted with Nall addressing the proposition of the "Passages and Atrocities of Humanity."

In the text of the book that accompanied the exhibition, Tommy McPherson, former director of the Mobile Museum of Art, provides this perspective of Violata Pax:

Many find Nall's work to be disturbing and misunderstand his need to juxtapose the seedy and the sacrosanct, the beautiful with the ugly or sublime. Nall is a surrealist, a fantasist, an alchemist, and a genius among us. He sees our world perhaps as angels do, a world of sin and shame and death and beauty and renewal and celebration without judgment. His is an art of super-realism, even super-spiritualism, and his discourse with our souls can help enflame and purify them, preparing us for less shameful futures than human frailty remembers.

In this challenging and powerful exhibition, a combination of new work and a Nall retrospective encompasses themes such as war, terrorism, racism, global warming, media control, and other atrocities. An unusual element of this overall project was the customized exhibits for a group of five cities in multiple venues. The most dramatic and unlikely setting was the Sacred Convent and both Lower and Upper Basilicas at Assisi, one of Europe's most iconic and historically significant sites. With the blessing of Pope Benedict XVI and Father Vincenzo Coli, head of one of the Franciscan orders, fifty-two portrait icons and the two large outdoor bronze sculptures—*Peace Frame* and the *Wounded Peace Dove*—were installed in the Assisi complex to greet the millions of annual pilgrim visitors. The *Dove* would come to represent not only the theme of the exhibition but Nall's call for world peace. It should be noted the Basilica

is both the burial tomb of Saint Francis and the location of the historic frescoes of Giotto and Cimabue, two of the most important painters of the early Renaissance. The visual juxtaposition of the Old Masters and Nall is, on one hand, an extreme aesthetic contrast, while on the other, a masterful matching of time, history, and artistry.

The Violata Pax tour included the cities of Assisi and Pietrasanta, Italy; Menton, France; the Principality of Monaco; and Mobile, Alabama, where it concluded at the Mobile Museum of Art. Each city showcased different Nall installations and creations. The tour began at Assisi with a motorcade of buses carrying Nall's Alabama friends, public officials, a CNN correspondent, travel writers, and art critics. The European phase of the project ended with a grand celebration at the N.A.L.L. Art Association in Vence. With this high-profile project, Nall secured prominence among the Alabama expatriates in the European art world. It would be hard to argue that an Alabama artist has ever had as much international impact and depth of accomplishment as Fred Nall Hollis from Troy, Alabama. Other Alabama artists such as Harper Lee, Tallulah Bankhead, Hank Williams, and Lionel Richie may carry more international fame than Nall, but none has his volume of achievement.

The year following Violata Pax, the Alabama State Council on the Arts presented Nall with its Distinguished Artist Award, the most prestigious recognition given to an artist by the State of Alabama. The award cited

Nall's exceptional promotion of art and individual artists in the state; for opening cultural exchange between specific cities in Alabama, France, and Italy; and for the creation of art that has gained critical recognition nationally and internationally. Nall was especially praised for his contributions and overall generosity to nonprofit arts organizations as well as his ongoing work with college students at two major state universities, Troy University and the University of Alabama.

IN THE MIDST OF his high-profile projects, Nall's reconnection with his roots in Alabama took shape in different forms, most notably his two-semester residency at Troy University. His passion for creating art is the only endeavor that surpasses his love of teaching and inspiring young aspiring artists. His ongoing relationship with Troy provided perfect opportunities to work with and mentor students. Students are amazed, motivated, and stimulated by Nall's dynamic personality and his unique process of making art. These students often say they were in the company of a genius at work. In addition, Nall donated artwork to be auctioned at fundraising events for Troy University, enabling an annual scholarship for a gifted art student to be established in his name.

Nall's connection to Troy and the University was enhanced by a growing relationship with Chancellor Jack Hawkins Jr. and his wife, Janice. Early on, Mrs. Hawkins recognized Nall's special talent and the potential

BELOW:
International Arts Center, Bronze Sculptures by Huo Bao Zhu

CENTER:
Troy University now occupies the former bank building where Nall's father once worked.

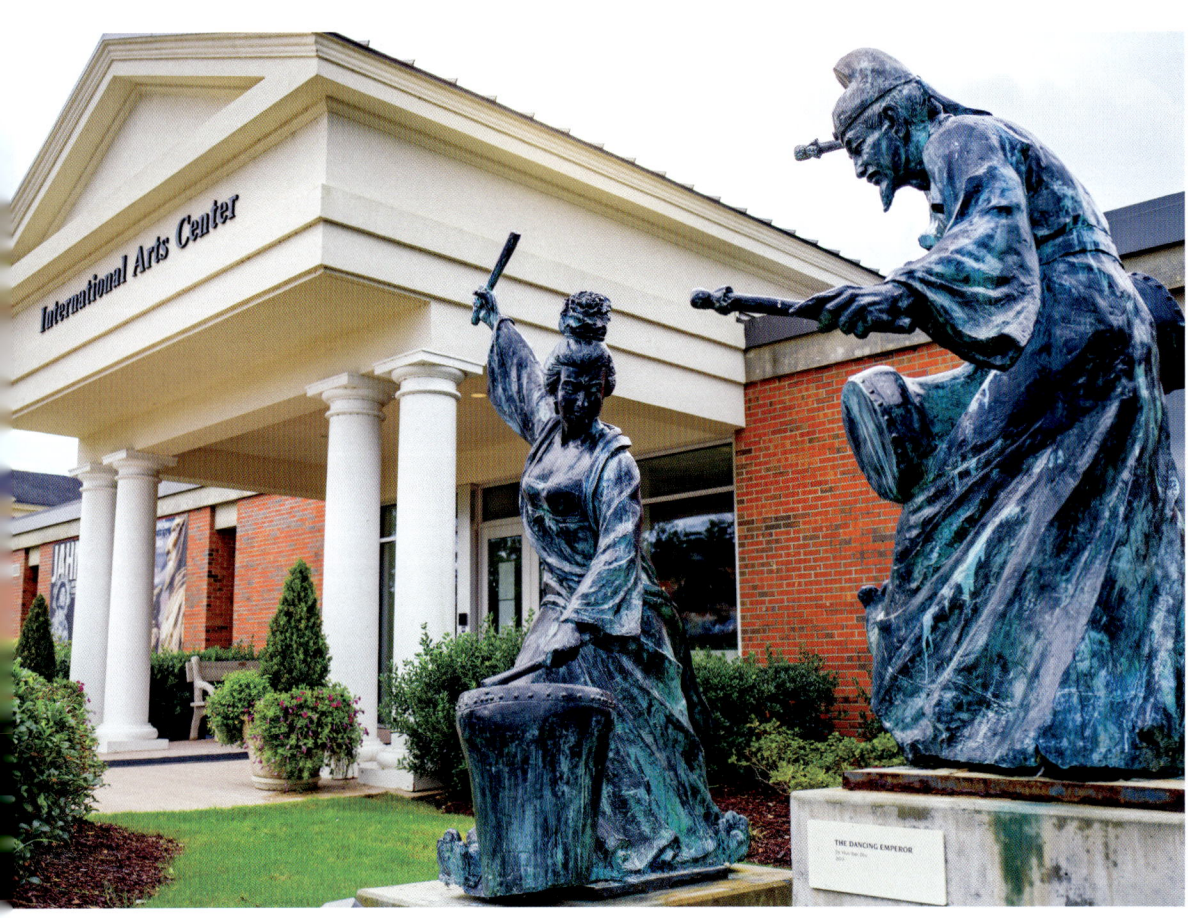

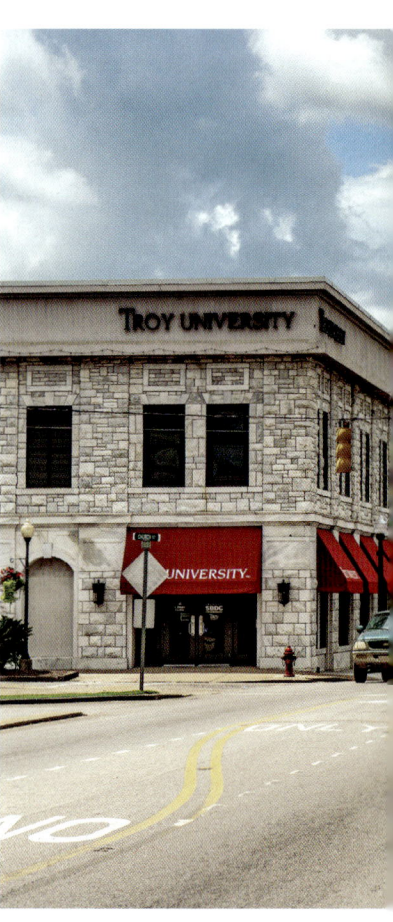

impact he could have on students, faculty, the University, and not only the City of Troy but the entire State of Alabama. That relationship produced many ideas and visions bonding the University and Nall. An abundance of creative thinking combined with a commitment to make dreams become a reality would set the table for major projects in the years to come.

In 2015–16, ten years after *Violata Pax*—arguably the pinnacle of an illustrious career—Nall found himself living in Fairhope, Alabama, surrounded by friends, Troy cousins, and fellow artists. In recent years, a realization has come to Nall and those who know his work best that the period of his producing physically demanding art has passed. His hands are not quite as steady, his eyes not quite as sharp, and his back not quite as strong as the artist who created the *Peace Dove* and *Alice in Wonderland.* Nall's collection—his own and that of fellow artists purchased over many years—is vast. His generous spirit has been consistent, and he continues to donate work for worthy fundraisers. With warehouses of art, large pieces and small, new and old, Nall's protection of his legacy and finding an appropriate home for his art are everpresent in his thoughts at this phase of life.

If "home is where the heart is," then Nall's looking toward Troy as a permanent repository for his work is not surprising. The rekindling of fond memories of home, the need to establish an appropriate Nall legacy, and a vision shared with his

CENTER:
Example of Town and Gown in Downtown Troy

BELOW:
Historic sign on Troy Square

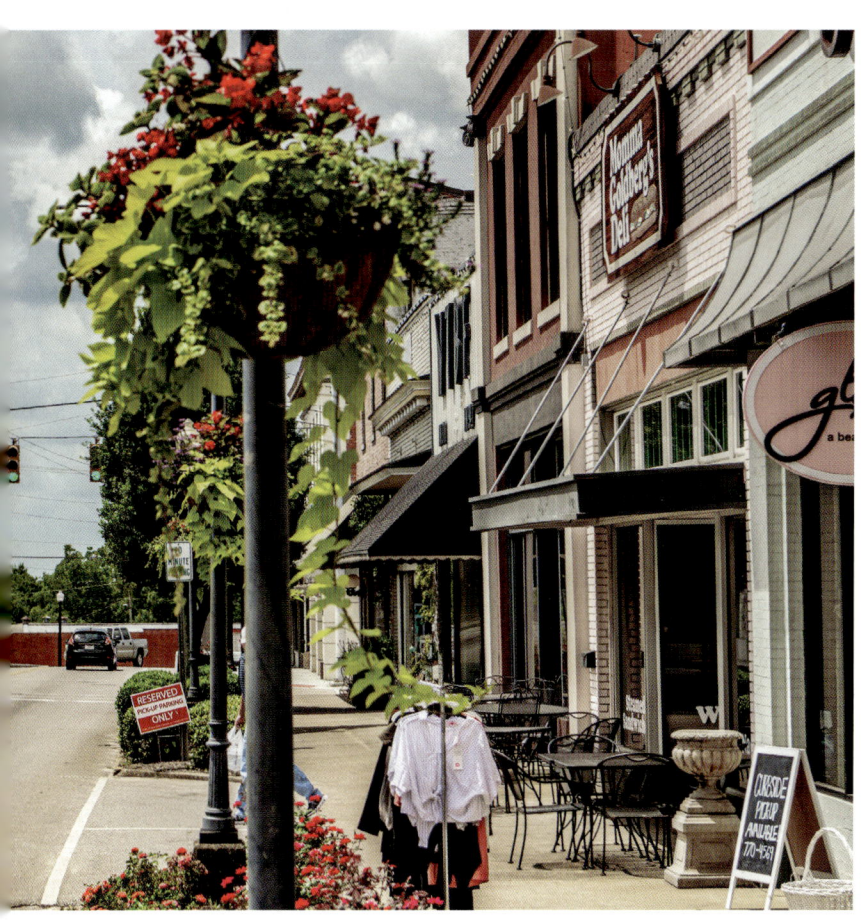

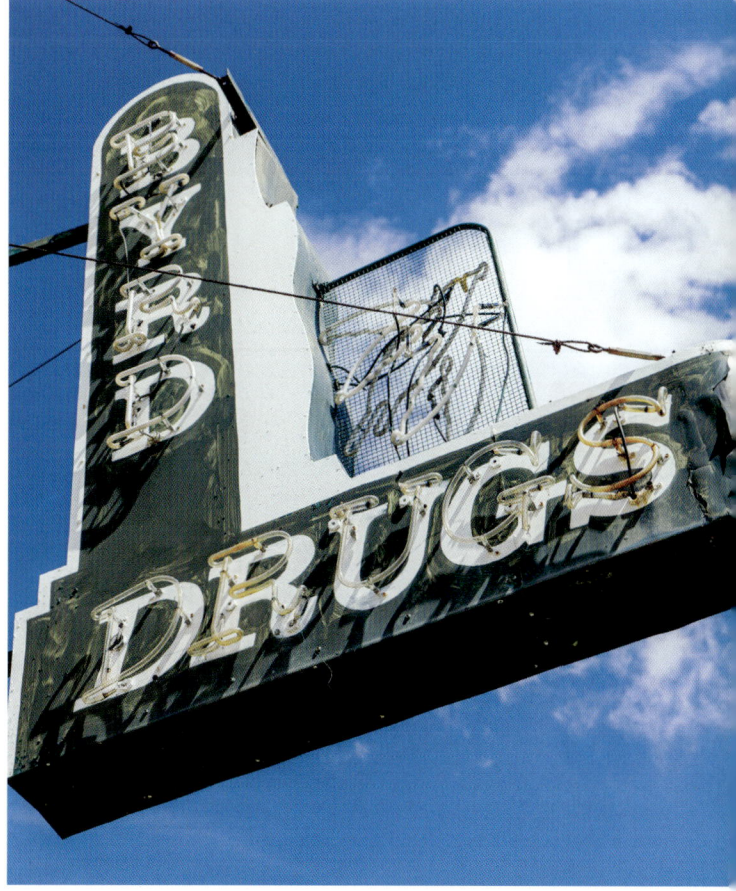

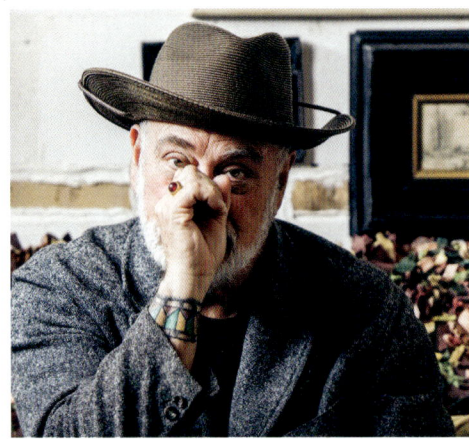

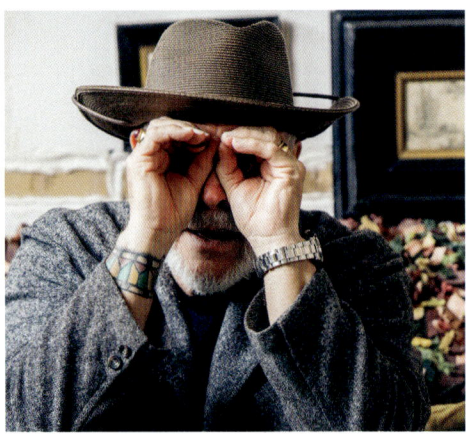

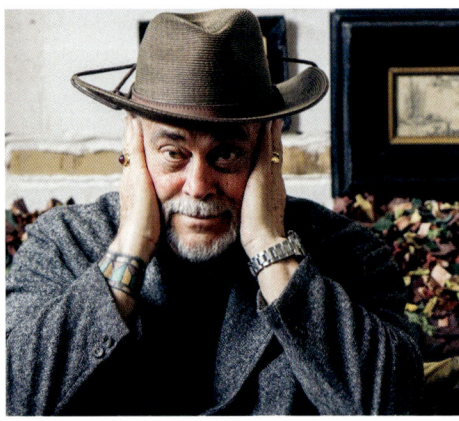

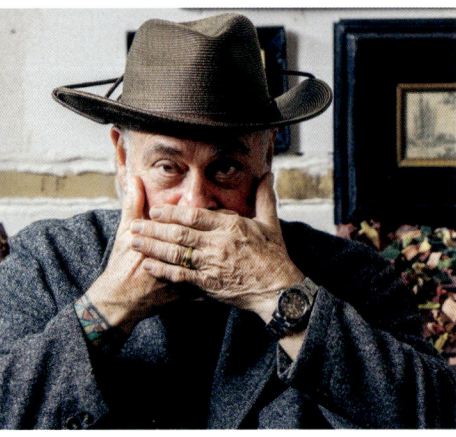

close friend Janice Hawkins for the arts on Troy University's campus were like the stars, the moon, and the sun finally aligning. To build an international arts center, a Nall museum, and a park housing an amphitheater on the campus seemed beyond ambitious. But for visionaries like Nall and Janice Hawkins, anything was and is possible. Mrs. Hawkins, in fact, had discussed with her husband renovating the old Stewart Dining Hall, scheduled for demolition, for the purpose of showcasing art. This would include significant pieces by up-and-coming artists, art students, art faculty, and recognized art professionals from all over the state and world. One million dollars was an initial funding request; the final project would cost far more.

Nall's offer to contribute art valued at more than $4 million was a significant boost for phase one of the project. Nall did stipulate that an appropriate space would have to be constructed to house such a major collection. Enthusiasm and momentum grew for an extraordinary, multi-phase undertaking. Plans had to be finalized and funds had to be raised from private, public, and foundation sources, augmented with personal gifts. The leadership of the University, Chancellor Hawkins, the Board of Trustees, and Troy's extended family was critical to the implementation and completion of the project. Amazingly the concept continued to gain broad support and the dream becoming a reality was in sight.

On November 4, 2016, the Janice

Hawkins Cultural Arts Park was dedicated. The park includes the International Arts Center, the Nall Museum, a landscaped park, and an amphitheater with two hundred terracotta replica warriors designed and donated by Chinese sculptor Huo Bao Zhu. Nall's *Violata Pax Wounded Dove* is overlooking the park from the Daniel Foundation Plaza directly behind the Center complex. In describing the project at the dedication, Chancellor Hawkins said, "A kudzu-covered ravine has been transformed into a beautiful park. We believe preserving the past is progress." The park also reflects Hawkins's long-held goal for the University to exist as a "global village," a place where the East meets the West in a manner that enhances an international environment for learning. The profile of this new space combines the cultures of China, France, Italy, and Alabama, greeting students and visitors at the west entrance to the campus with a spectacular view. While many generous people made it possible for this project to become yet another focal point of a beautiful campus, the presence of Nall, the artist, the visionary, the patron, and the partner was instrumental in the Park's overwhelming success. For Nall, the project is another part of a lasting legacy that reflects his long and unique journey. One might say it is a grand finale in the act of returning home to Troy.

Once the Nall Museum was in place and opened to the public, Nall was asked to talk about the pieces in the Museum, many going back to the mid-1960s. Nall said:

Most of my best and favorite pieces I did not sell. I wanted these pieces to be shared and seen by a large number of people. I wanted to find a special place for these special pieces to be on display permanently and available for touring. At this point in my life I decided that special place was Troy, my home. The University made that possible by providing that special place.

A final piece of the puzzle that is Nall needs to be shared for one to fully grasp the man and his art. This important piece of clearly a multi-layered individual is the personal energy force that lies behind the art and a colorful personality. The personality is also a complicated one that has produced much beauty, tension, insight, reflection, sense of place, and a vision of the future. This personality needs to be appreciated before one can fully understand the accompanying images in these pages. Shedding a little brighter light on Nall, the person, provides a clearer perspective and context for his truly unique story. That said, Nall the person and Nall the artist are mostly one and the same. Nall is an artist first. But looking a bit deeper into the various ingredients that make Nall tick can be enlightening.

For those observing Nall from afar, he is a bit of an enigma—that is to say, somewhat mysterious, strange, hard to understand, and/or difficult to describe. For those fortunates who spend time with him, it becomes

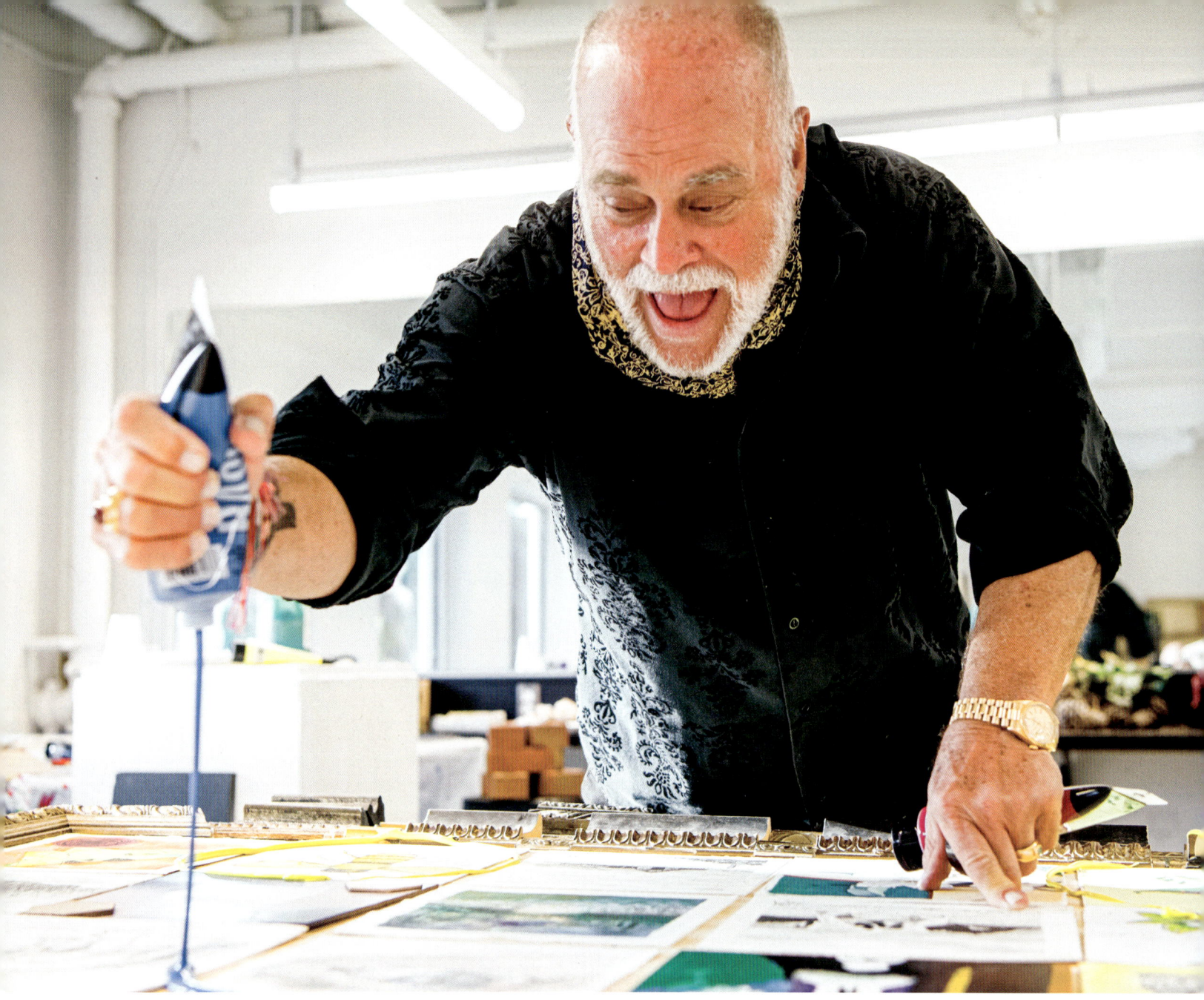

clear he is one of a kind, authentic to the bone, a maker of art with a very big heart. In describing his friend on "Nall Day" in Troy in May 2019, Chancellor Hawkins said, "On the surface Nall can be flamboyant but there is another dimension to him. He is introspective, he is kind, he is generous. He has a legacy at Troy University. What he has done for the arts here at Troy University can't be measured." Other friends at "Nall Day" echoed the warm, generous, and kind side of the otherwise hard-driving artist. His personal and professional passion can at times conflict with his heartfelt expressions for a better quality of life for everyone worldwide.

Visiting his studio or visiting a Nall "space" is a 100 percent arts experience to, one might say, an art wonderland with all the fantasy and fun of such a visit. He creates art constantly or, if not making it physically, is thinking about making it. Nall will create a portrait on a place mat after a dinner overlooking the piazza in a small Italian town. He will draw portraits at a dinner party to help raise funds. And he will create and give art as a wedding present. He paints, sculpts, draws, and designs china, furniture fabric, carpets, decks of cards, and covers of cookbooks. It is hard for Nall to be idle. He is above all else prolific.

This is an artist who does not seek being alone or need solitude to create work; in fact, much of his creative process is performance-like. Even if his company and audience happen to be one of his beloved dogs, Nall thrives on being surrounded by those who appreciate his work, including those who are furry. On many occasions one will not only have dinner with Nall but enjoy the company of his dogs as well. Where dogs provide unconditional love to their owner, Nall craves that love and returns it tenfold. His longtime relationship with and compassion for dogs says a lot about who he is. As a matter of fact, Nall will often half seriously describe himself as a mongrel from Alabama—"all of us from Alabama are," he enjoys saying. Dogs often find their way into his paintings and drawings, with distinct personalities always reflecting something important to the curious viewer. Biscuit will remain one of Nall's favorite mongrel friends.

In *Alabama Art,* noted Alabamian and award-winning author Fannie

Flagg adds a personal touch to the creative roots of our artist that could explain a lot about the pieces that make up the whole:

My friend Nall is as large and alive and as colorful as his work. Who he is in the art world is clear. He is a major presence, brilliantly reviewed and admired, who leaves awestruck all who see his work. But this book is not entirely about Nall the artist. It is about Nall the man, because no matter what heights he continues to climb in the art world, he will always be, first and foremost, lovingly and proudly, an Alabama boy. A true Alabamian who at the core just happens to be a great genius. A native son bursting at the seams with so much energy he wants to pull us all up with him.

It is little wonder that Nall developed a strong sense of place in Alabama, a cultural landscape that has influenced his work over an art-filled life. Even when traveling and living around the globe, Troy remained Nall's North Star for creative inspiration, personal fulfillment, finding a spiritual focus, and discovering peace with an identity

Student participants at Master Class Nall Day, May 2019.

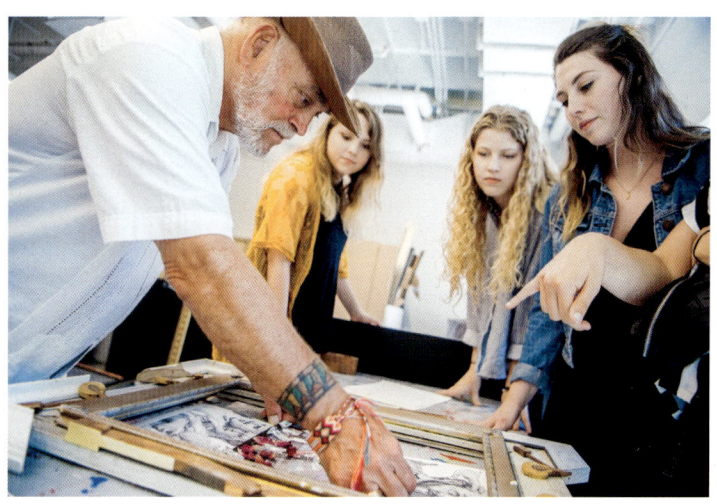

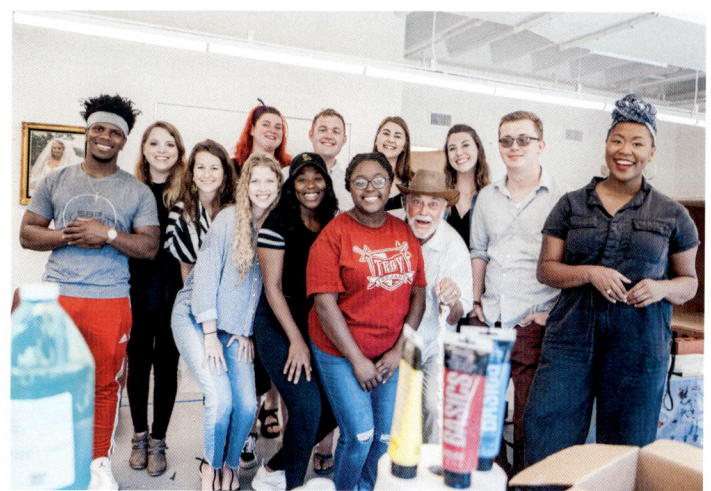

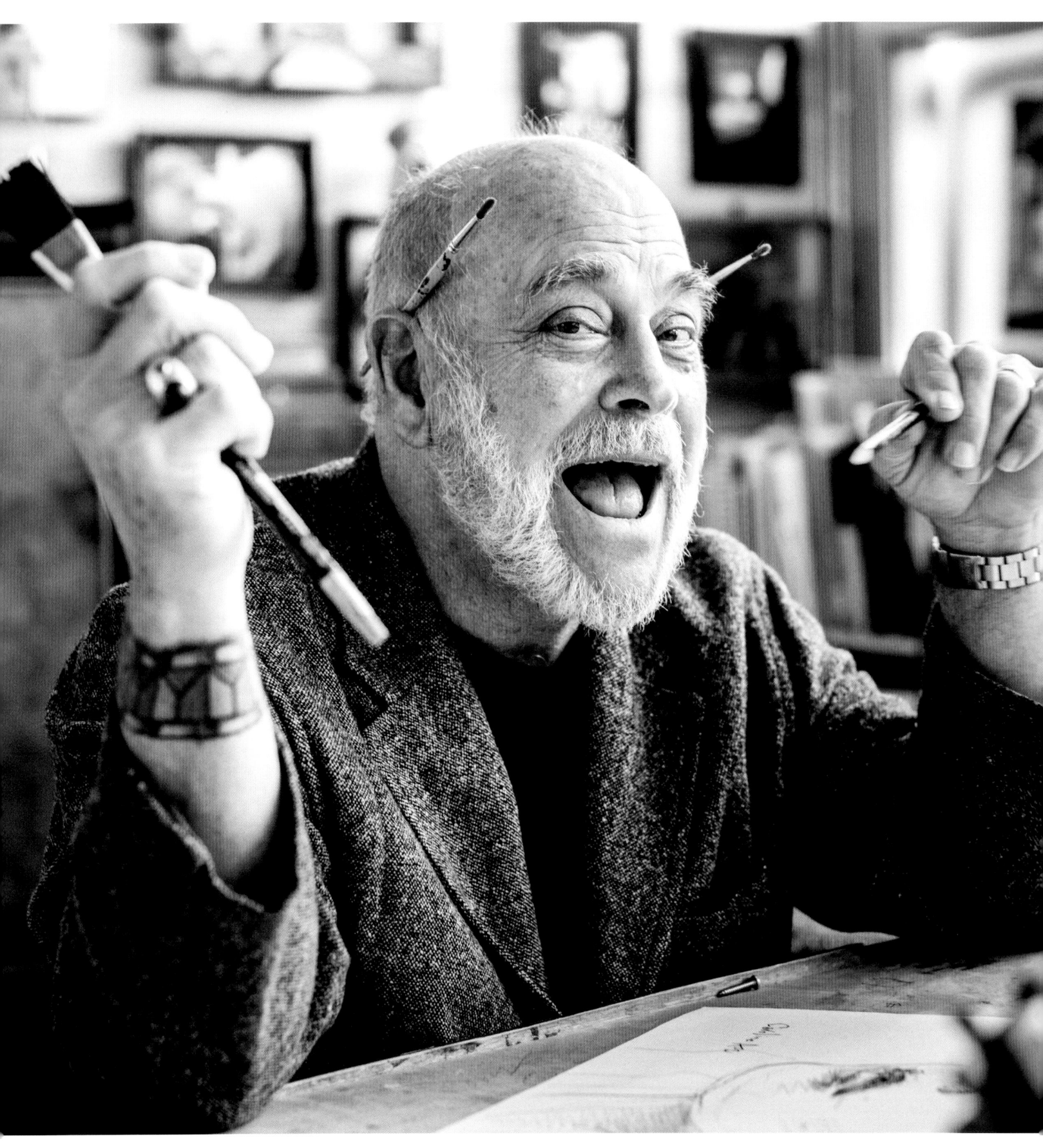

that can only be found by coming to terms with one's true home. Thanks to Troy University, all of those elements come together at the Nall Museum, a space of fantasy, wonder, and incredible art.

In *Alchemy*, a comprehensive 2006 biography-retrospective, the artist's identification with the title is clear. A more contemporary definition of alchemy suggests "an existence and presence of a magical process of transformation, creation and/or a combination of the two." In that sense Nall could easily be known as a present-day alchemist with the magical powers to create beauty in his own world of wonderment. Somewhere along his journey he may even have turned a few pieces of lead into gold. Just maybe, for our purposes, we will give him credit for turning the red clay of his hometown Troy, Alabama, into gold. And finally, Nall may go down in history as one

of the really important stars that fell on Alabama, forever transforming our cultural landscape.

ALBERT B. HEAD is executive director emeritus of the Alabama State Council on the Arts. He retired at the end of 2018 after serving thirty-three years as the agency's director. He is a 1971 graduate of Troy University with a degree in Art History and Aesthetics. He holds a Master of Liberal Arts degree with a concentration on Southern history and literature from Auburn University at Montgomery. He is proud to claim Troy as his hometown.

Biscuit napping after a long day of art directing.

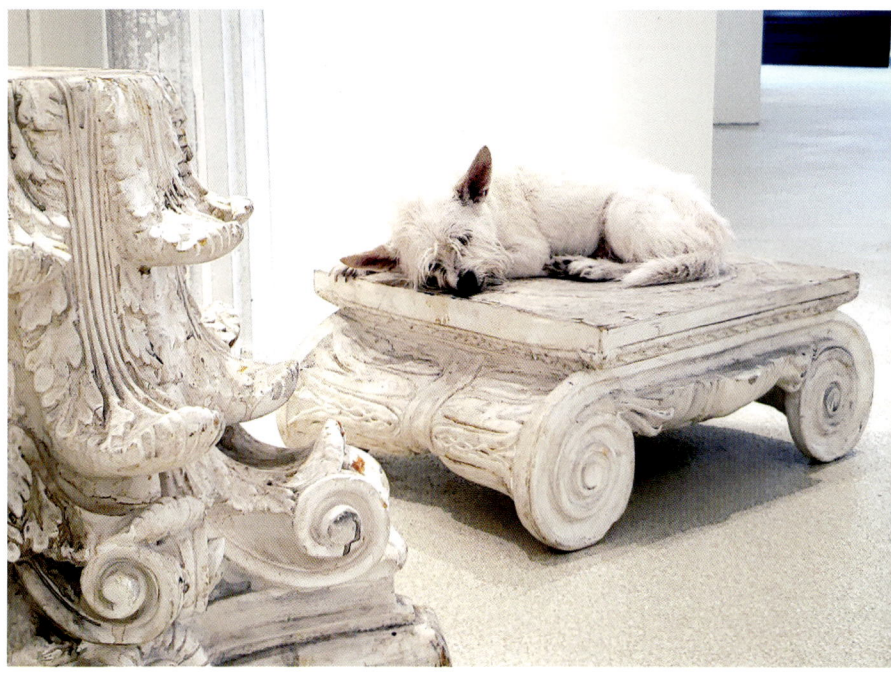

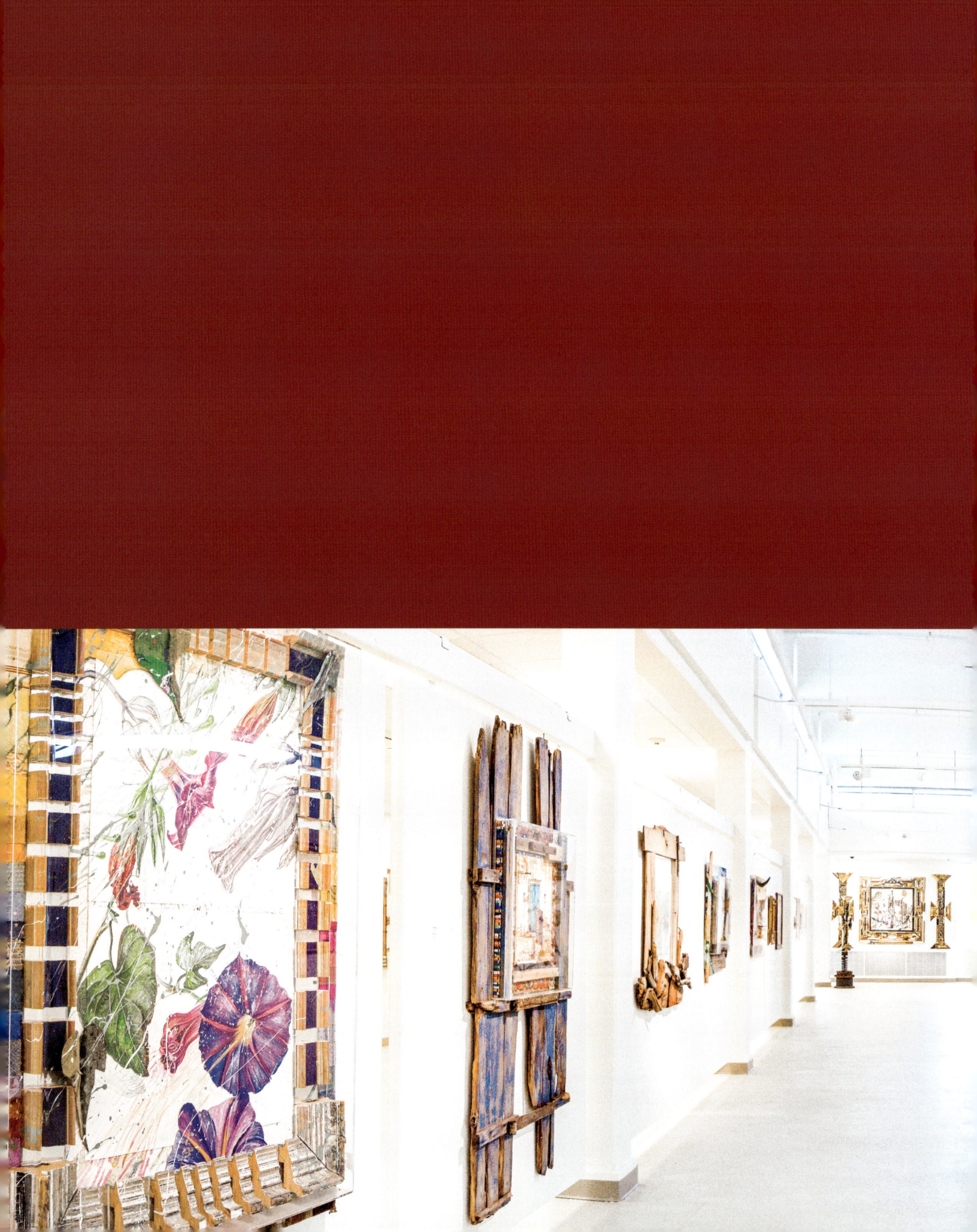

The Collection

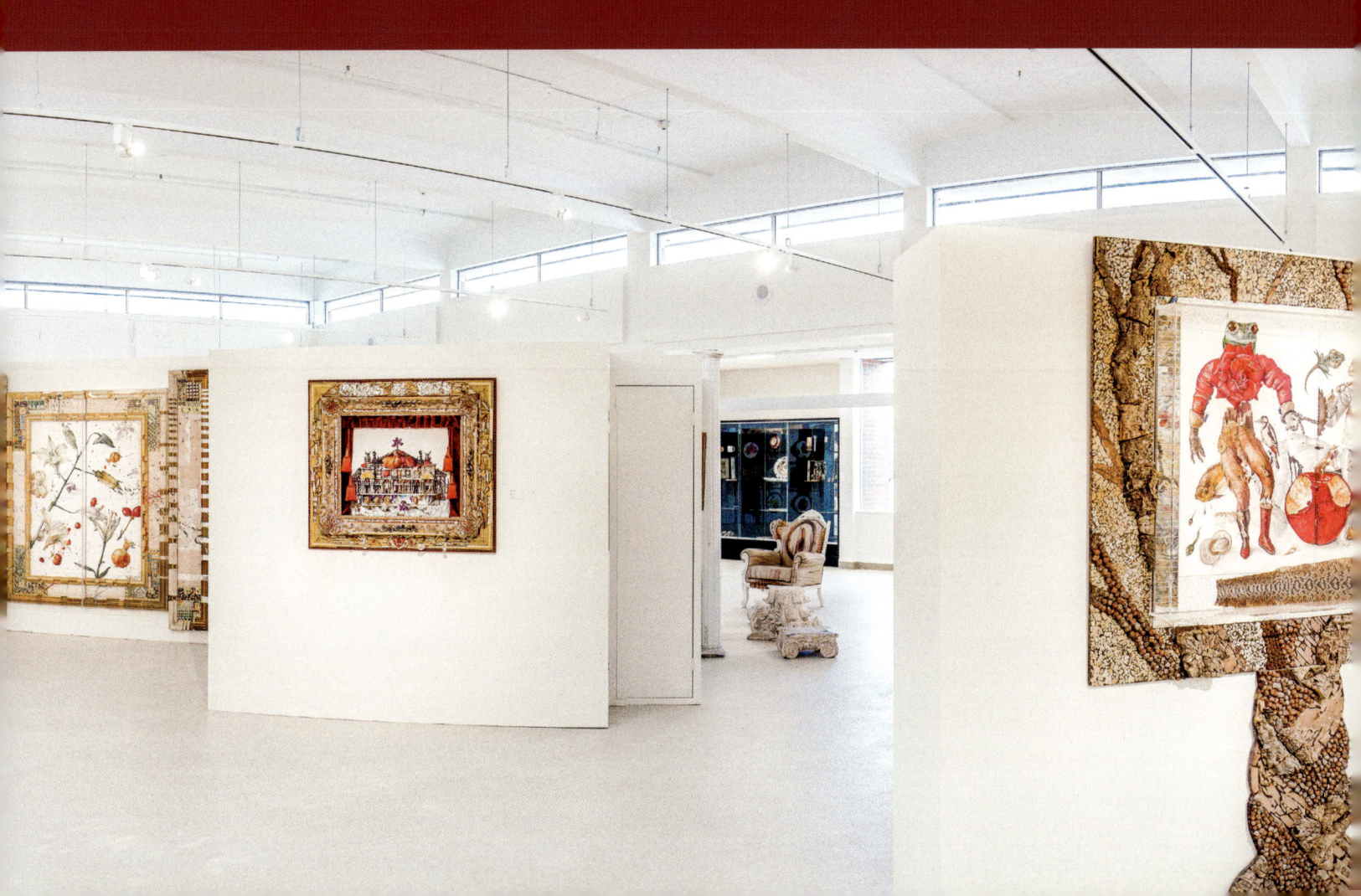

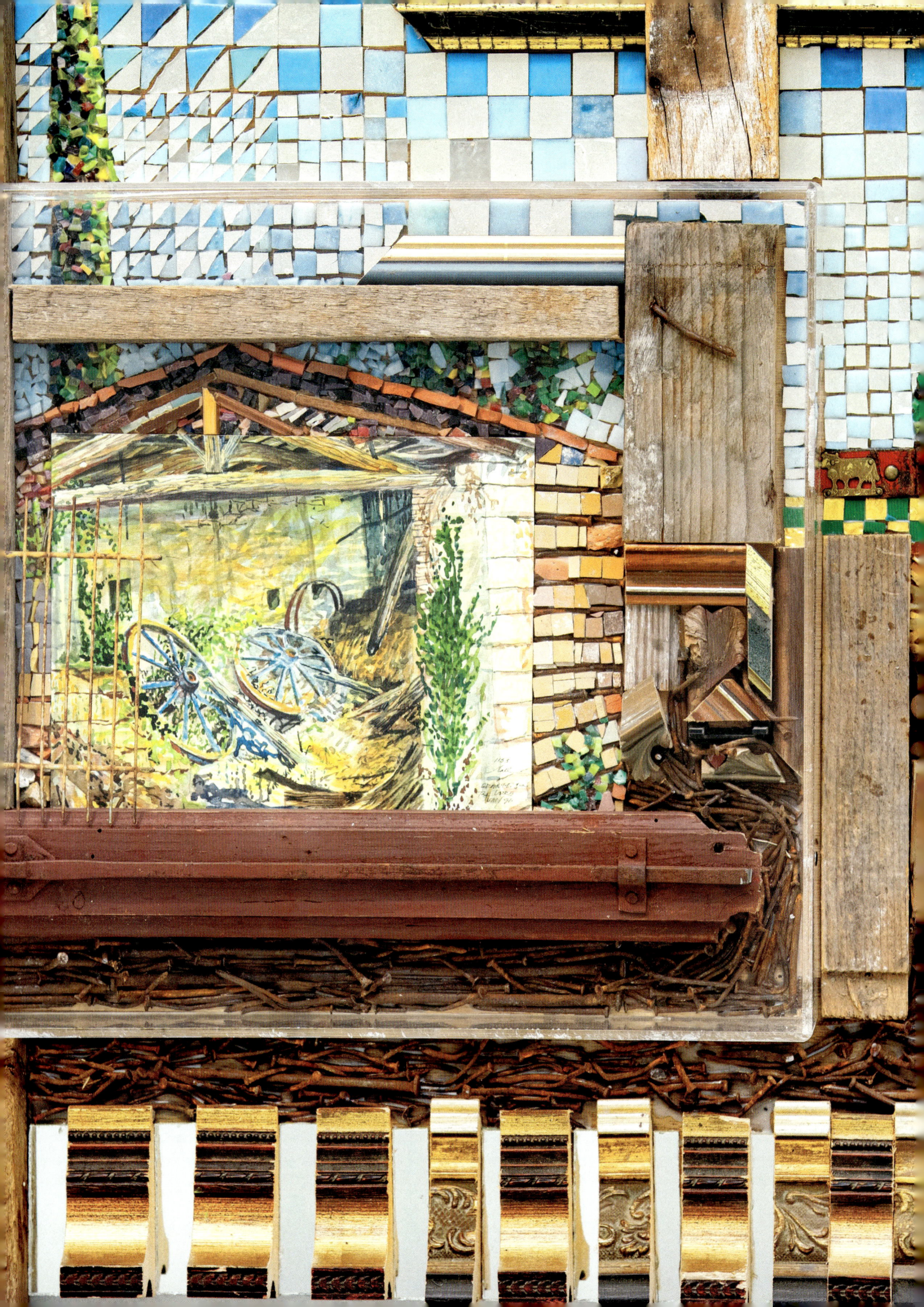

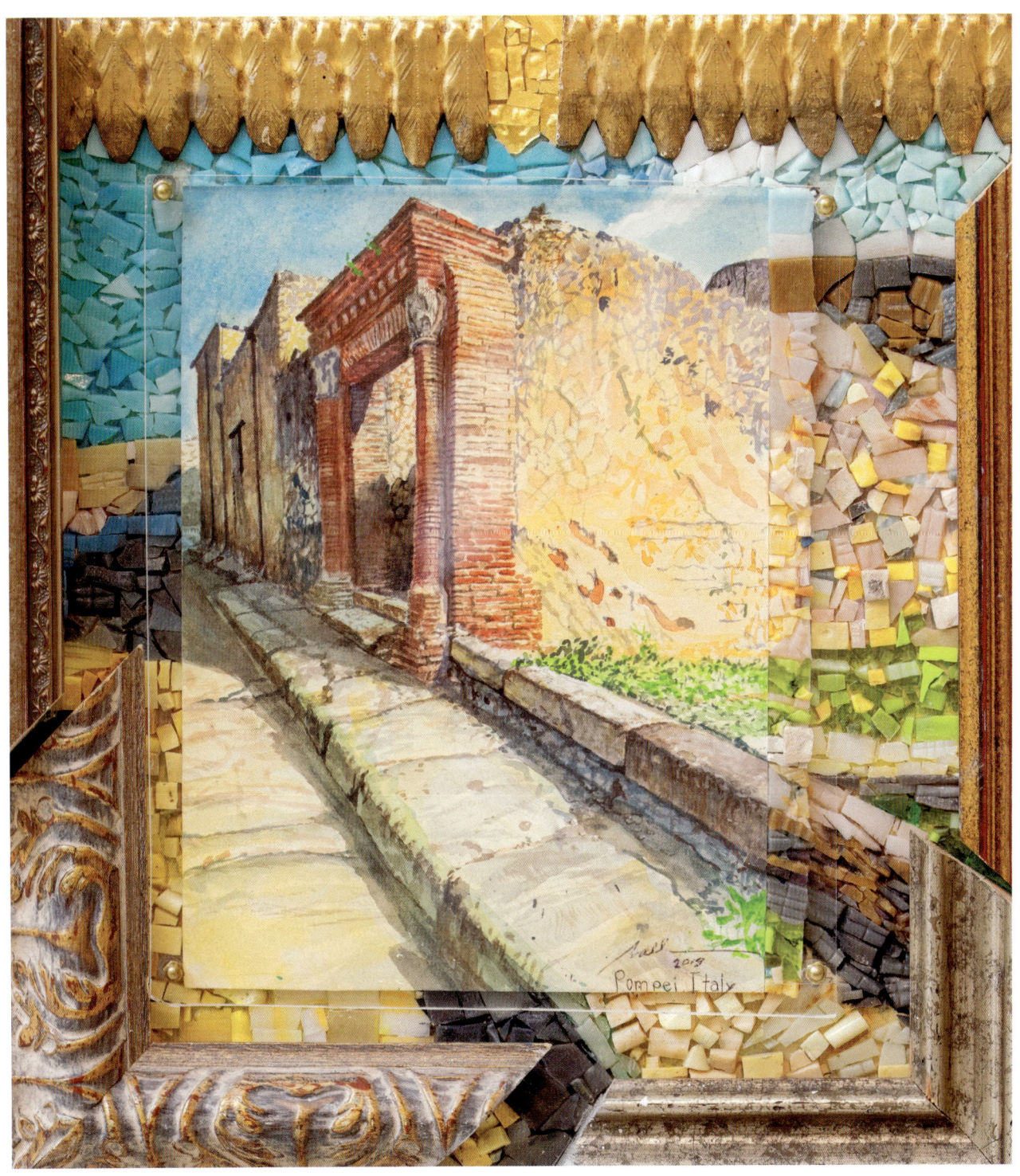

POMPEII II
MIXED MEDIA
18.125" x 16.5"
ca. 2000

GRANGE DANS LA GERS
MIXED MEDIA
26.5" x 32"
1996–2007

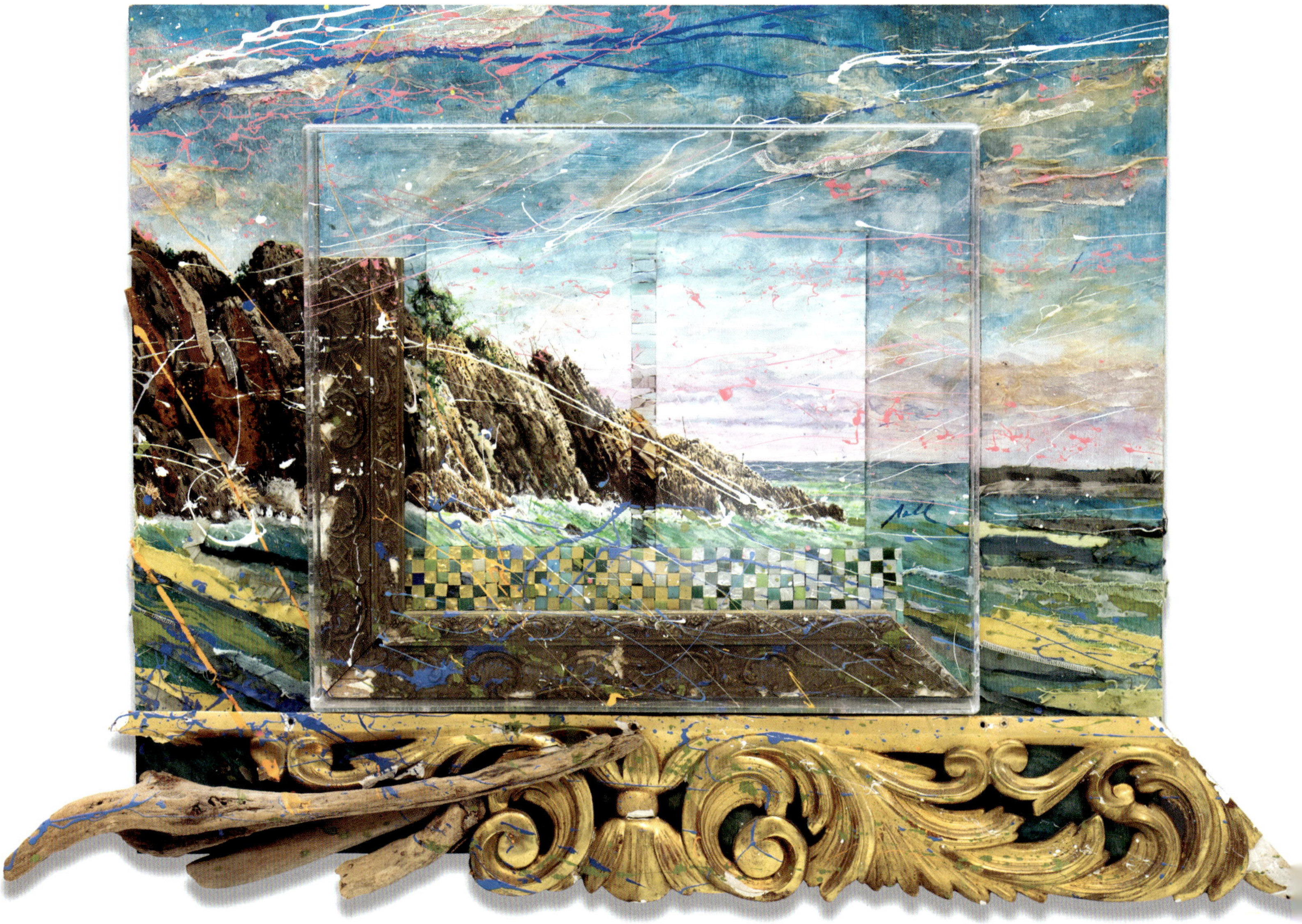

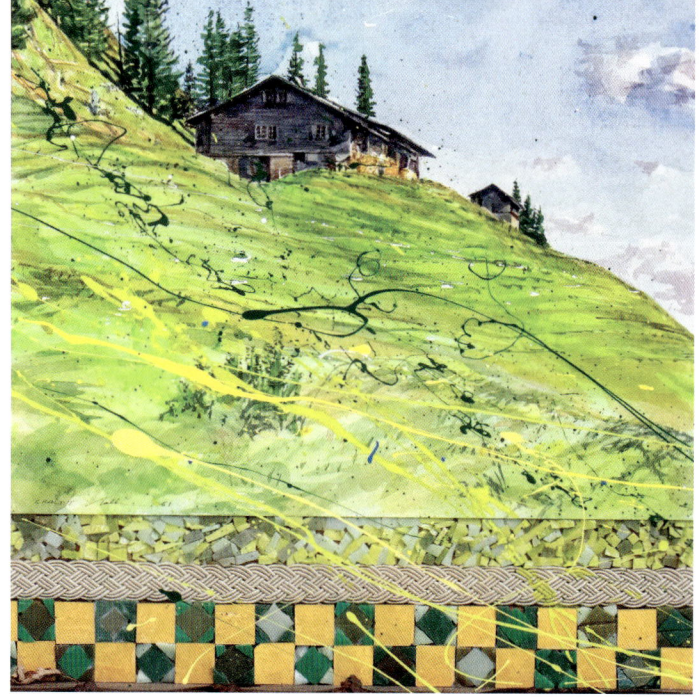

ABOVE:
RABAU CAPAU
MIXED MEDIA
29" X 42.5"
ca. 2000

LEFT:
**CHALET IN
SWITZERLAND**
MIXED MEDIA
40" X 35"
ca. 2000

OPPOSITE PAGE:
POMPEII
MIXED MEDIA
23.5" X 19.5"
ca. 2000

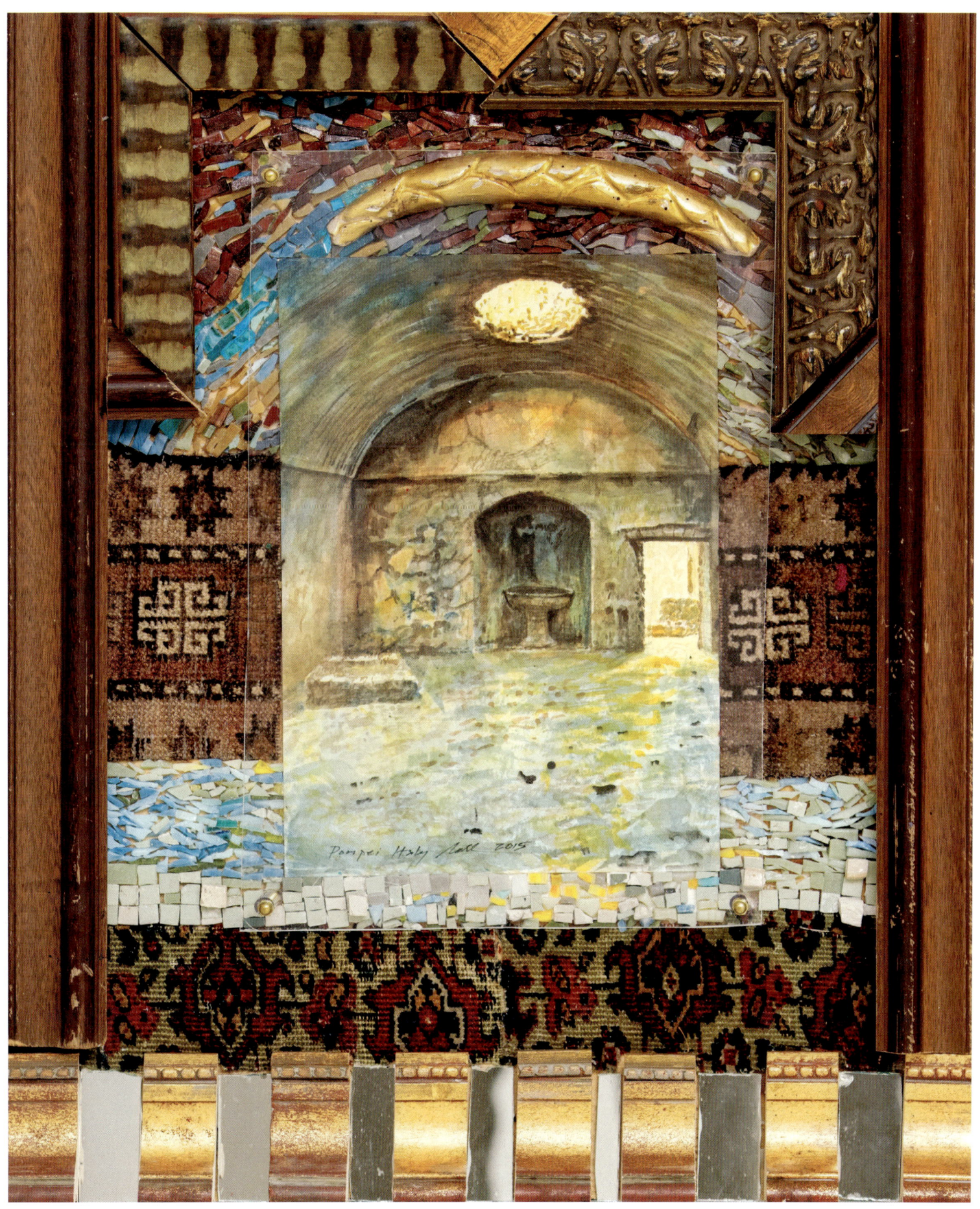

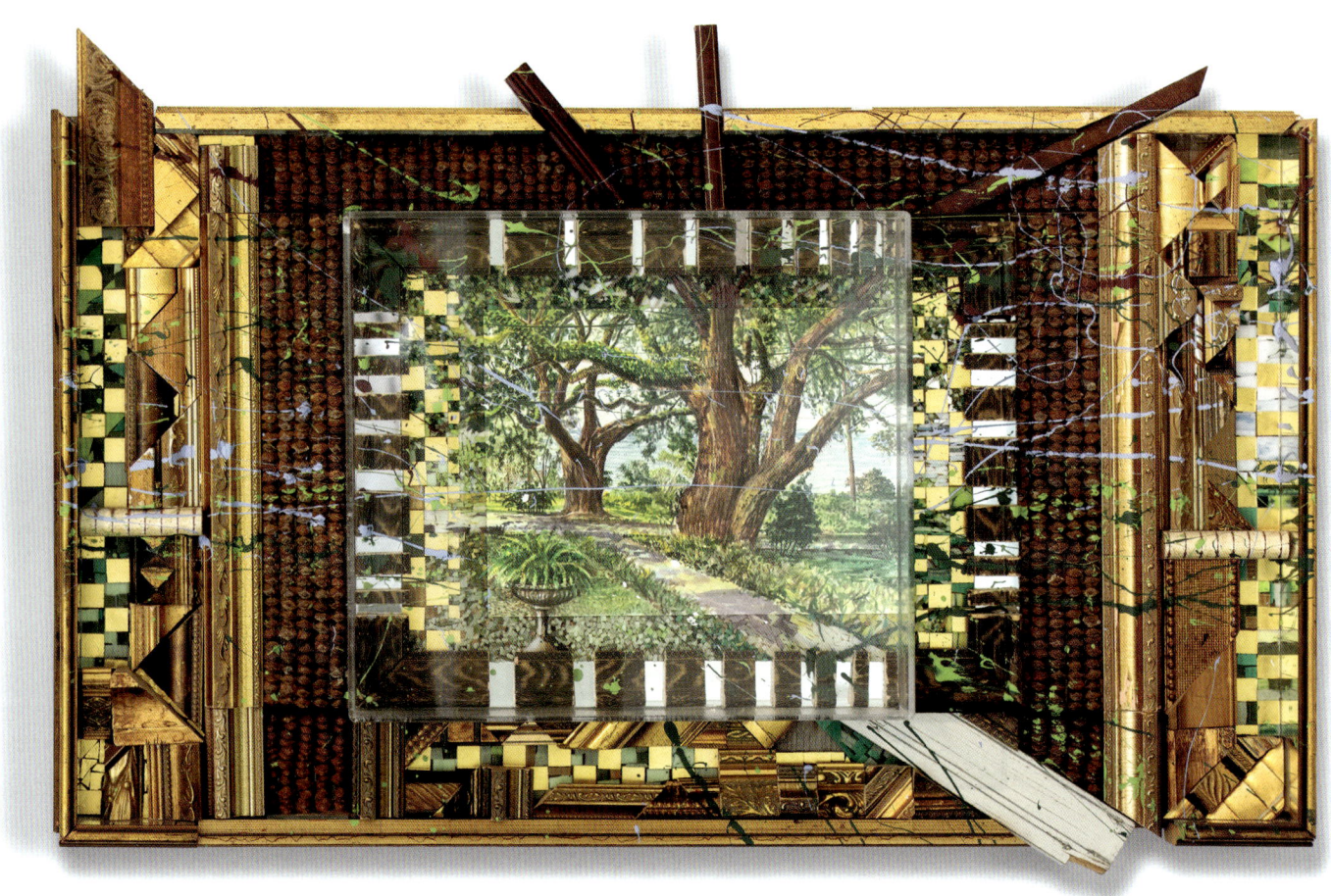

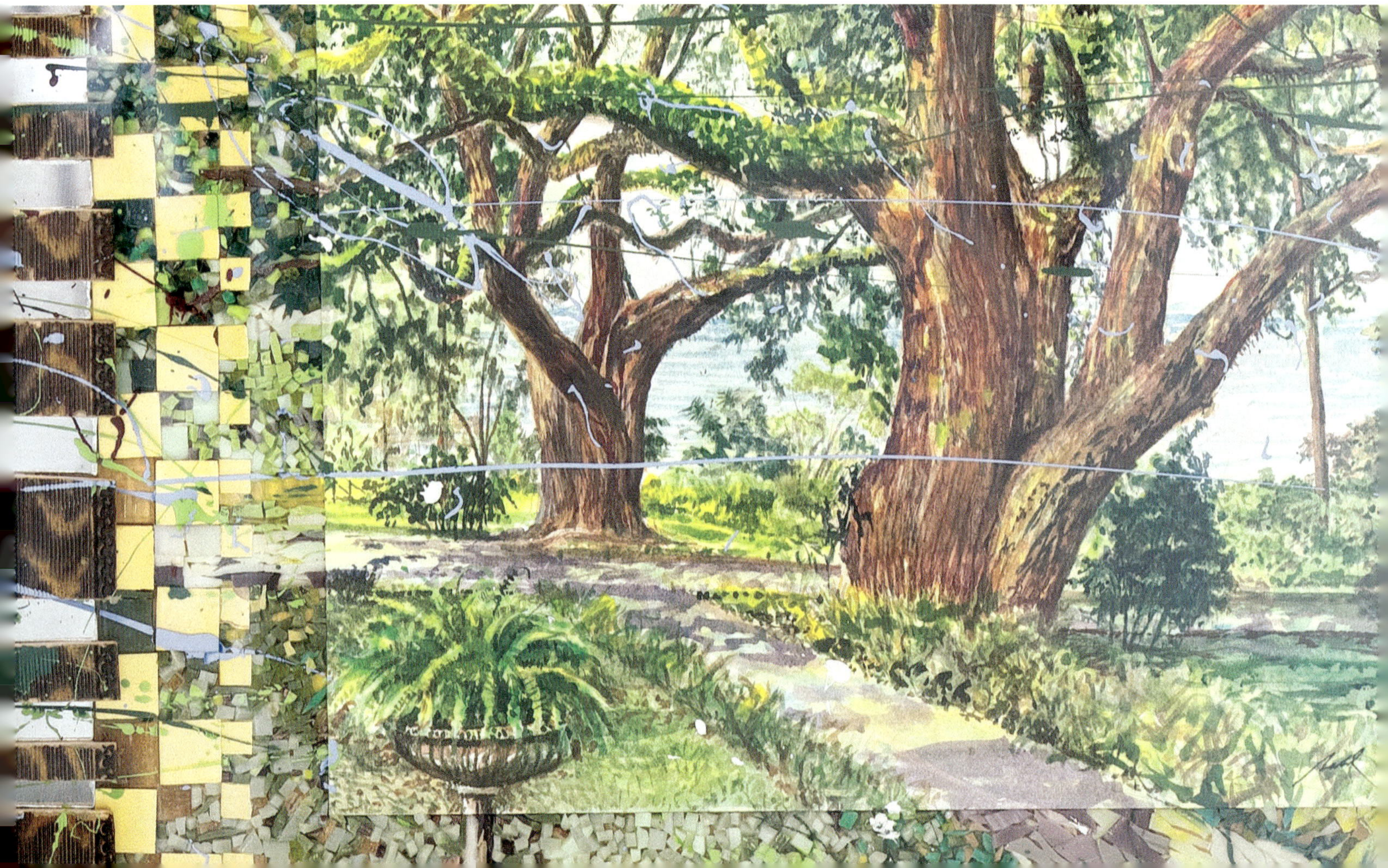

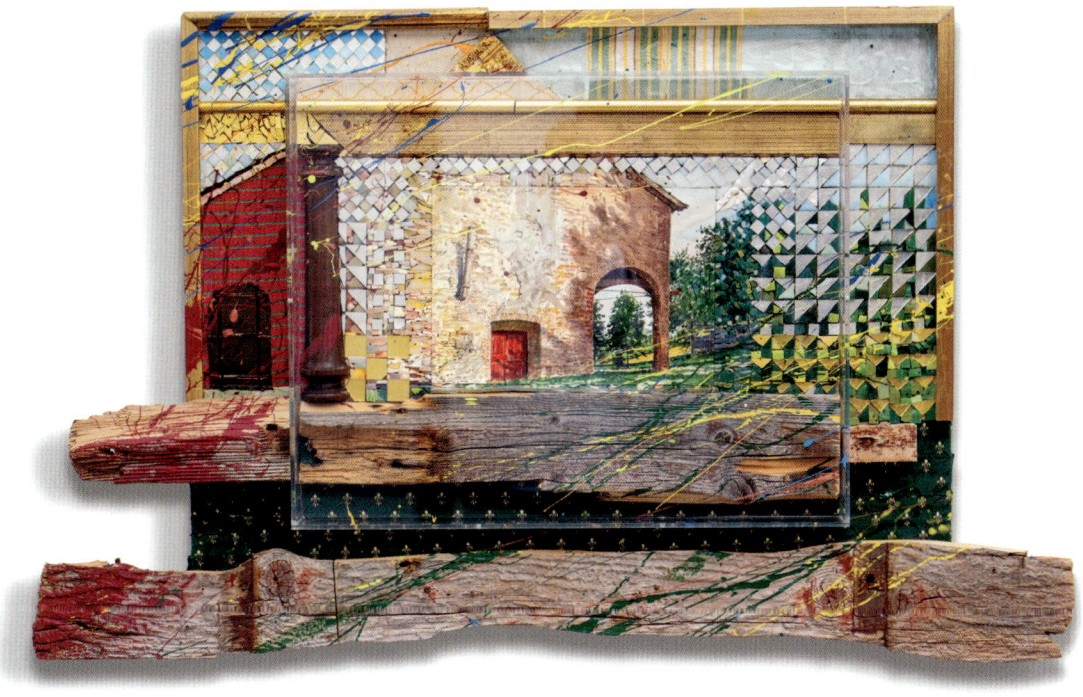

OPPOSITE PAGE:
**204 Bay View Oaks
Fairhope, Alabama**
Mixed Media
29" x 43"
2004

OPPOSITE PAGE BOTTOM:
204 Bay View Oaks
detail

LEFT:
**Red Door at the
Barchessa**
Mixed Media
22" x 37.5"
2004

BOTTOM:
**Red Door at the
Barchessa**
detail

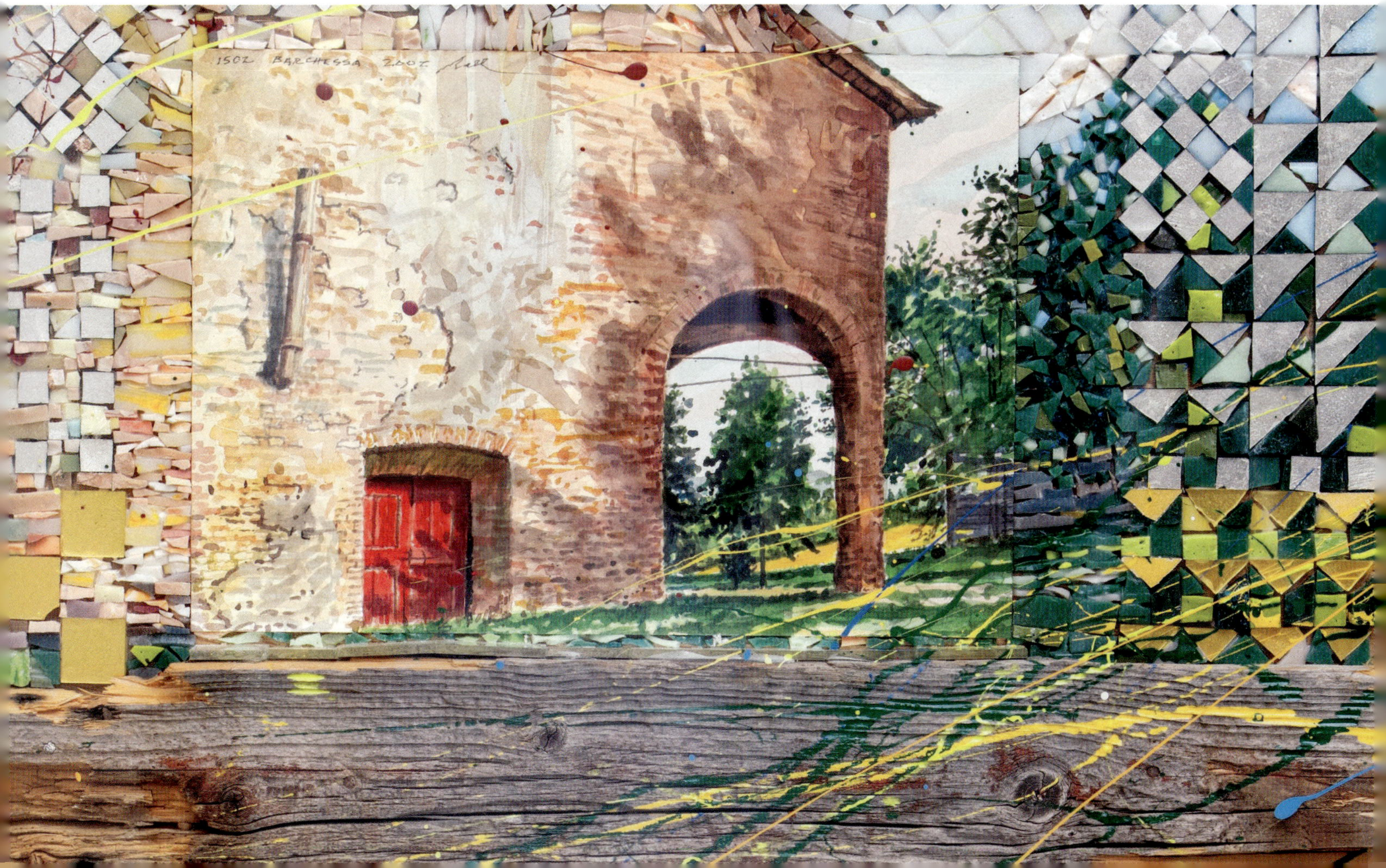

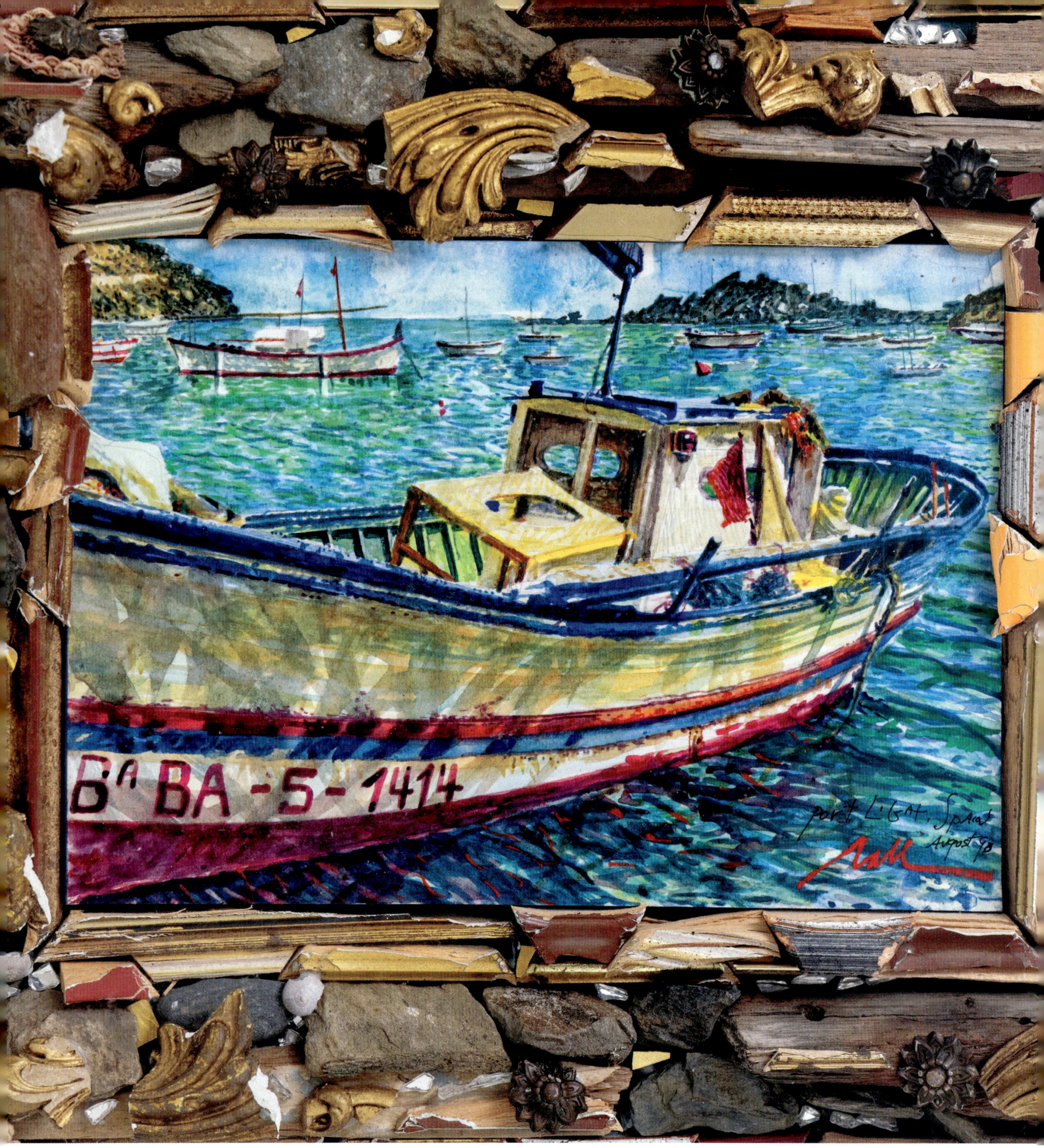

Port Ligat, Spain
Mixed Media
11.5" x 14"
1990

OPPOSITE PAGE:
Adam, Eve and Darwin
Mixed Media
88" x 63"
2009

VIDEO

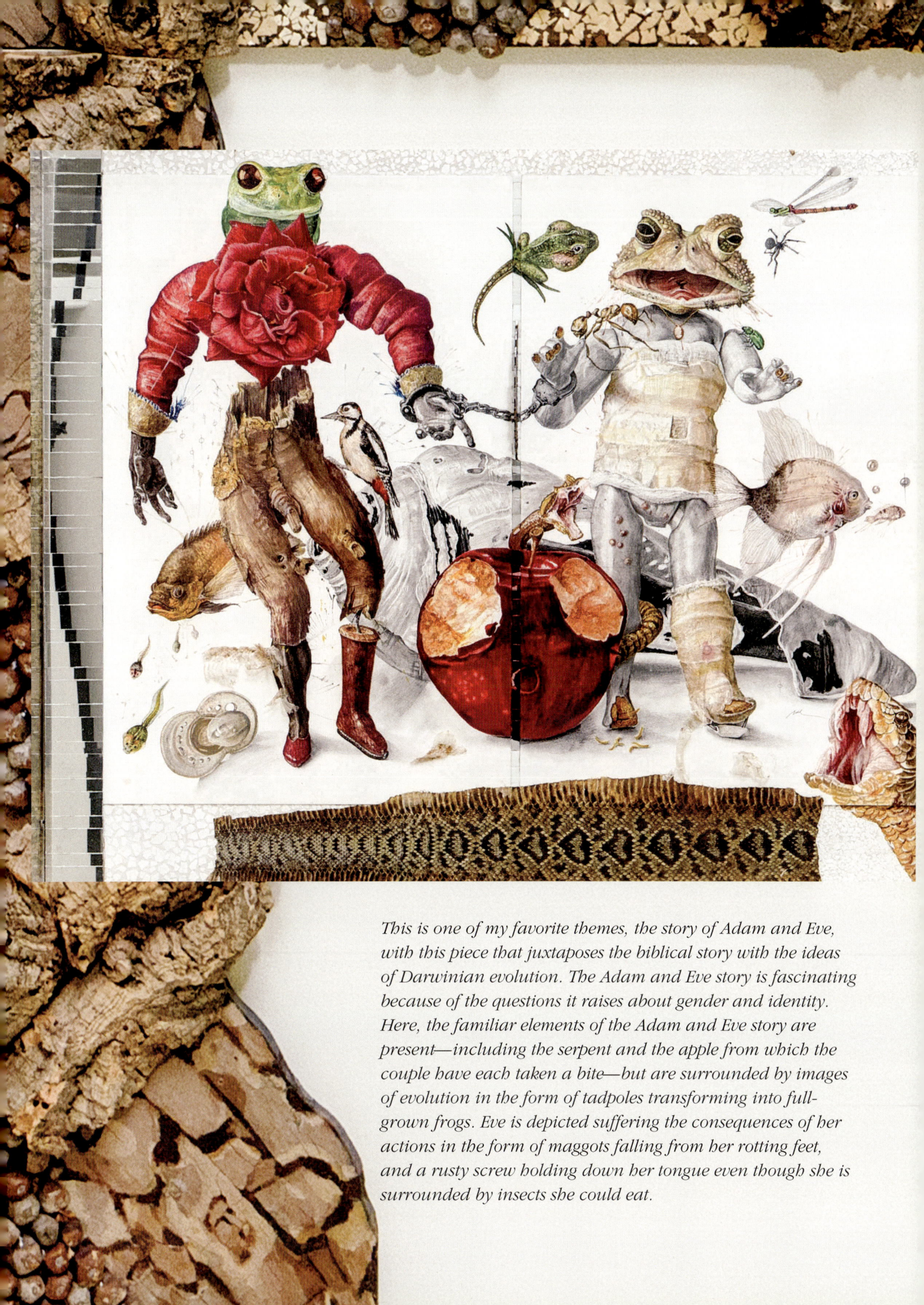

This is one of my favorite themes, the story of Adam and Eve, with this piece that juxtaposes the biblical story with the ideas of Darwinian evolution. The Adam and Eve story is fascinating because of the questions it raises about gender and identity. Here, the familiar elements of the Adam and Eve story are present—including the serpent and the apple from which the couple have each taken a bite—but are surrounded by images of evolution in the form of tadpoles transforming into full-grown frogs. Eve is depicted suffering the consequences of her actions in the form of maggots falling from her rotting feet, and a rusty screw holding down her tongue even though she is surrounded by insects she could eat.

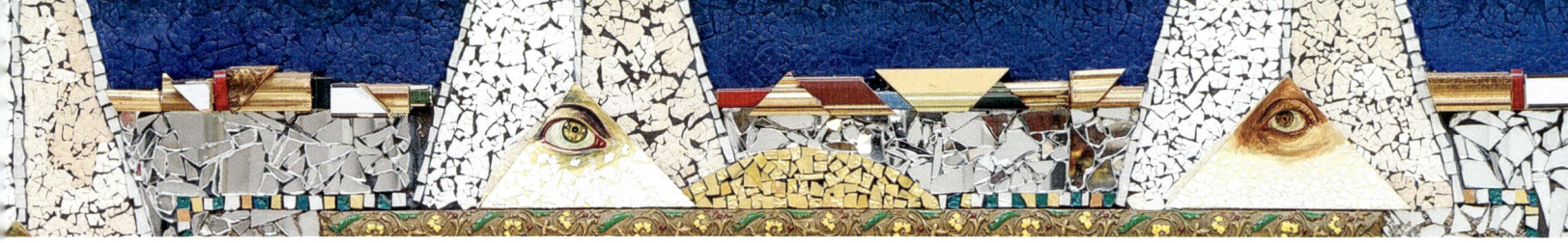

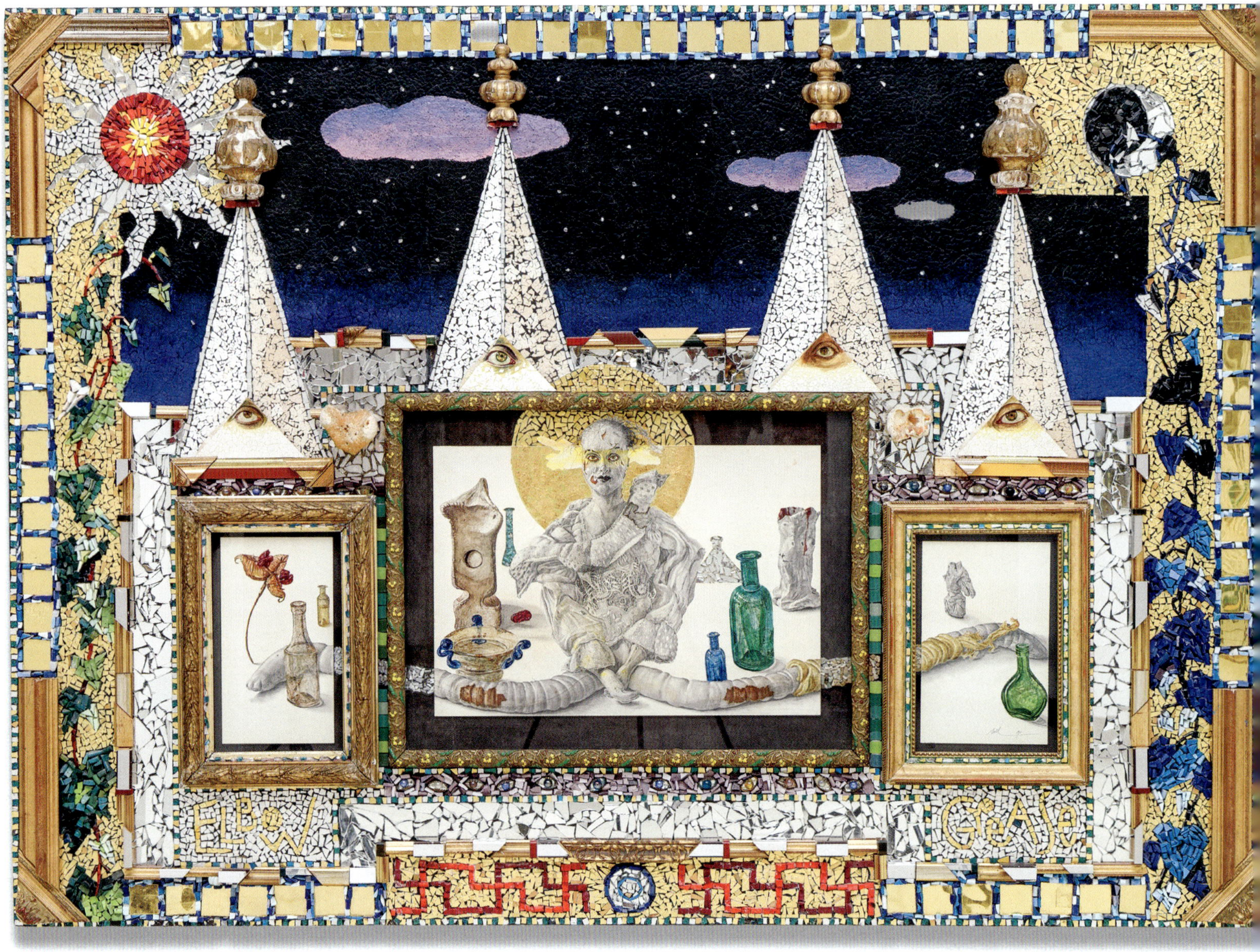

Elbow Grease
Mixed Media
59" x 83"
1990

The four eyes inside the spires are inspired by the iconography of the Freemasons, while the sun, moon, and ivy evoke Catholic symbolism. The title alludes to both work ethic and artistic generosity.

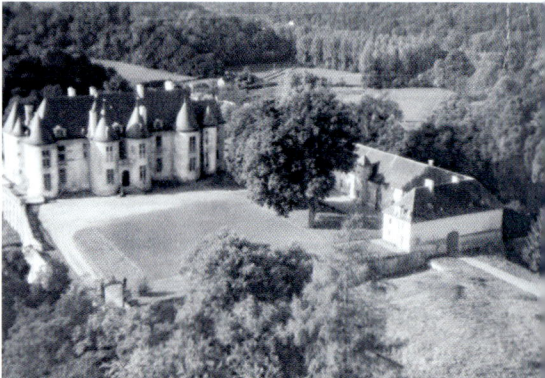

The composition was inspired by a chateau near Compiègne, France, where Nall spent many Christmases and New Years in the company of a local count and countess.

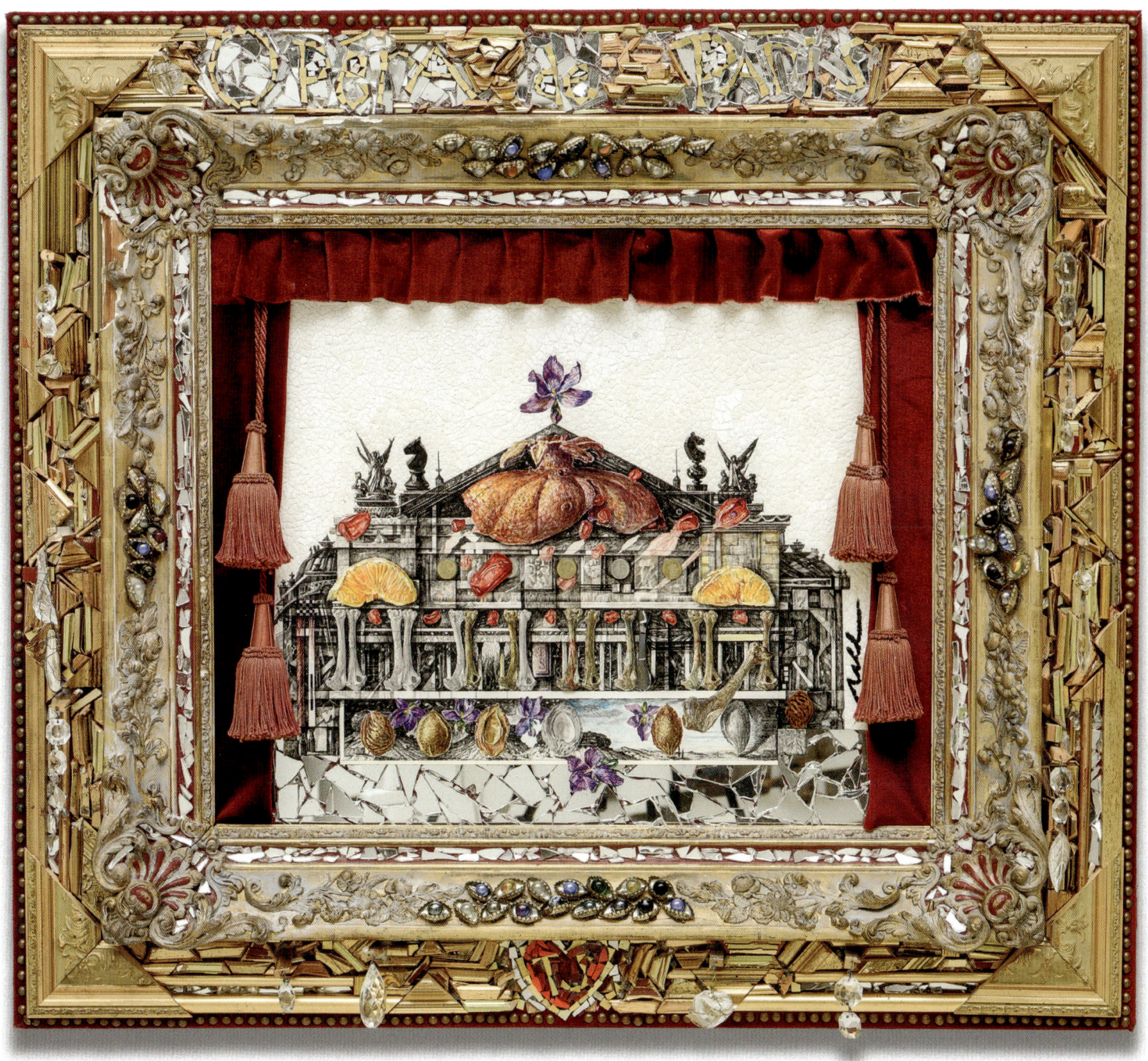

OPERA DE PARIS
MIXED MEDIA
44" X 39"
1991

I was commissioned by former French President, then Mayor of Paris, Jacques Chirac to create a series of paintings for the Paris guest guide capturing famous architectural landmarks from the city, including this one featuring the Opera of Paris. Shortly before receiving the commission, I had spent time in Calcutta volunteering with Mother Teresa and was struck by the stark contrast between the poverty I witnessed and the wealth in Paris. This piece evokes the opulence of France and Europe through imagery of luxurious fruits, including pomegranate seeds, orange slices, and peach pits. Columns on the building are depicted as chicken bones, which were inspired by the bones my mother used to feed to stray dogs while I was growing up in Troy.

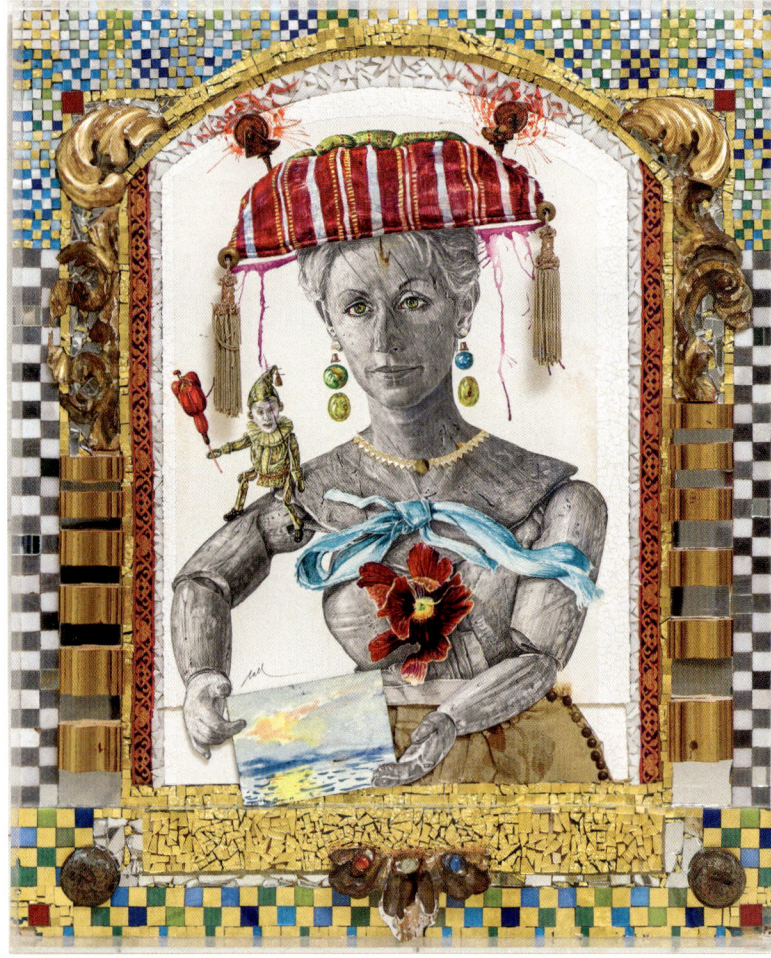

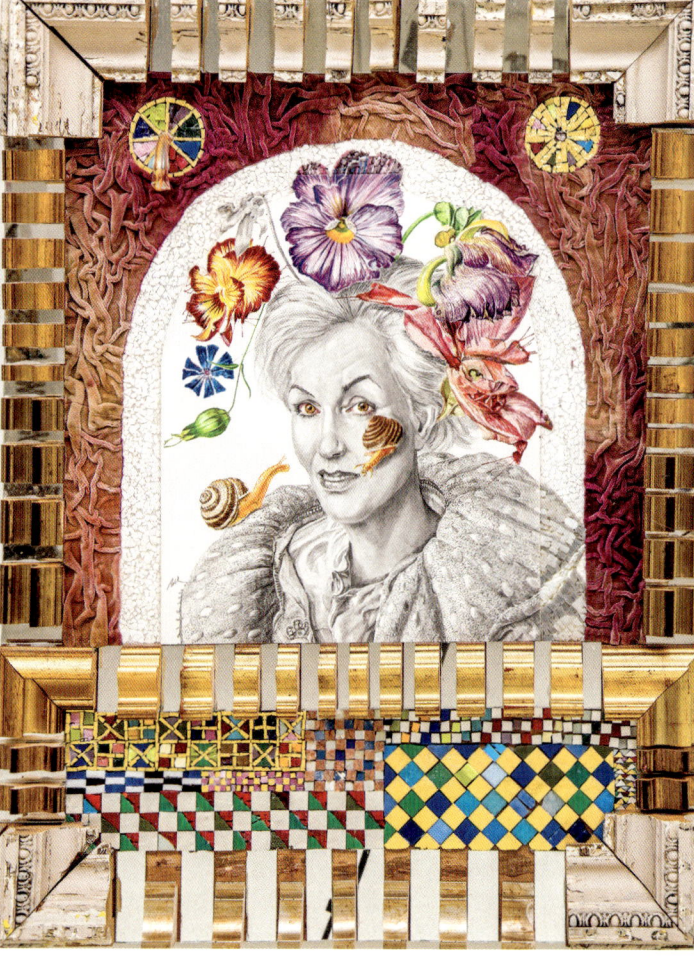

Barbara Tober
Mixed Media
38" x 29"

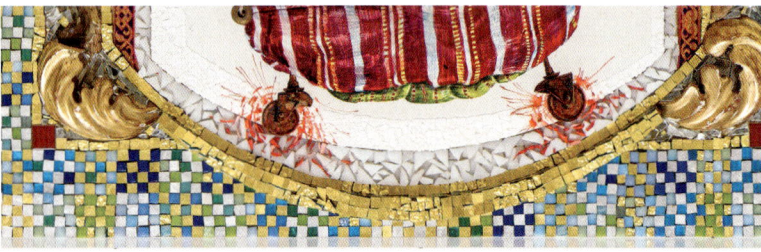

The Collectioneuse Sylvie Autef
Mixed Media
38" x 32"
2007

Sylvie Autef is a Parisian art collector and gallerist with whom I worked for many years. In this portrait, she is depicted with distinctive headwear reminiscent of a matador because of her remarkable ability to outmaneuver both clients and artists. I painted myself into the piece as a conscience riding on her shoulder, ever reminding Sylvie that "the artists have to be paid first."

The frame incorporates a variety of collected items, included sari fabric from India, Venetian gold, and pieces from an eighteenth-century frame.

Androgen
Mixed Media
39" x 31.5"
1994

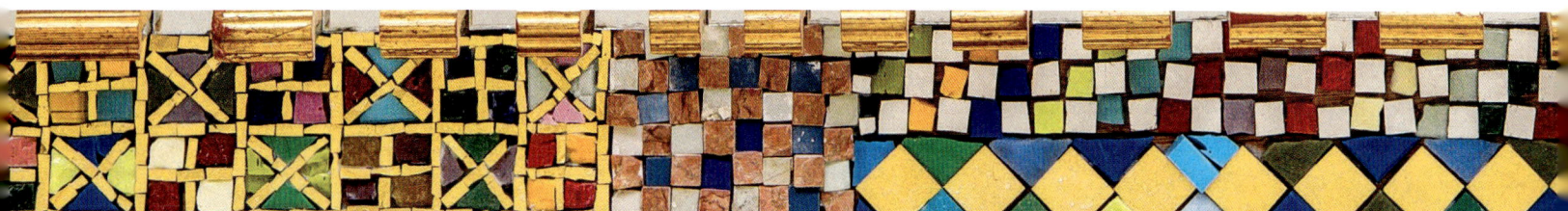

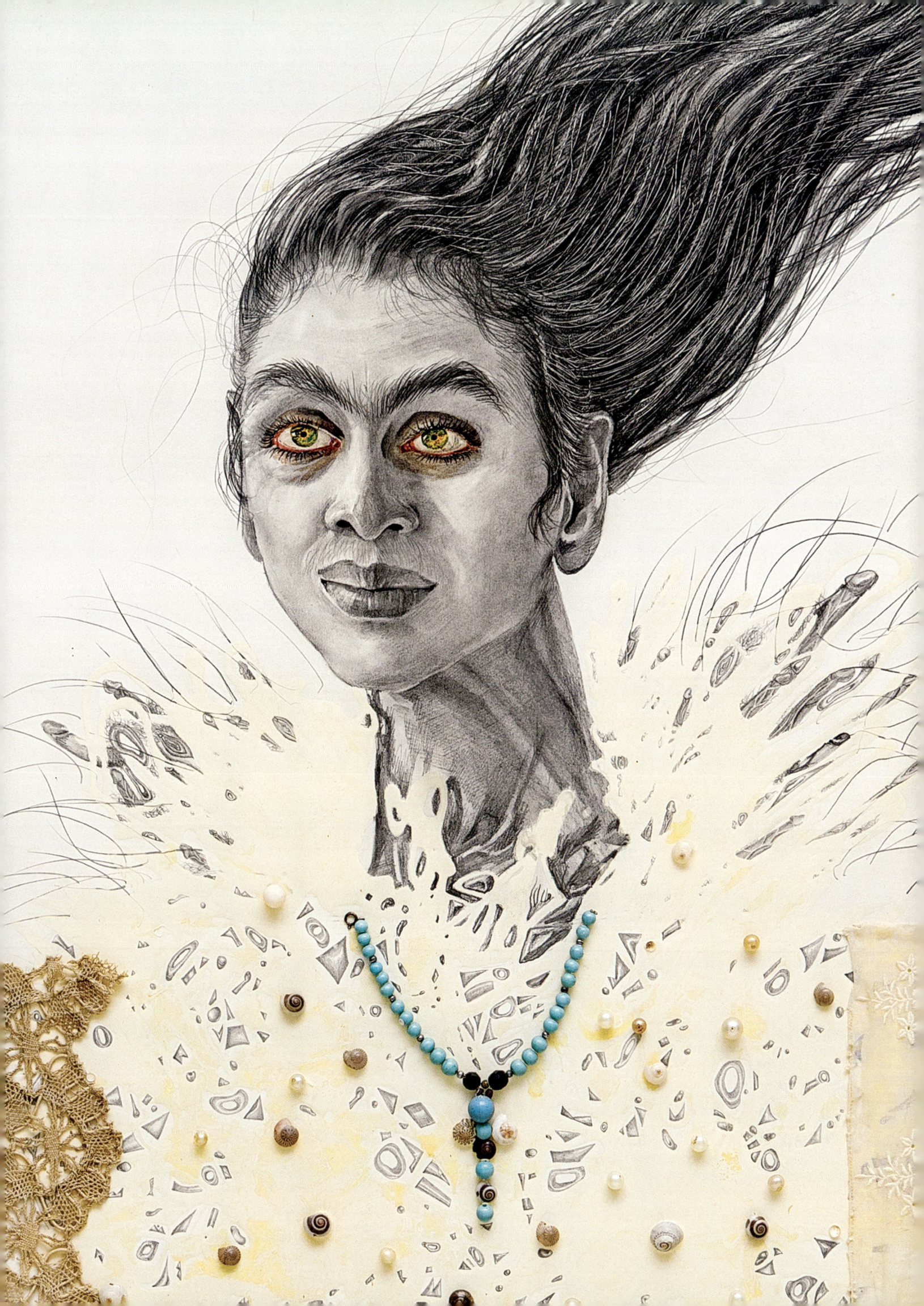

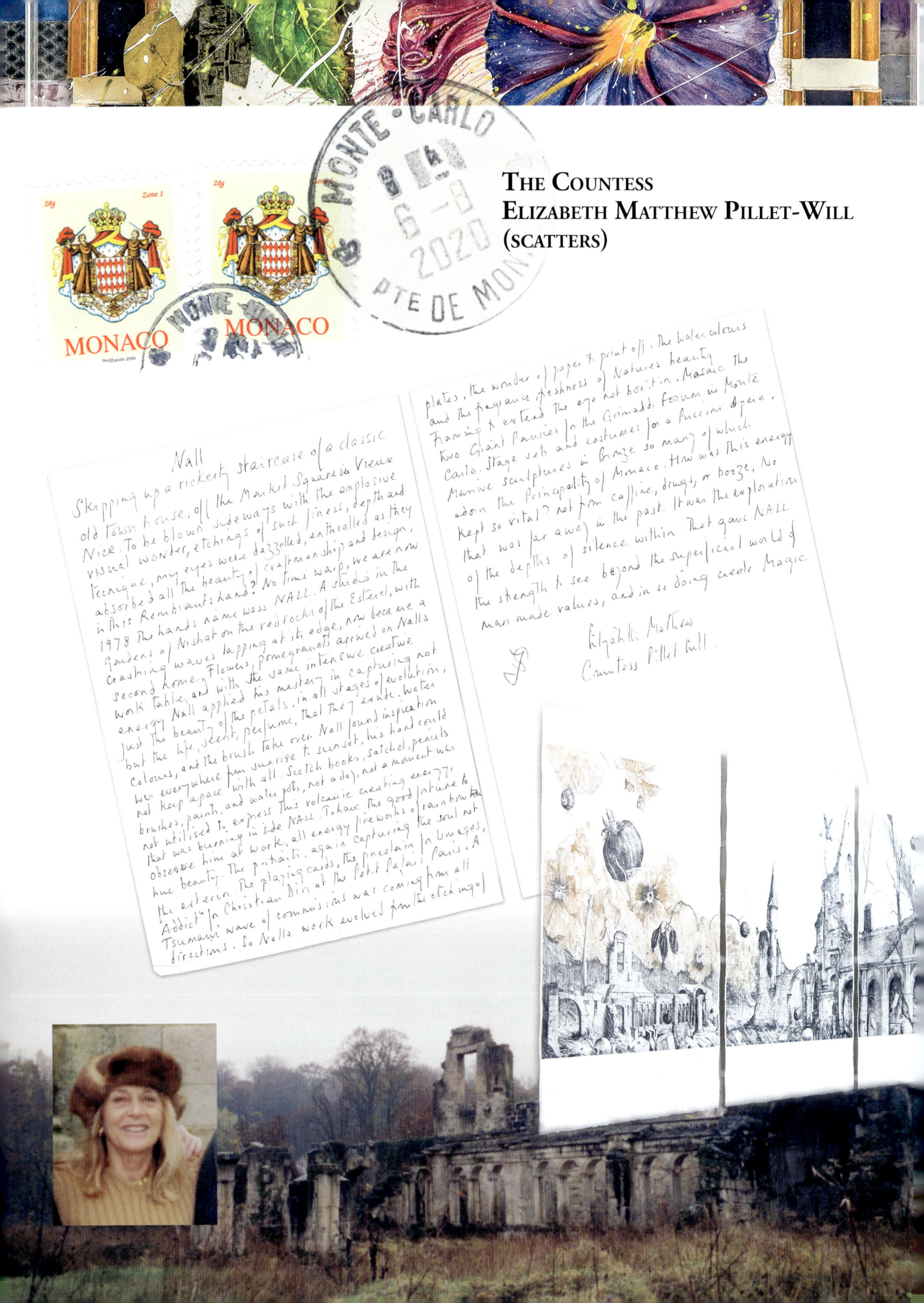

The Countess
Elizabeth Matthew Pillet-Will
(scatters)

Nall

Skipping up a rickety staircase of a classic old town house, off the Market Square in Vieux Nice. To be blown sideways with the explosive visual wonder, etchings of such fineness, depth and technique, my eyes were dazzelled, enthralled as they absorbed all the beauty of craftmanship and design, in this Rembrants hand? No time warp, we are now in 1978 The hands name wass NALL. A studio in the Gardens of Nishat on the red rocks of the Esterel, with crashing waves lapping at its edge, now became a second home. Flowers, pomegranets arrived on Nalls work tables, and with the same intensive creative energy Nall applied his mastery in capturing not just the beauty of the petals, in all stages of evolution, but the life, scent, perfume, that they exude. Water colours, and the brush take over. Nall found inspiration everywhere from sunrise to sunset, his hand could not keep apace with all. Scetch books, satchel, pencils brushes, paints, and water pots, not a day, not a moment was not utilised to express this volcanic creating energy' that was burning inside NALL. To have the good fortune to observe him at work, all energy fireworks of rainbow hue beauty. The portraits, again capturing the soul not the exterior. The playing cards, the porcelain for Limoges, Addict' for Christian Dior at the Petit Palais Paris. A Tsunami wave of commisions was coming him all directions. So Nalls work evolved from the etching of

plates, the wonder of paper & print off. The water colours and the fragrance freshness of Natures beauty. Framing & extend the eye not box it in. Mosaic. The two Giant Pansies for the Grimaldi forum in Monte Carlo. Stage sets and costumes for a Puccini Opera. Massive sculptures in Bronze so many of which adorn the Principality of Monaco. How was this energy kept so vital? not from caffine, drugs, or booze. No that was far away in the past. It was the exploration of the depths of silence within. That gave NALL the strength to see beyond the superficial world of man made values, and in so doing create Magic

Elizabeth Mathew
Countess Pillet Will.

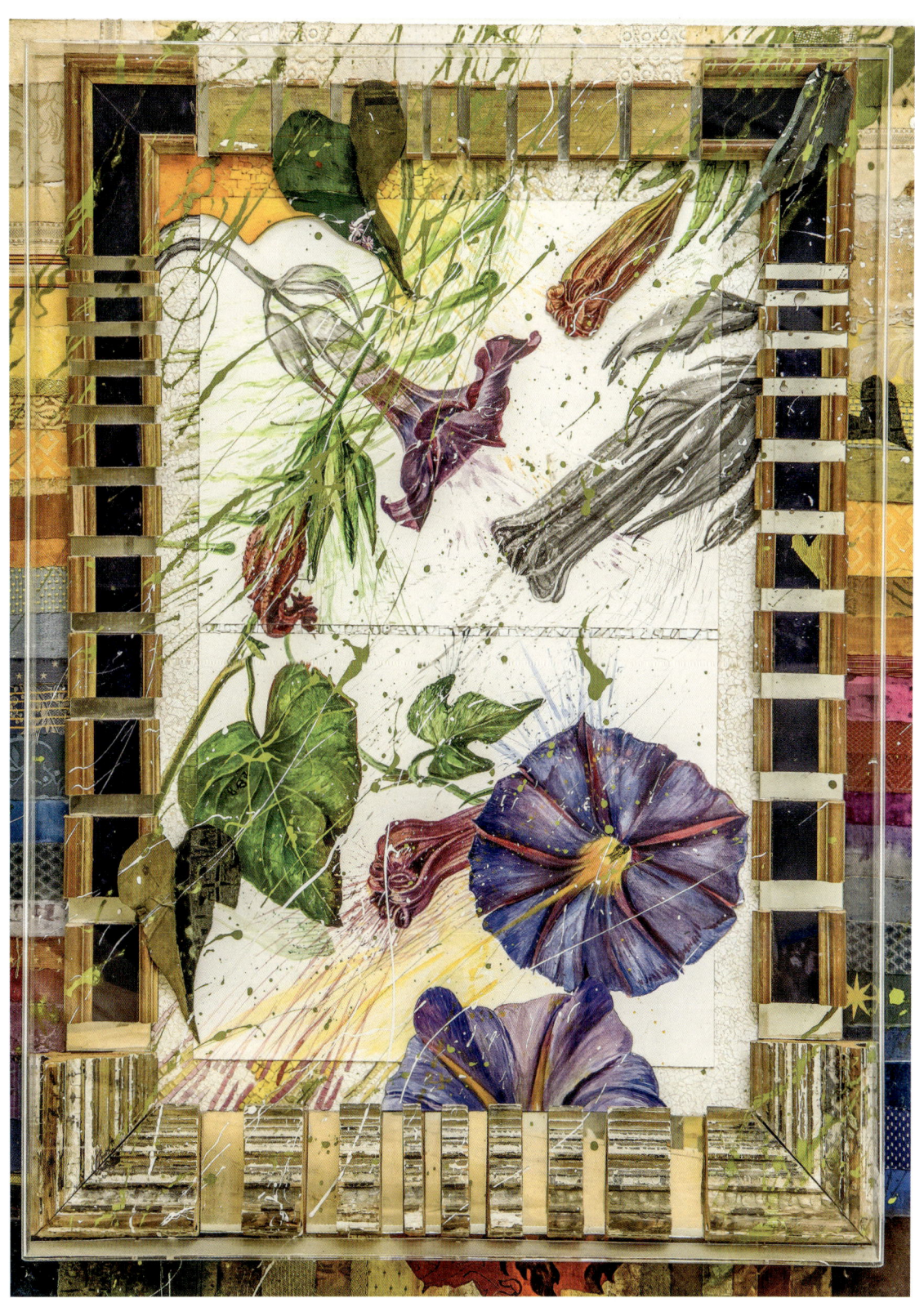

TOVE'S MORNING GLORY
Mixed Media
38" x 33"
2007

One of my old friends had a home in the south of France. I would often walk through the woods around her estate and was struck by the beauty of her morning glory flowers. The trumpet shape of the flowers symbolizes the symphony of life in the forest. The painting depicts the morning glory in various stages of life, from a bud, to open flower, and in death.

Also known as "Homage to Princess Grace of Monaco," this piece is a tribute to my dual life in Europe and Alabama. For many years I lived and worked in Monaco, while also frequently traveling back home to Alabama to show my work in galleries throughout the state. This painting was meant as a tribute to both of my homes, with the red and white of the orchid and pomegranate seeds evoking the colors of the Monaco and Alabama flags. The piece incorporates other items collected from my life and travels, including my grandmother's lace and crochet, egg shell from Mexico, and souvenirs from Istanbul and Tunisia.

ALABAMA RENAISSANCE
MIXED MEDIA
88" x 96"
2005

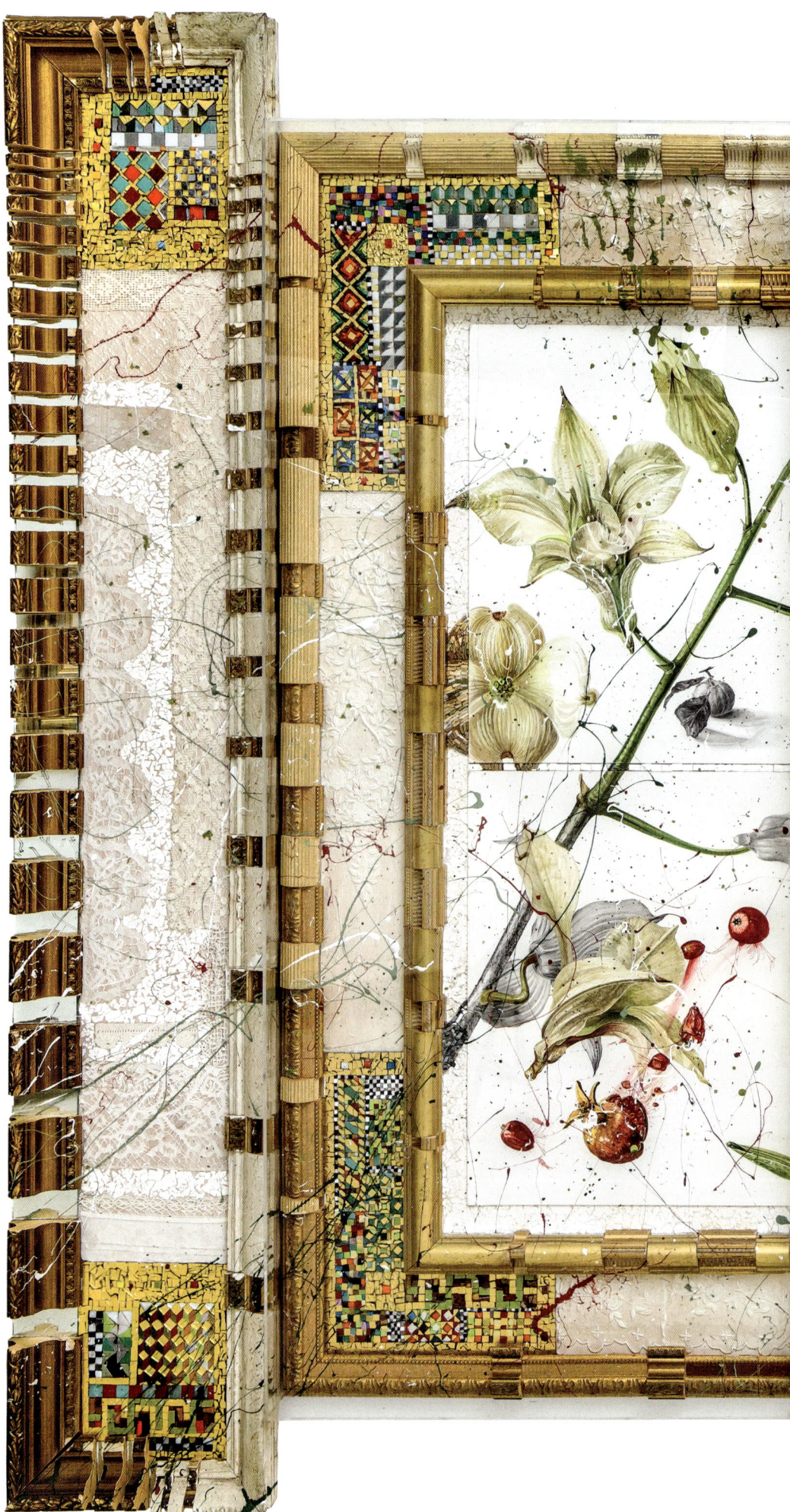

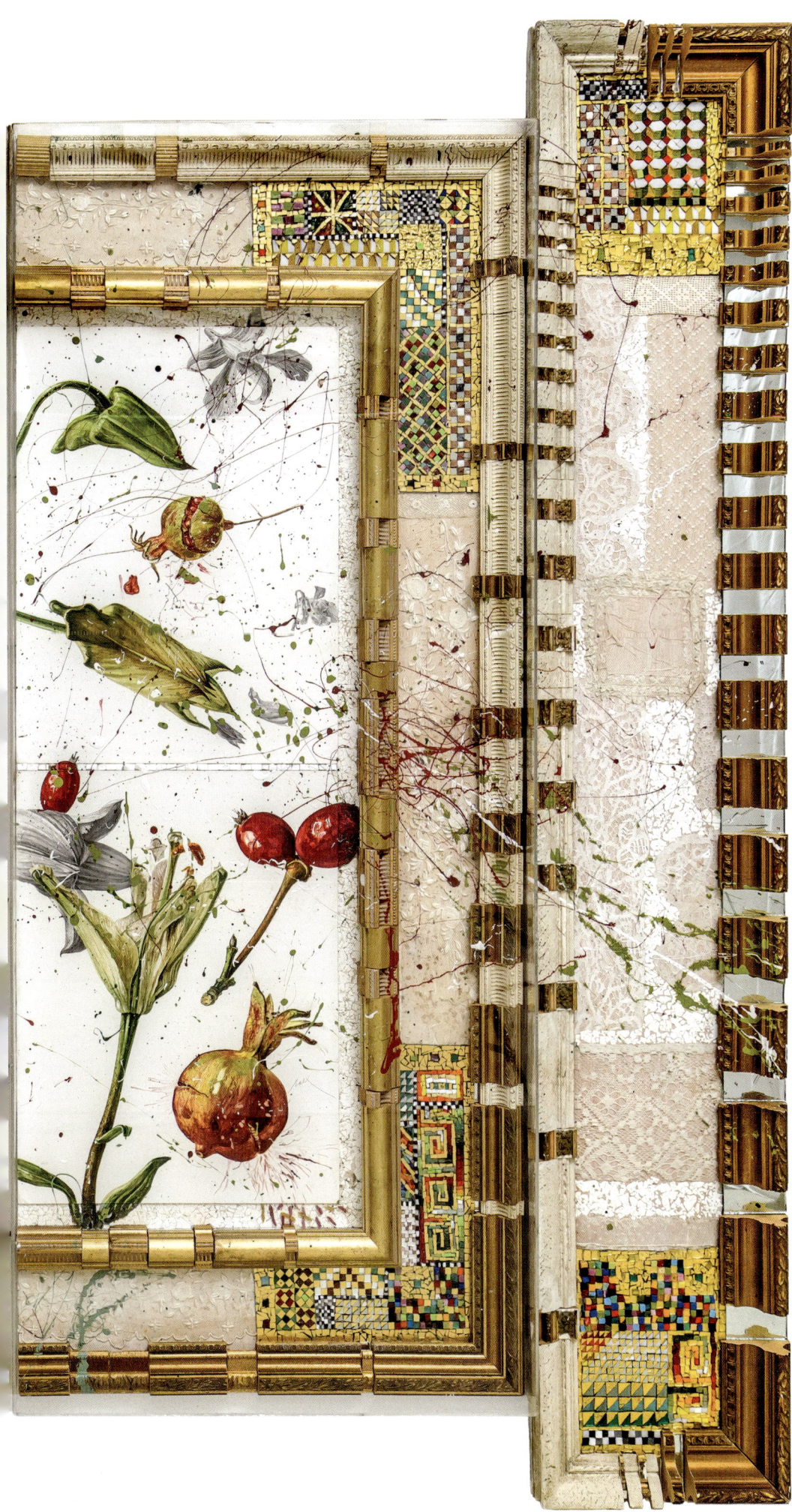

NEXT PAGE:
YELAPA DOGS
MIXED MEDIA
31" X 39"
ca. 1980

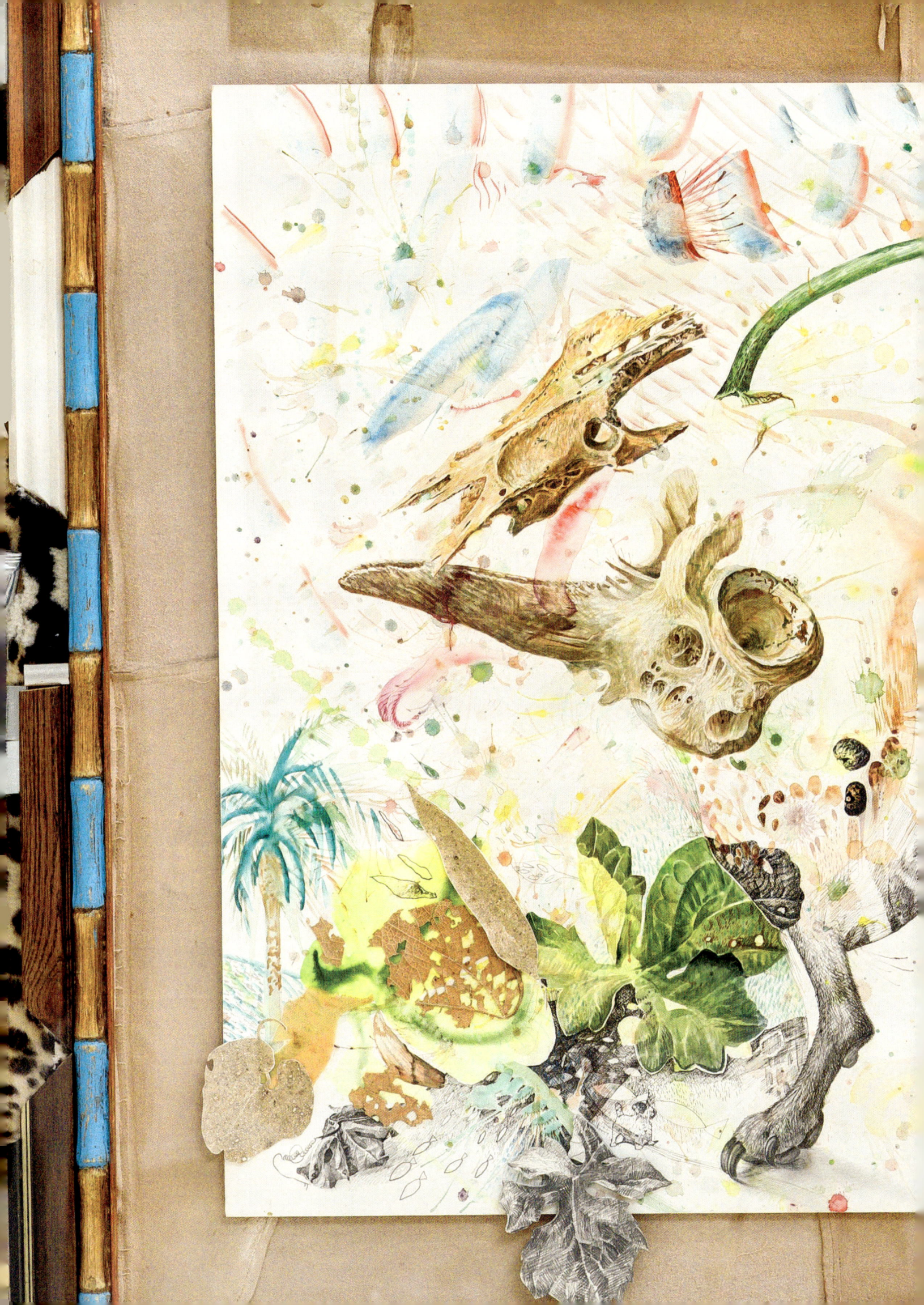

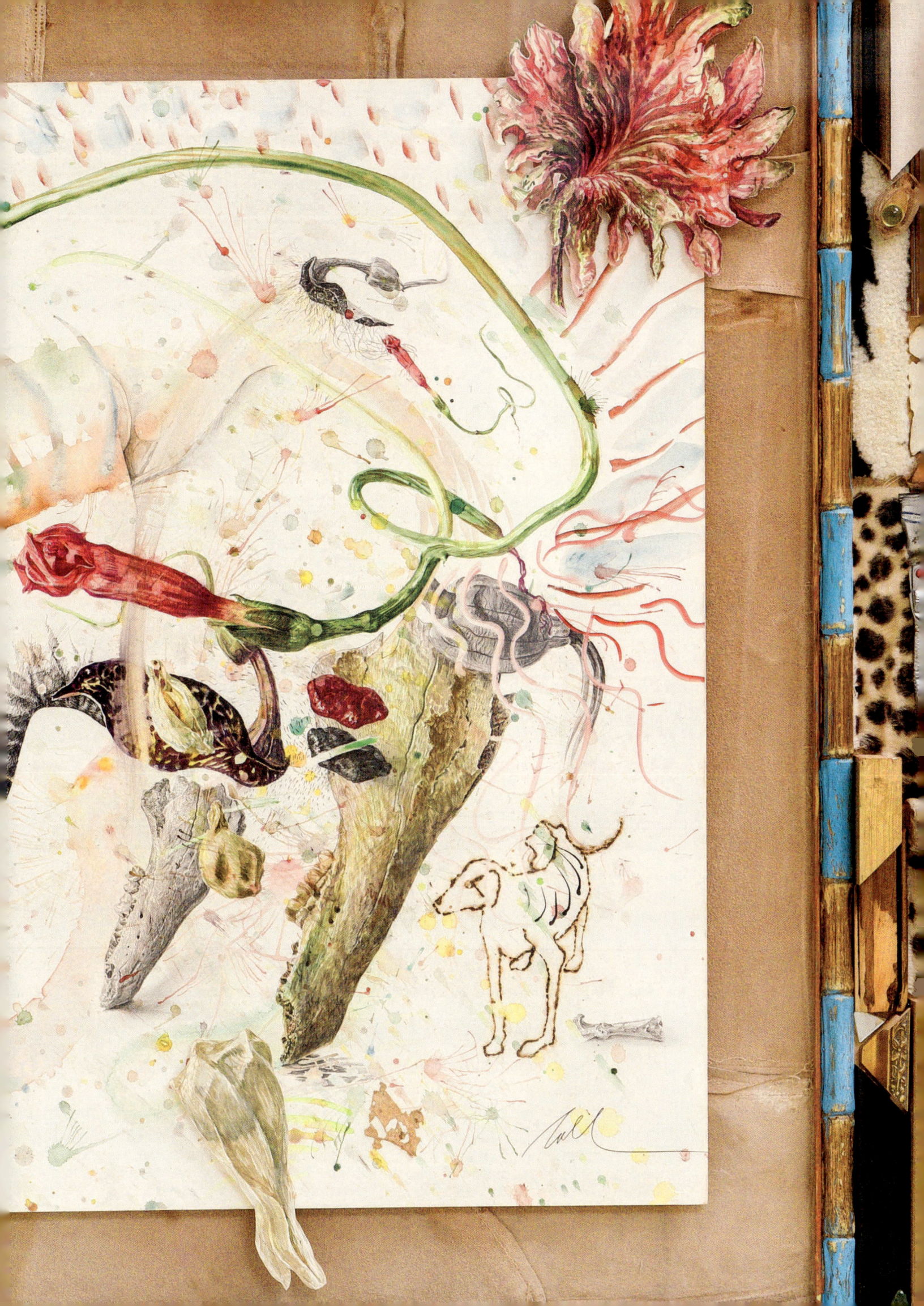

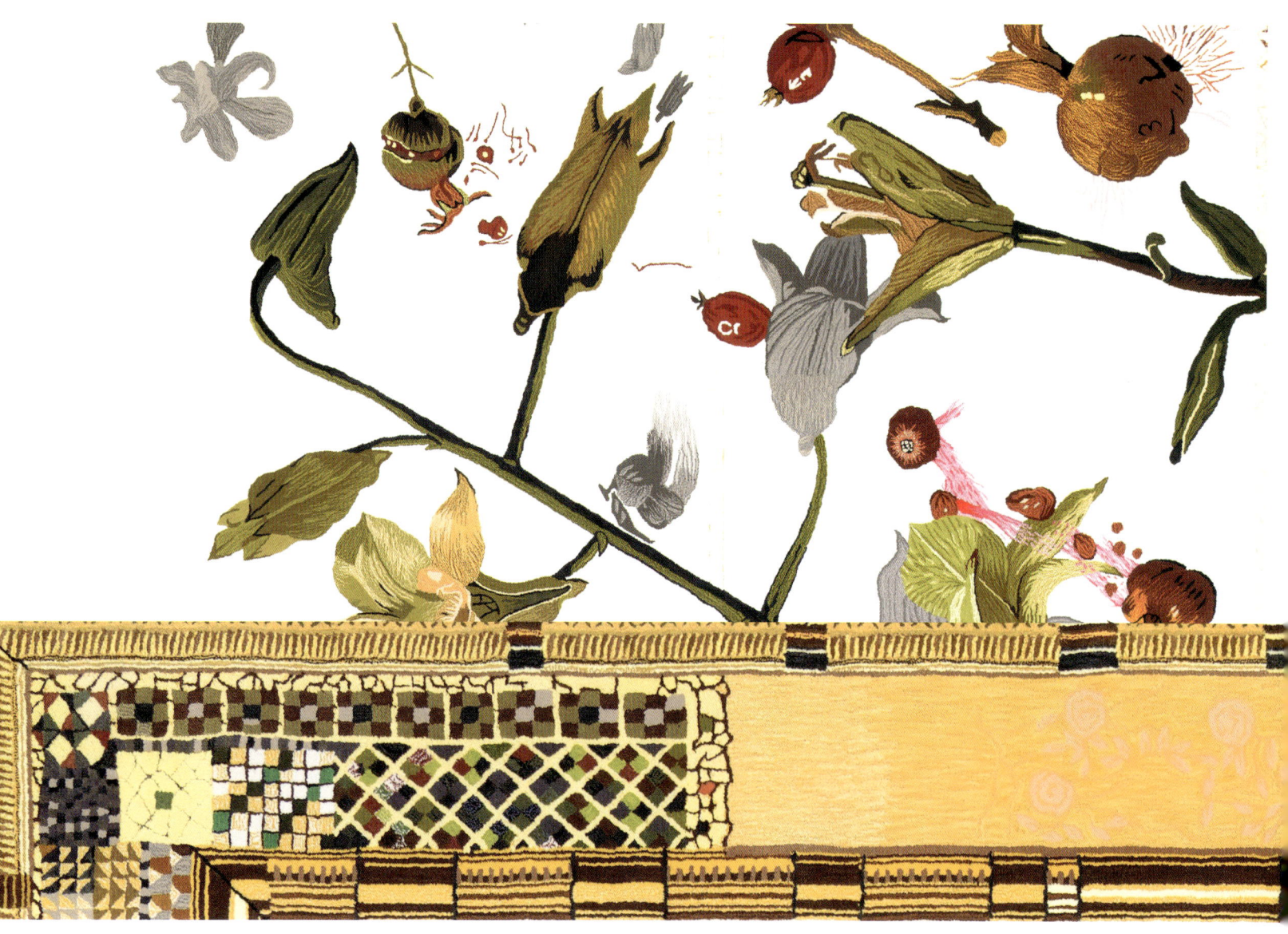

I have had a lifelong love of flowers, stemming from my memories of my grandmother's camellias. I will often incorporate a single flower into my more symbolic pieces as an "escape route" for the viewer but had avoided doing solely flower pieces out of a concern of being perceived as too commercial. But with the encouragement of a friend, I did the etching of a rose shown here, my first flower piece. It was well received, and an editor soon commissioned a full series of flower etchings in my distinctive style. The prints here are from the second edition made from those etchings.

Flowers evoke memories of my childhood in Troy and symbolize beauty, freedom and the peace movement of the 1960s.

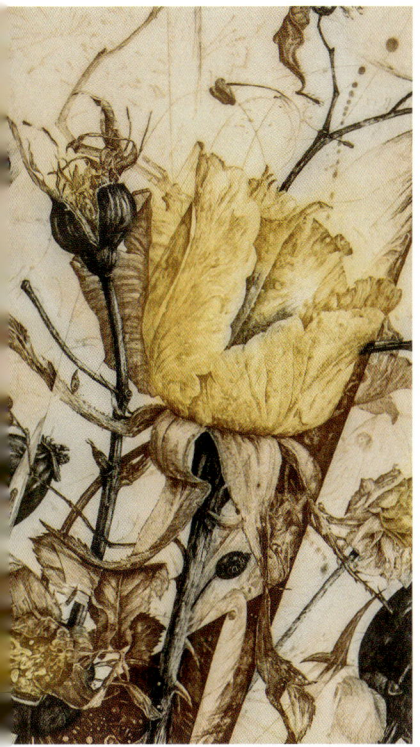
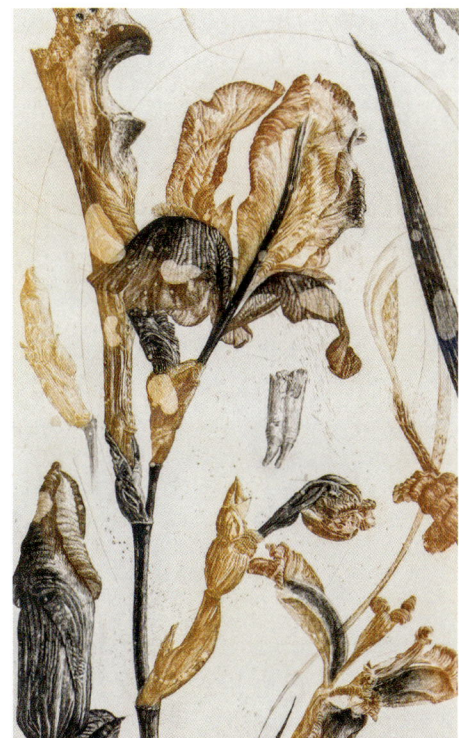
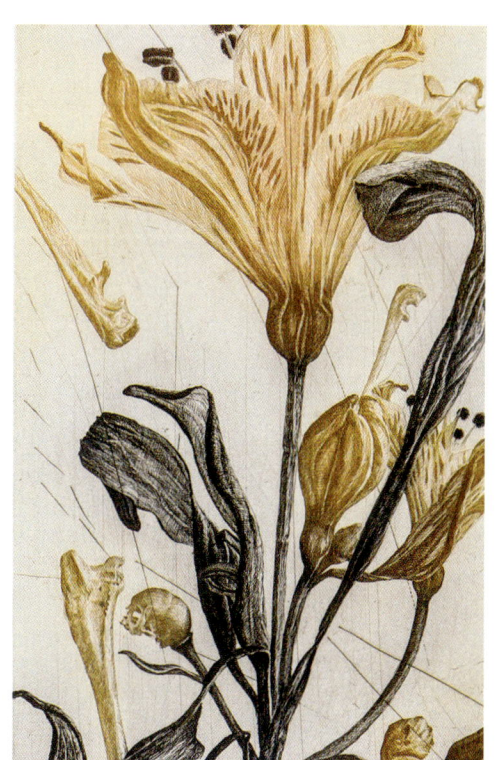
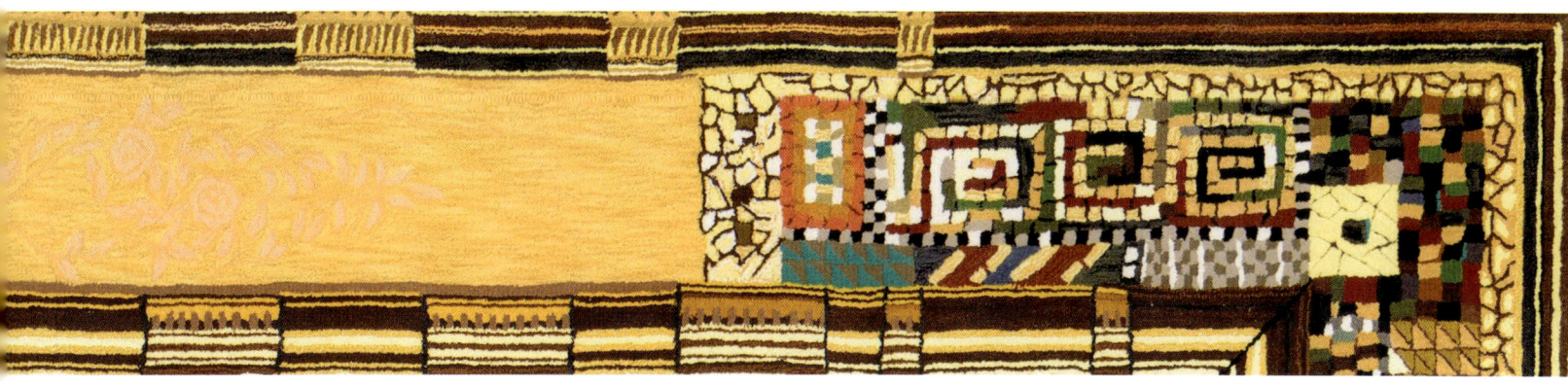
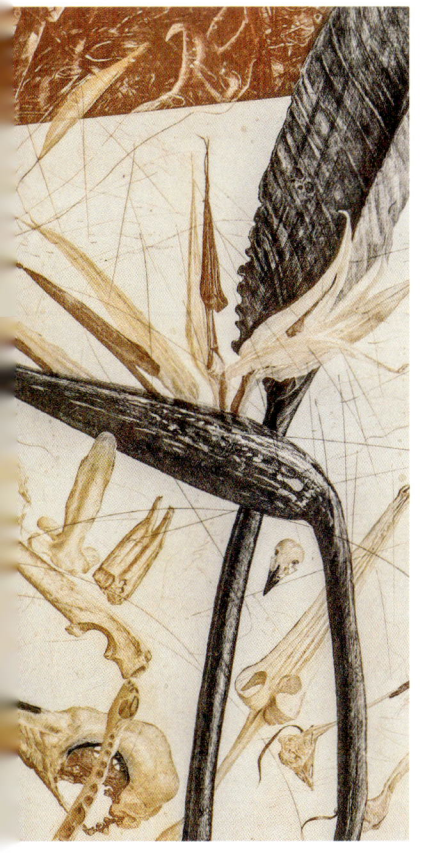
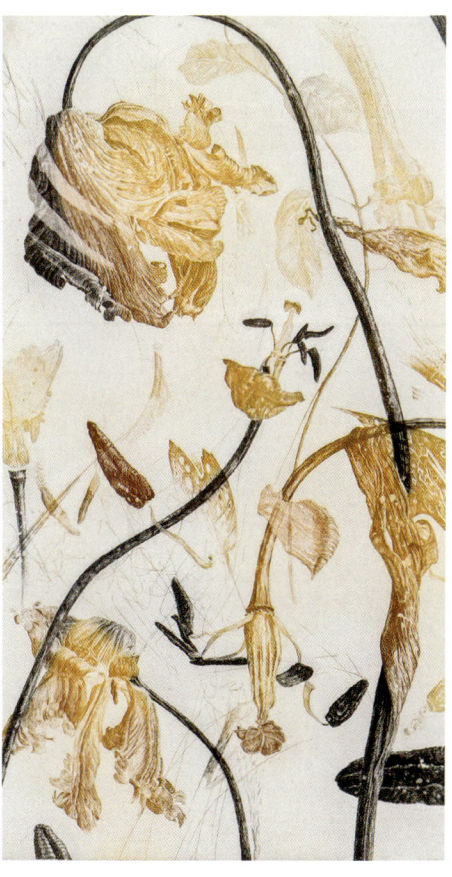
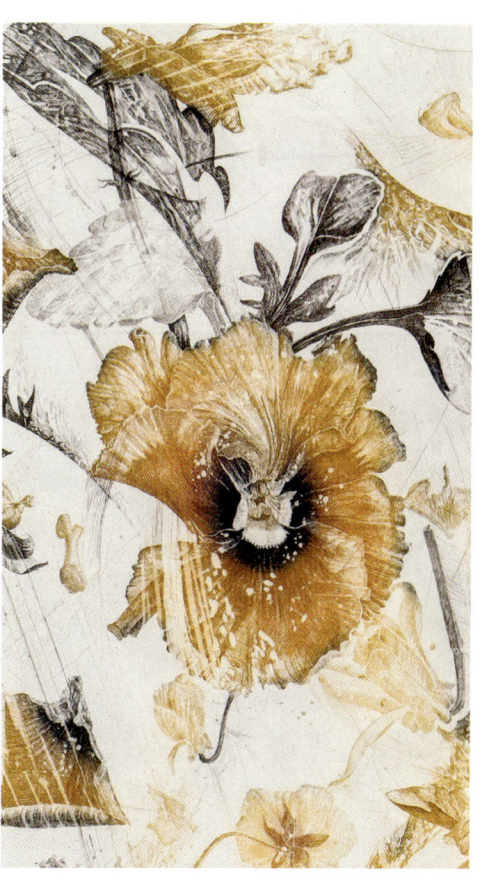

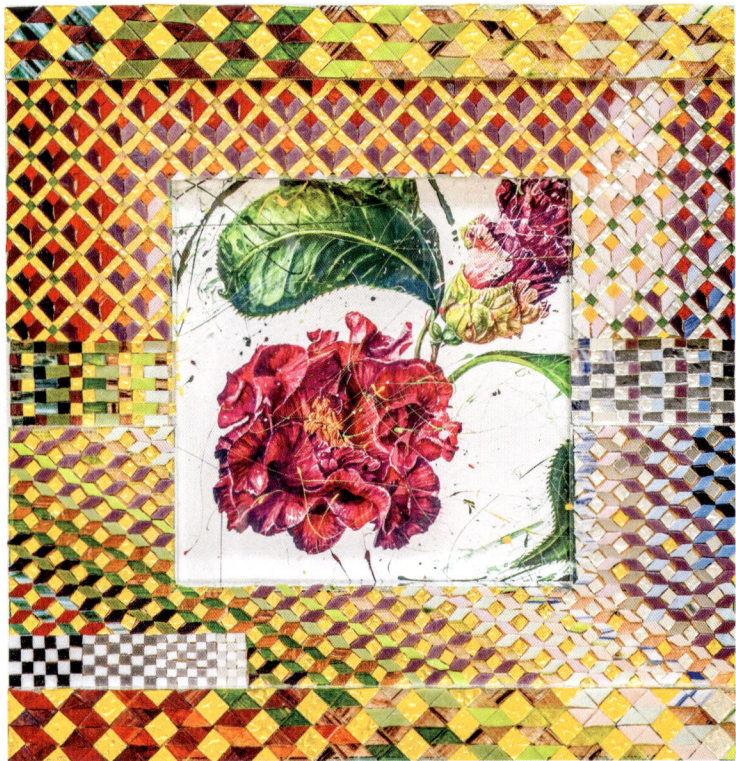

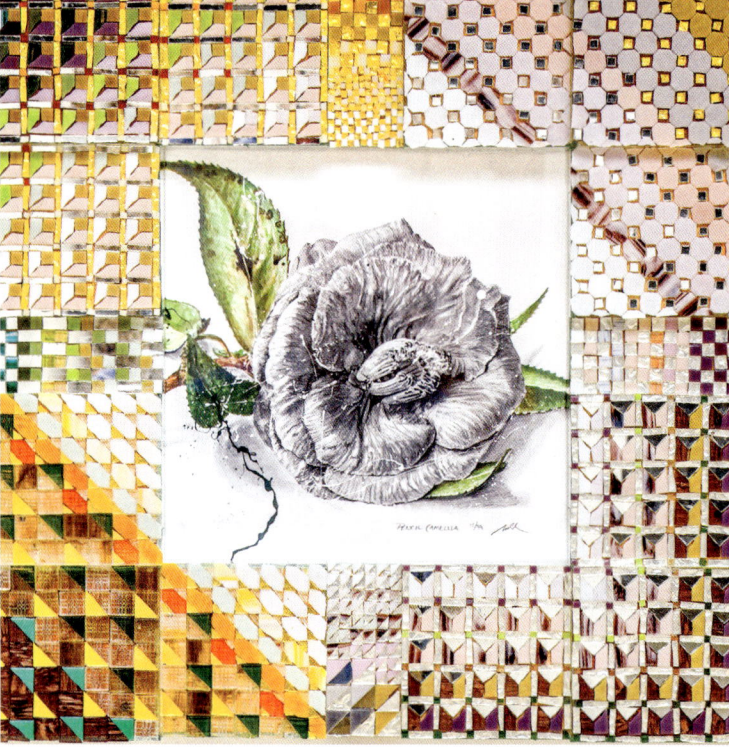

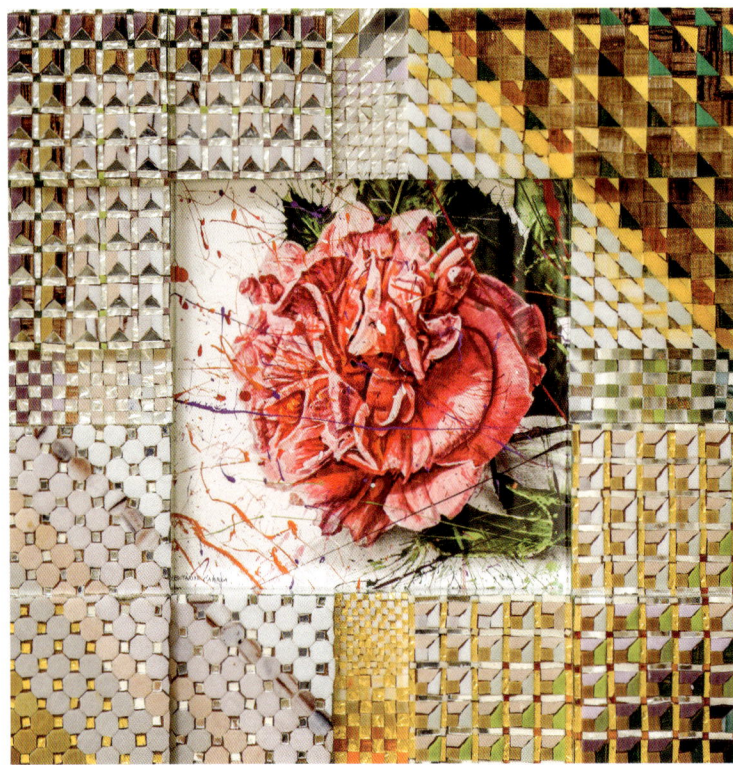

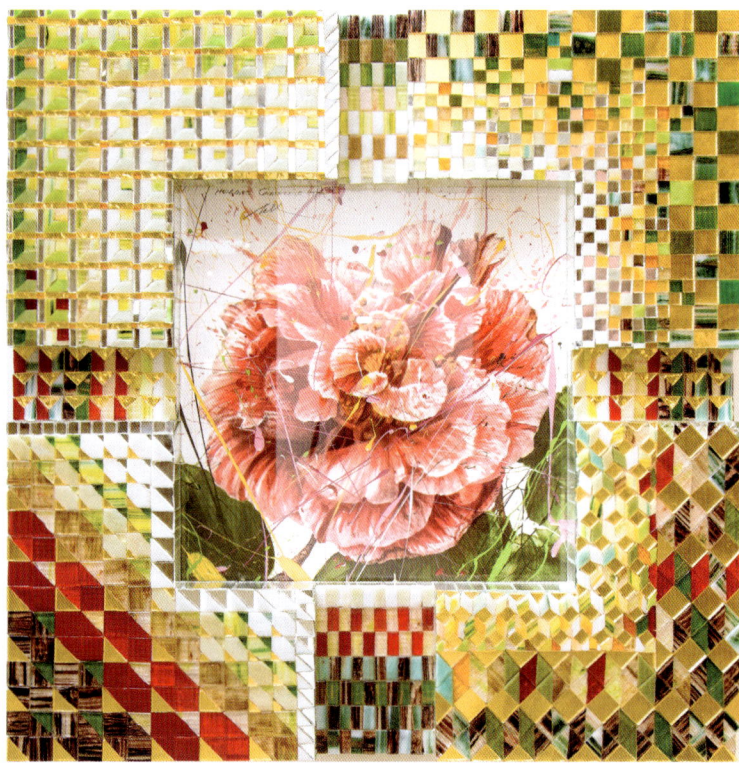

BLACK MAGIC
MIXED MEDIA
24" X 24"
2008

PENCIL CAMELLIA
MIXED MEDIA
24" X 24"
2008

DEBUTANTE CAMELLIA
MIXED MEDIA
24" X 24"
2008

HERMES CAMELLIA
MIXED MEDIA
24" X 24"
2008

VIDEO

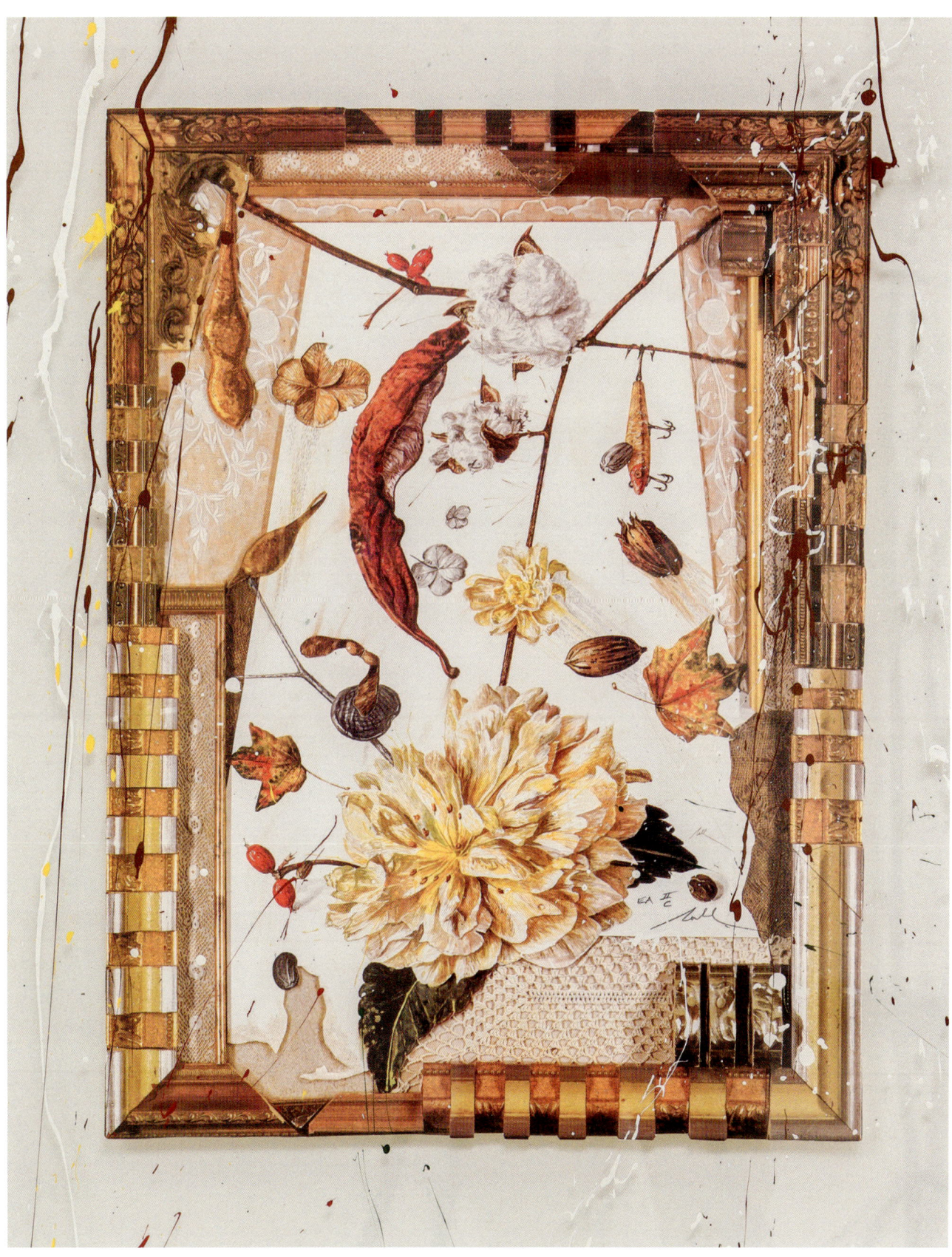

ALABAMA WHITE CAMELLIA
LITHOGRAPH
35" x 30"

An homage to Nall's beloved home state, this piece is filled with images that are evocative of Alabama, including a white camellia flower, dogwood blossoms, pecans, a fishing lure, and cotton. The sticks are arranged to indicate Alabama's river system. Surrounding the painting are bits of lace from Nall's grandmother's wedding dress.

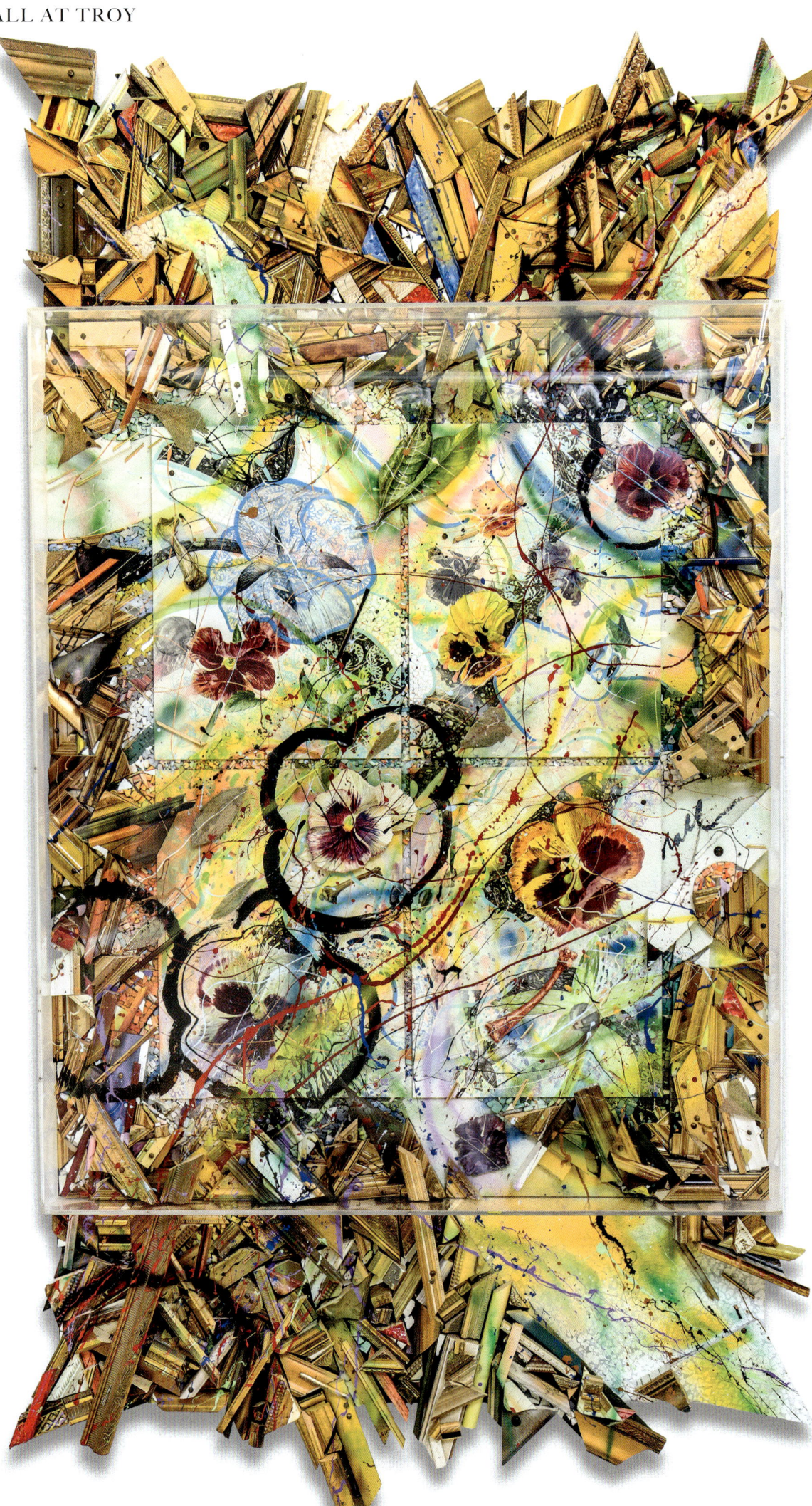

I recall that Ringo Starr was with me in the studio while I was painting a portrait of him. As I dripped black paint onto the canvas, Ringo cried out that I was going to ruin it. I replied: "What do you mean ruin it? It's my painting. Do I tell you how to drum?"

COSMIC HARMONIES
MIXED MEDIA
115" X 58"
1988

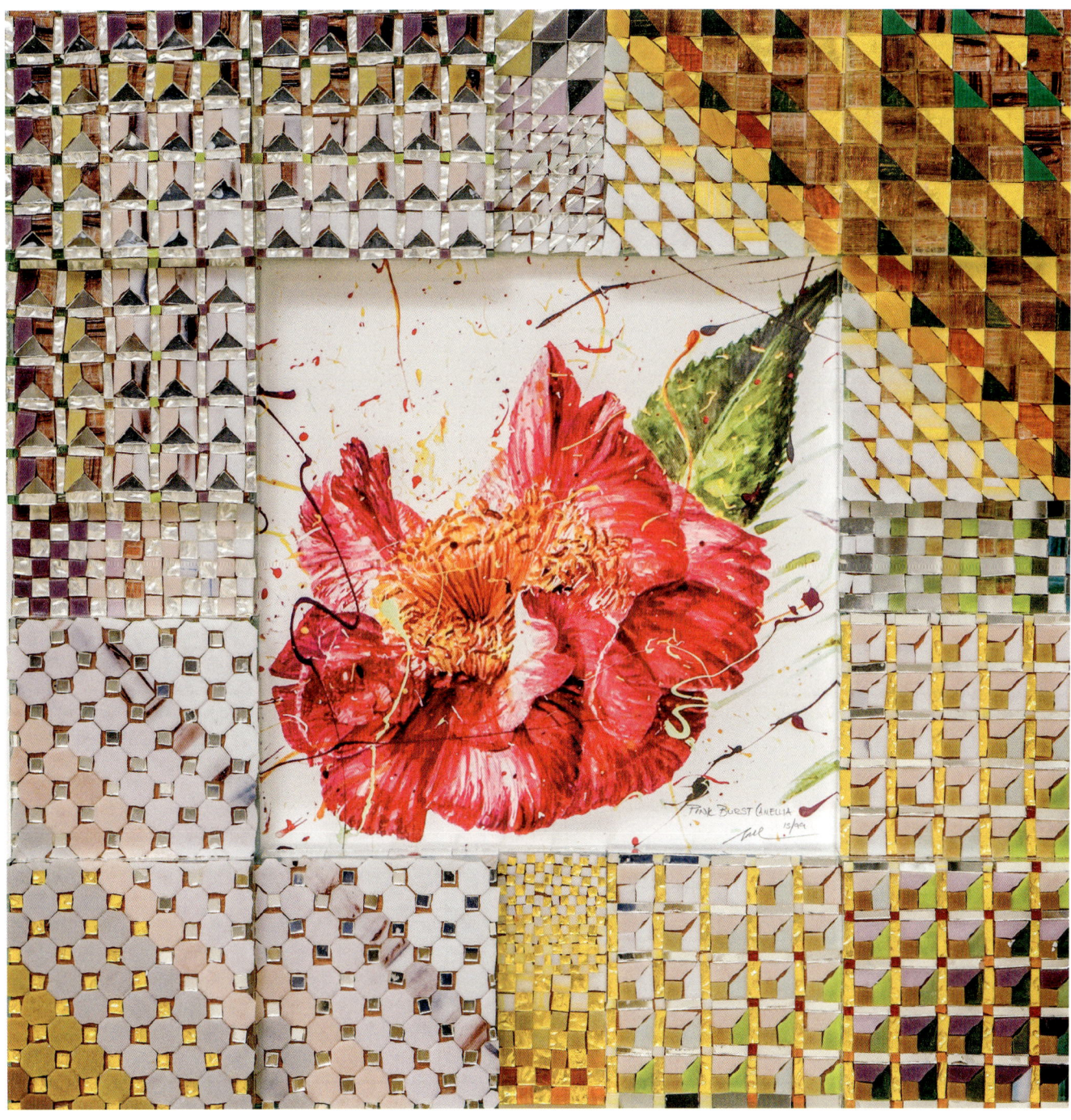

**Pink Burst
Camellia**
Mixed Media
24" x 24"
2008

*Sometimes the frame comes before the painting. These mosaic frames were started
in Monaco while I was working on a show for fashion house Christian Dior. The
frames originally contained images of flowers grown at the N.A.L.L. Foundation
in France. I credit the photographer Elmore Inscoe DeMott of Montgomery for
inspiring me to paint a new series featuring a flower more reminiscent of my
home state—the iconic southern camellia.*

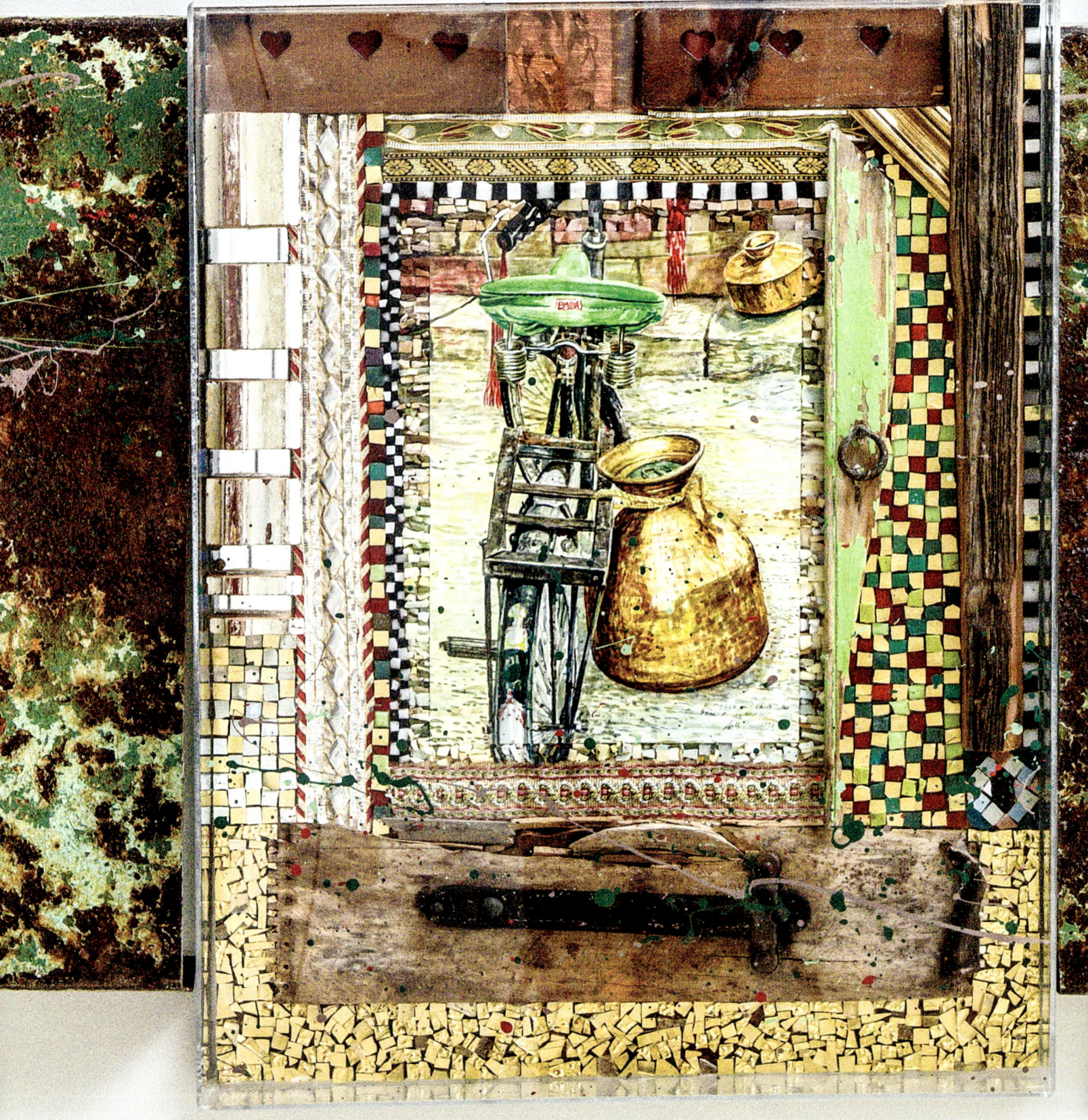

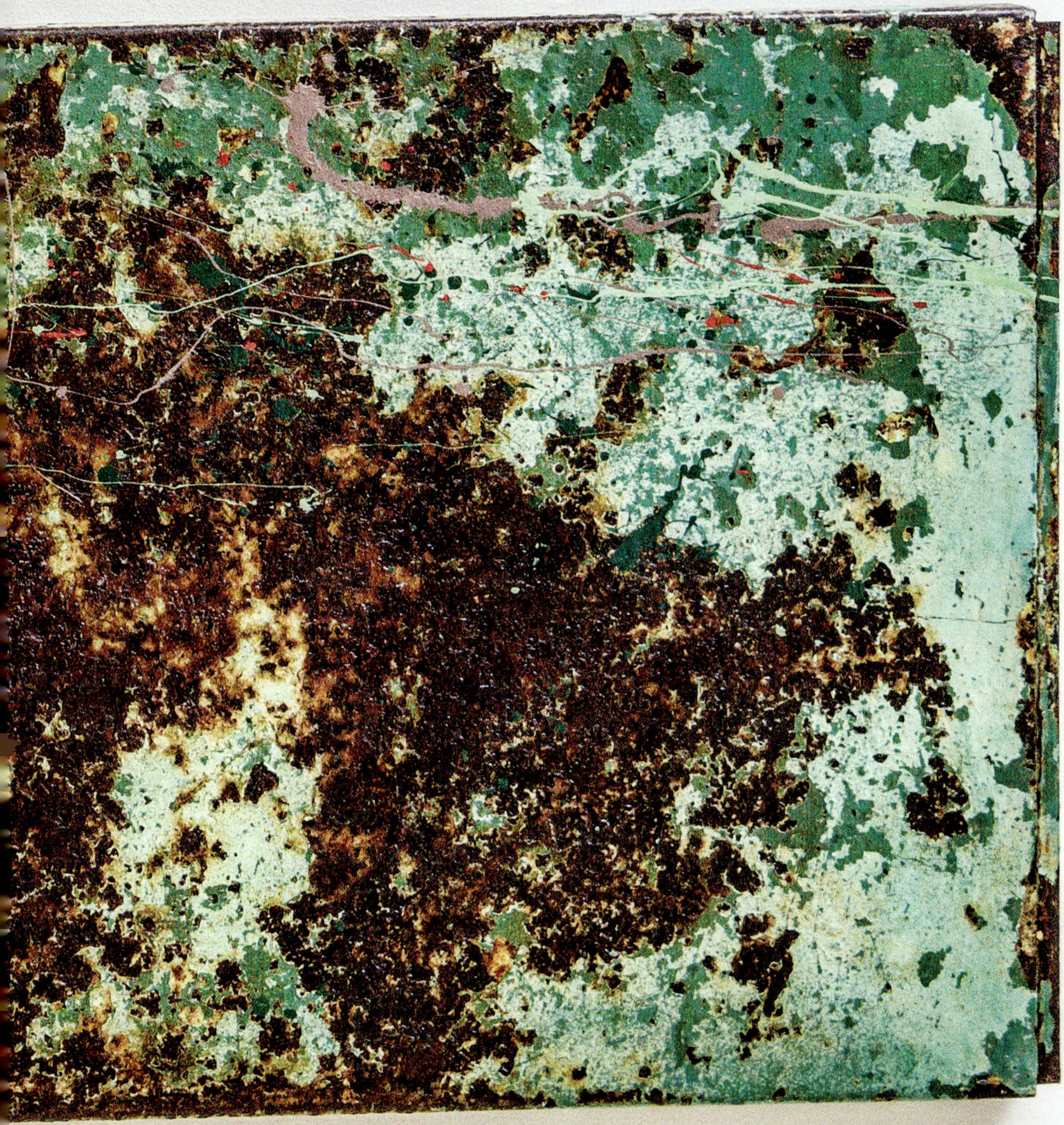

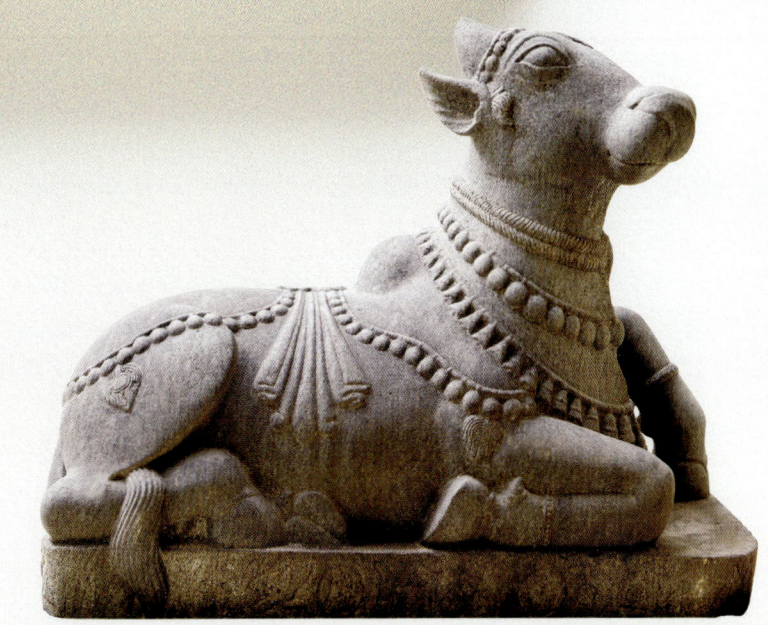

ABOVE:
INDIAN BICYCLE
MIXED MEDIA
26" x 74"
1996–2007

RIGHT:
NANDI BULL
MAHAKALI PURANA
GRANITE
43" x 53" x 25"
1996

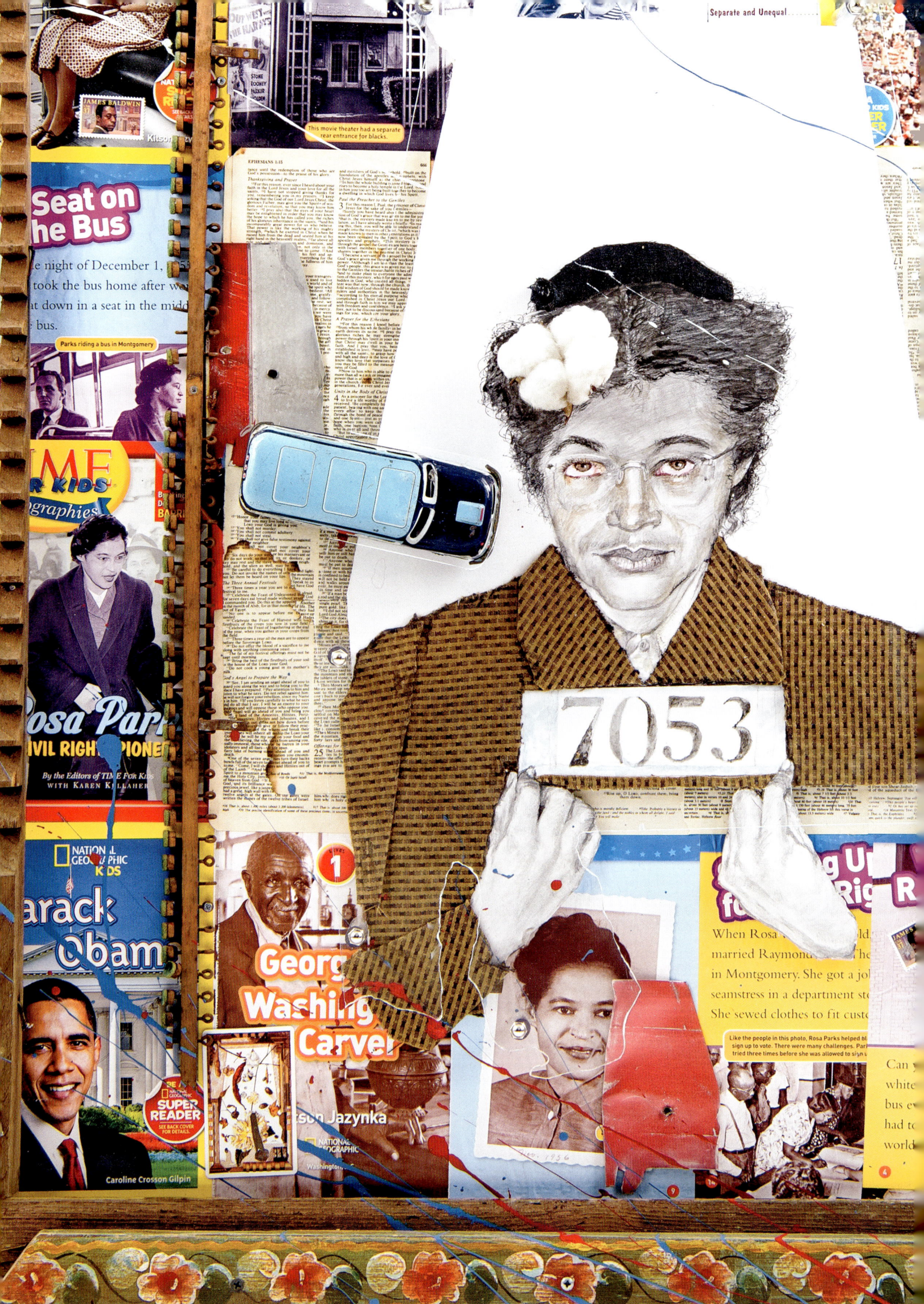

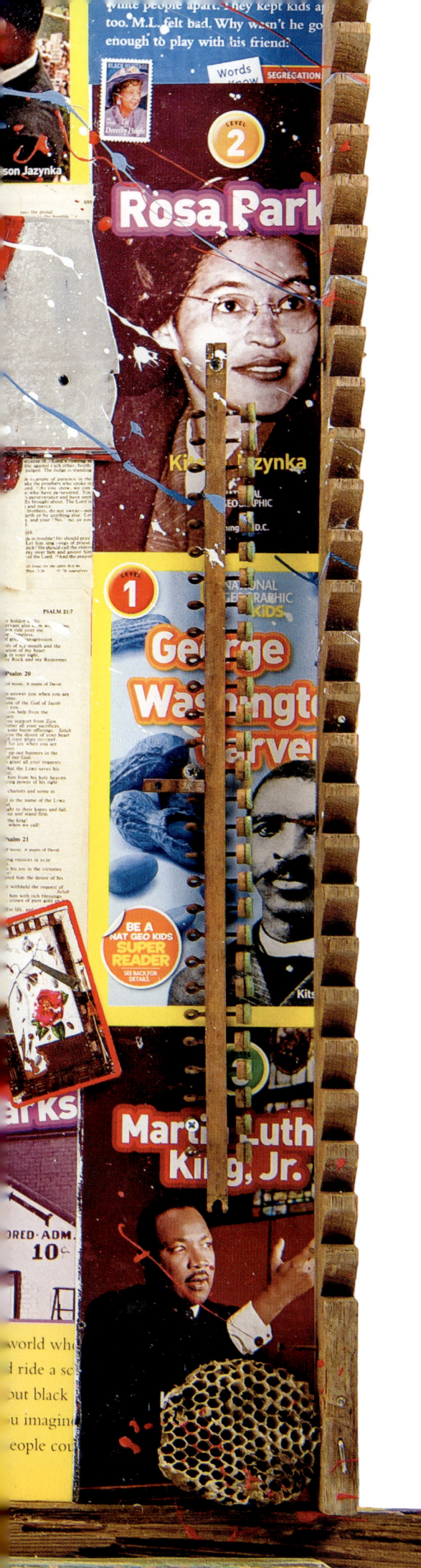

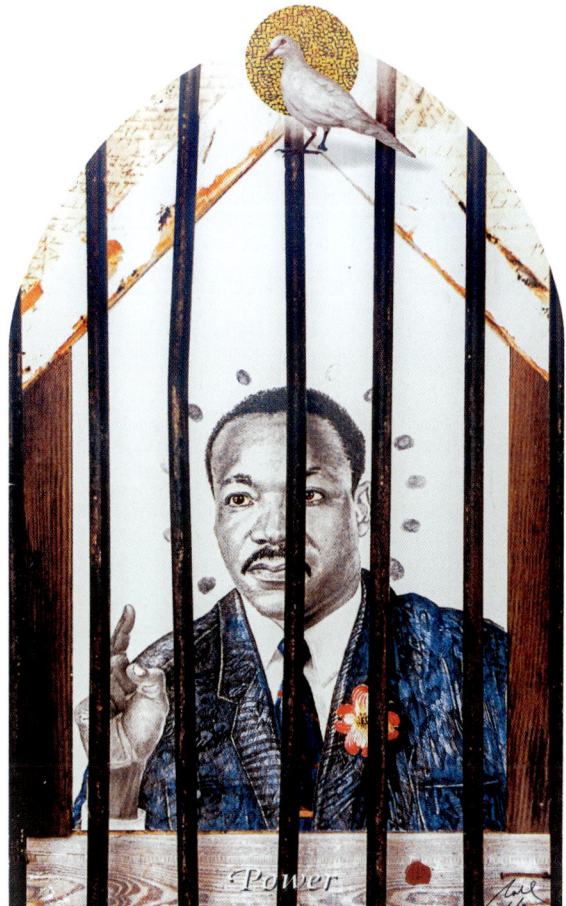

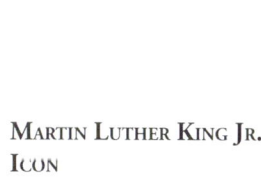

THREE WHO DARED:
CIVIL RIGHTS ICONS

MARTIN LUTHER KING JR.
ICON
MIXED MEDIA
FROM THE SERIES
"SINS OF HUMANITY"

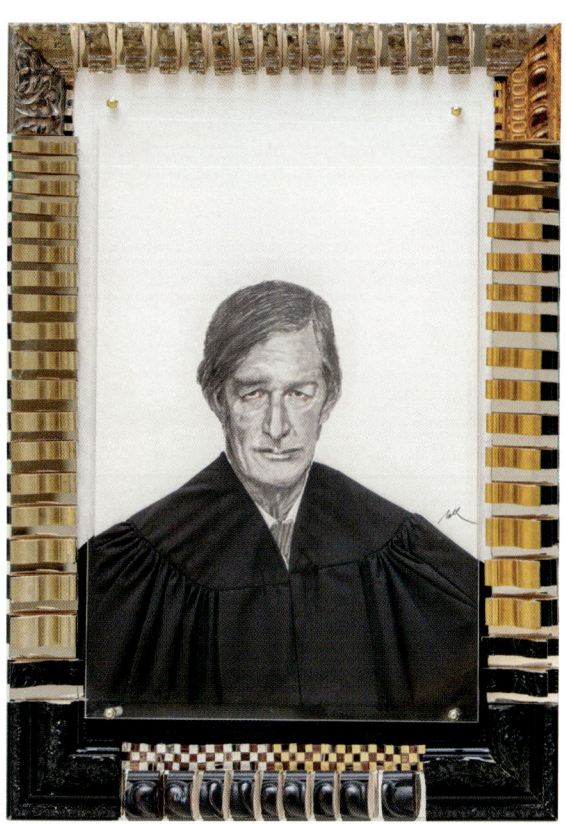

JUDGE FRANK M. JOHNSON JR.
MIXED MEDIA
41" X 28.5"
2018

PORTRAIT OF ROSA PARKS
MIXED MEDIA
35.5" X 47"
2017

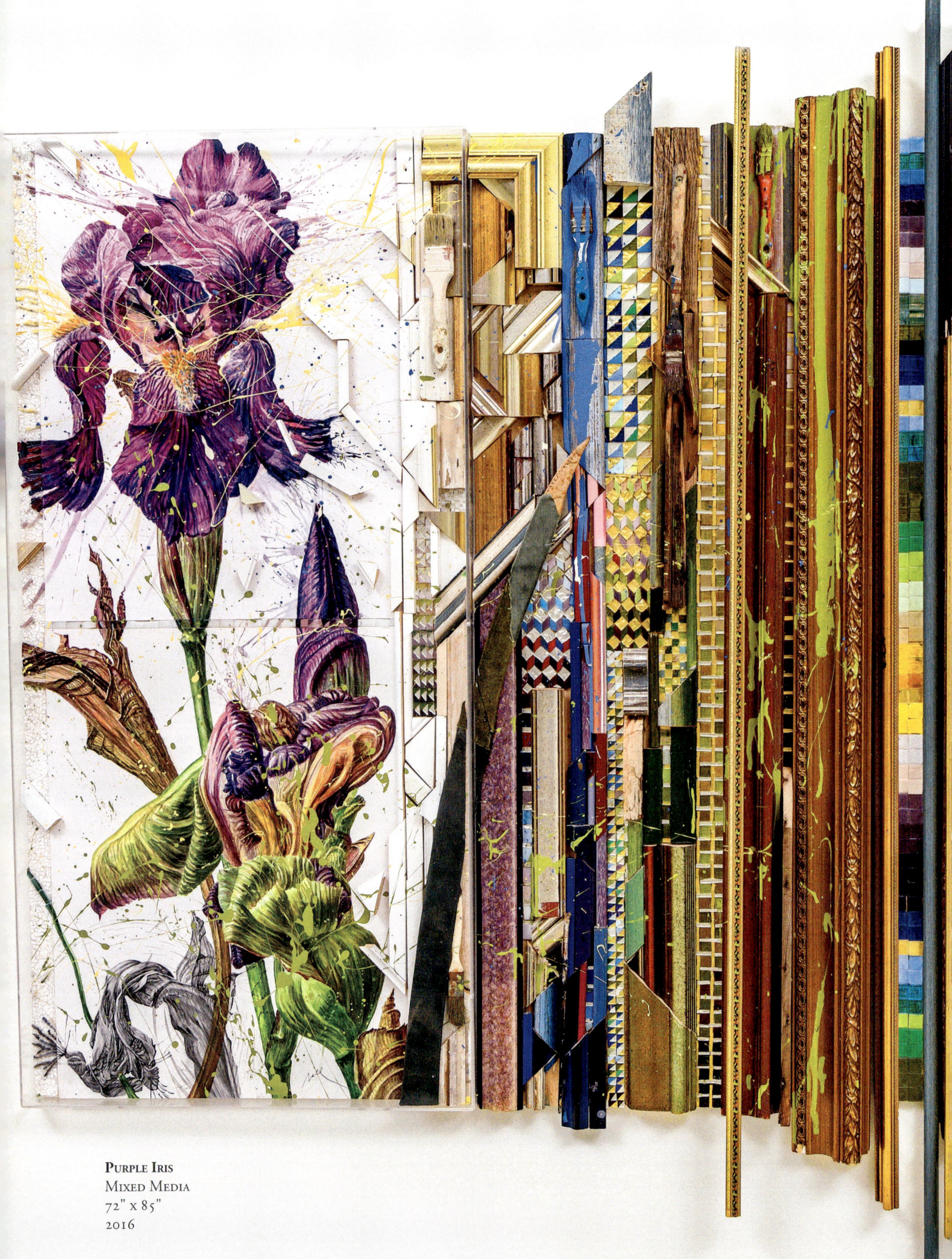

PURPLE IRIS
MIXED MEDIA
72" X 85"
2016

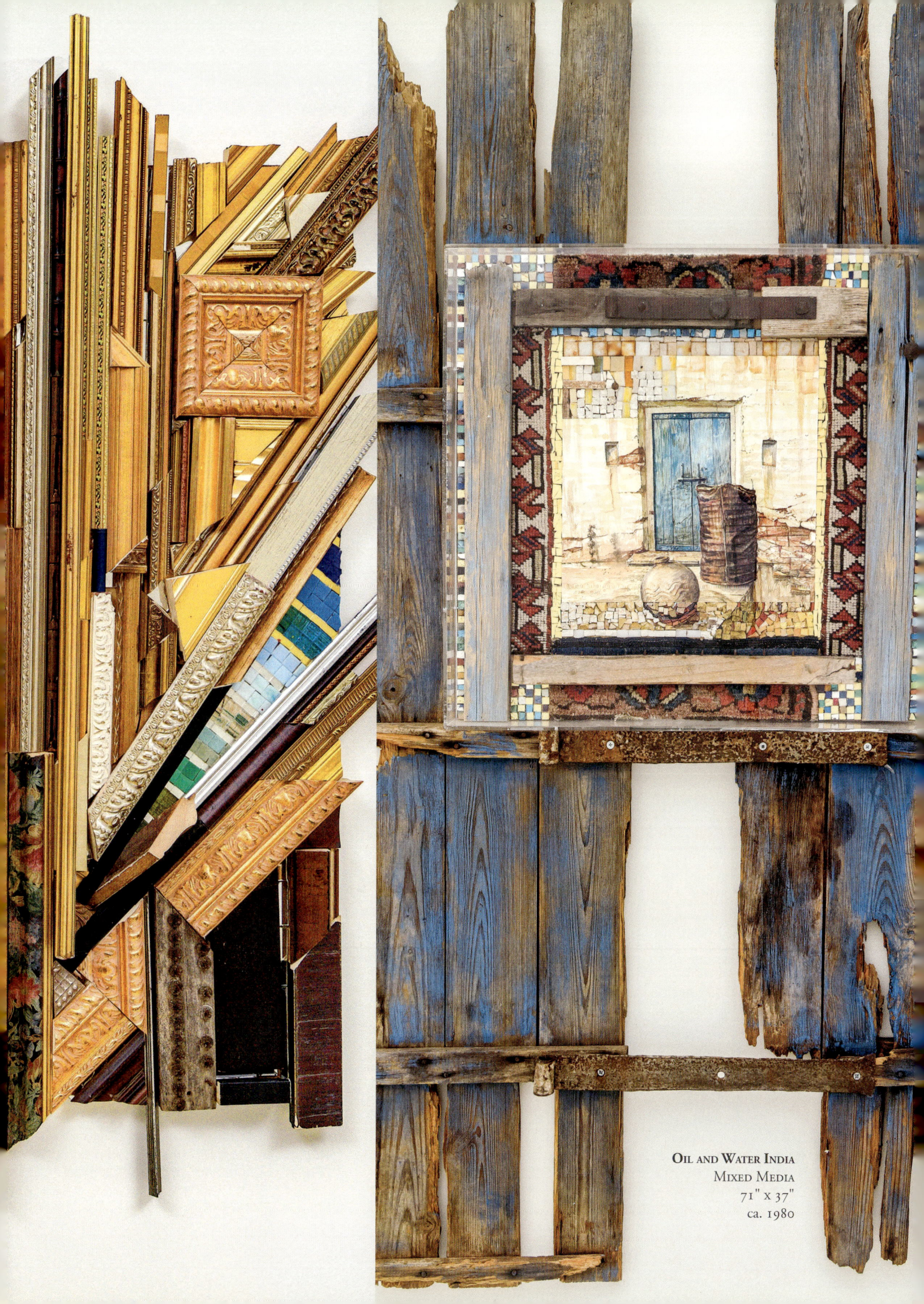

OIL AND WATER INDIA
MIXED MEDIA
71" X 37"
ca. 1980

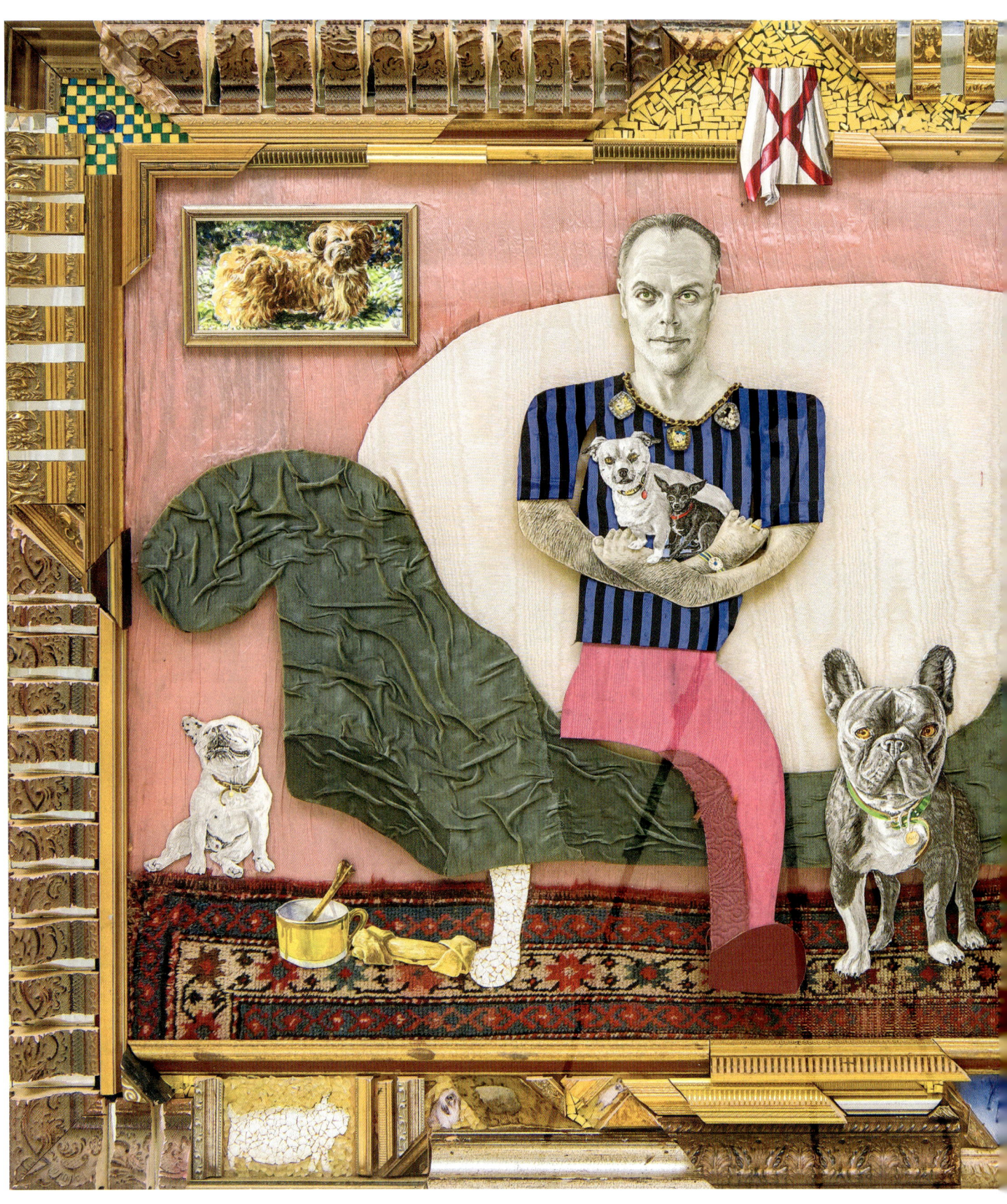

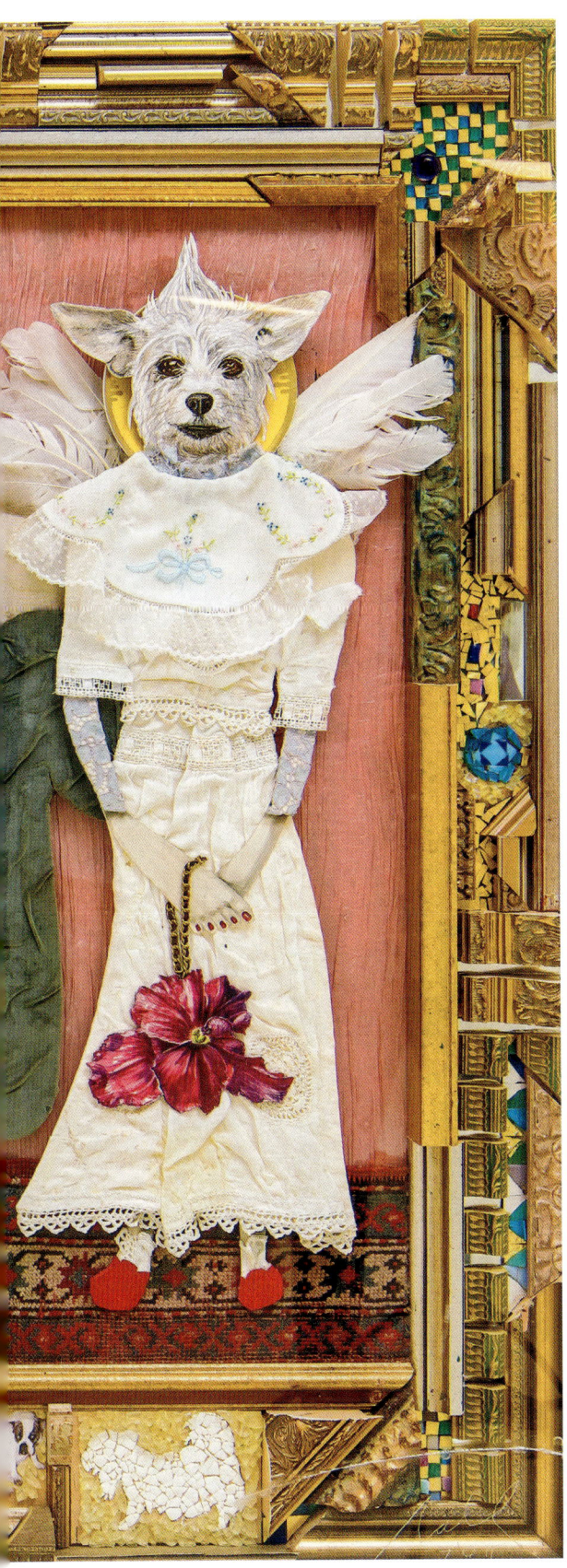

FAMILY PORTRAIT
NALL AND DOGS
MIXED MEDIA
49" X 65"
1998–2012

Palace of the Popes in Avignon, France, reflects Nall's fascination with iconic architecture and the use of symbolism at its best. During the fourteenth century, the home of the Catholic Church and Papacy was moved from Rome to Avignon. Here Nall depicts the grandeur and turmoil of this particular point in European history. Throughout the composition Nall references the reign of seven popes using the numerology and imaging of seven skulls, seven flowers, and seven bones. The coins surrounding the palace represent his view of the monetary power of the Catholic Church. The piece also attempts to make the leap to a much different time in the future where Thomas Jefferson is emphasizing the Constitutional "separation of Church and State," a pillar of the new republic in America. Growing up as a Southern Baptist, Nall's personal struggles with the history of church and state surface in a powerful way in *Palais des Papes*.

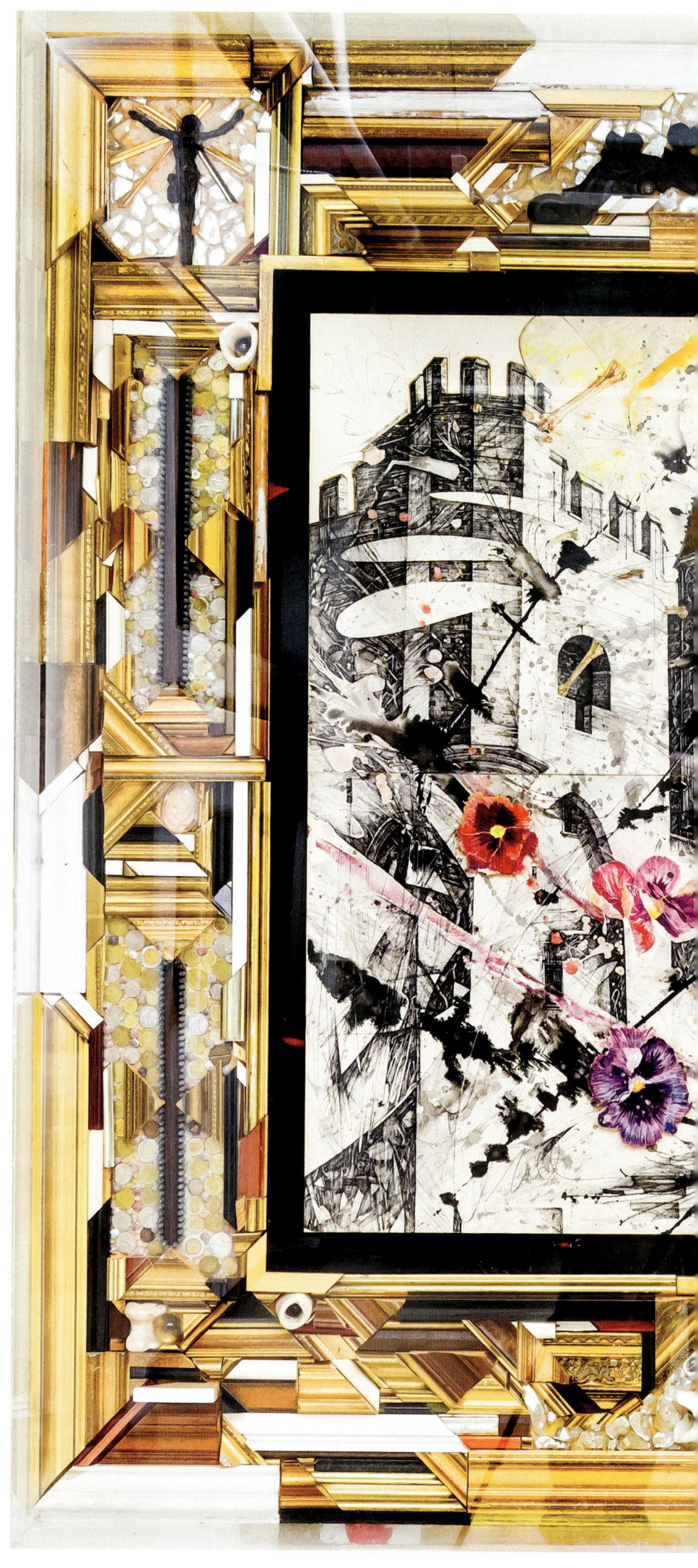

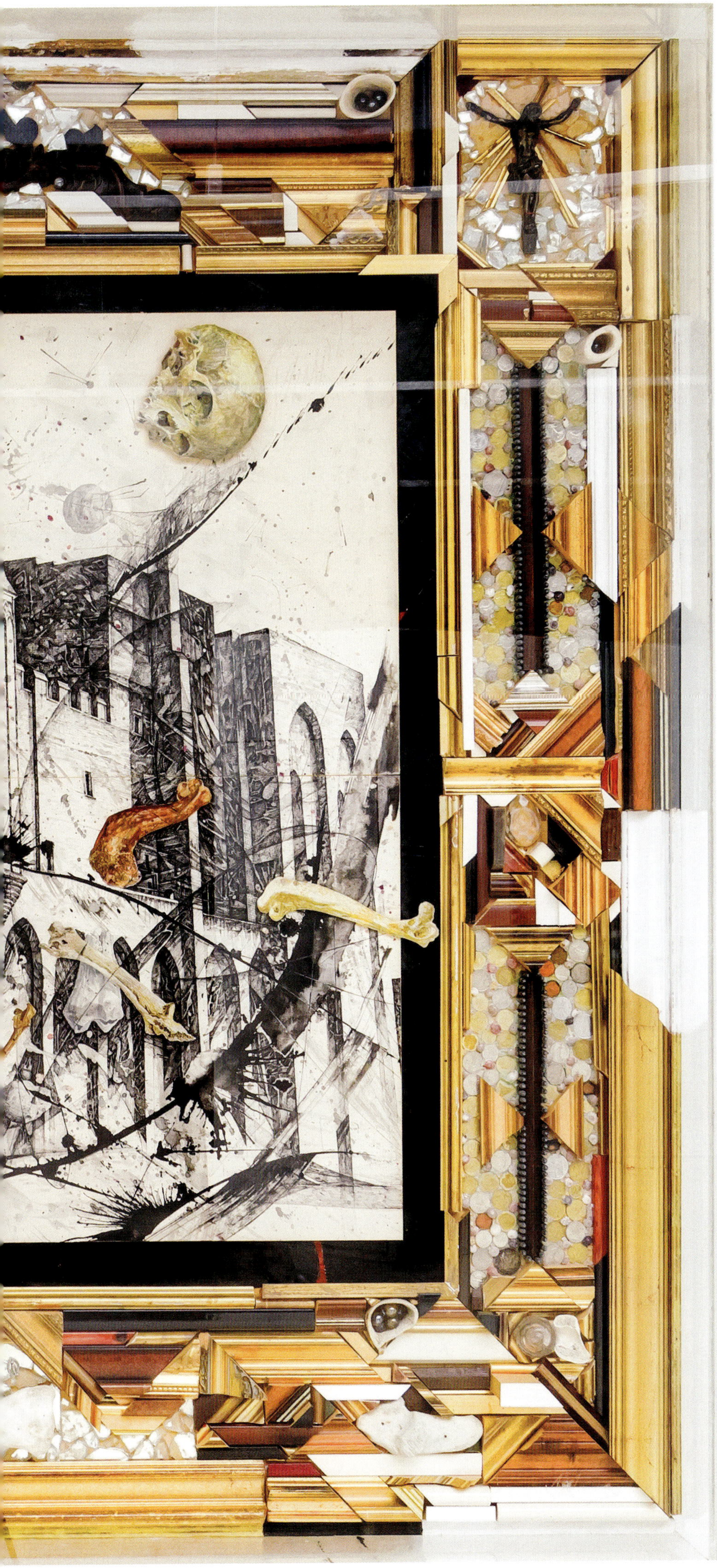

**AVIGNON,
PALAIS DES PAPES**
MIXED MEDIA
64" x 64"
1988

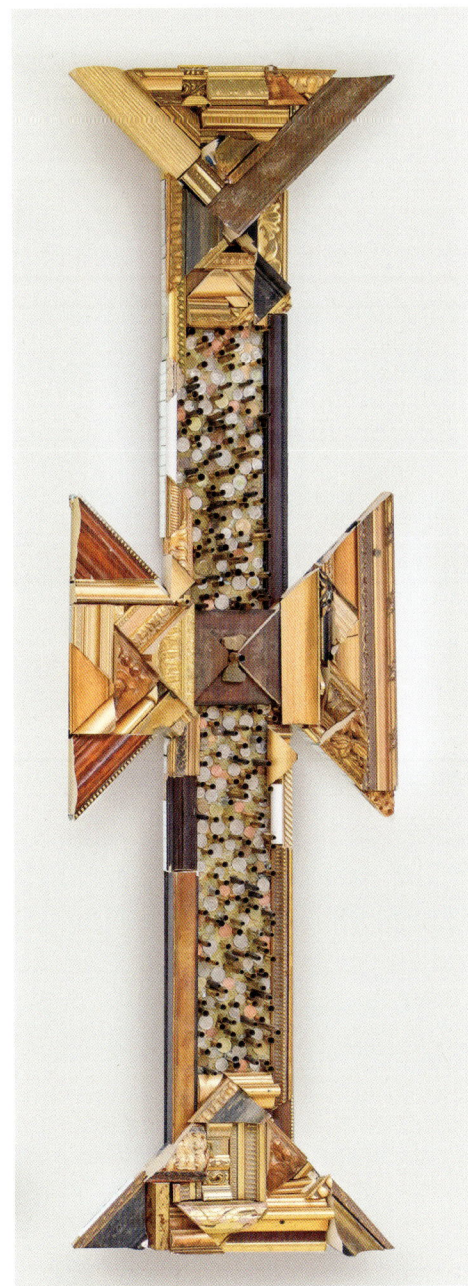

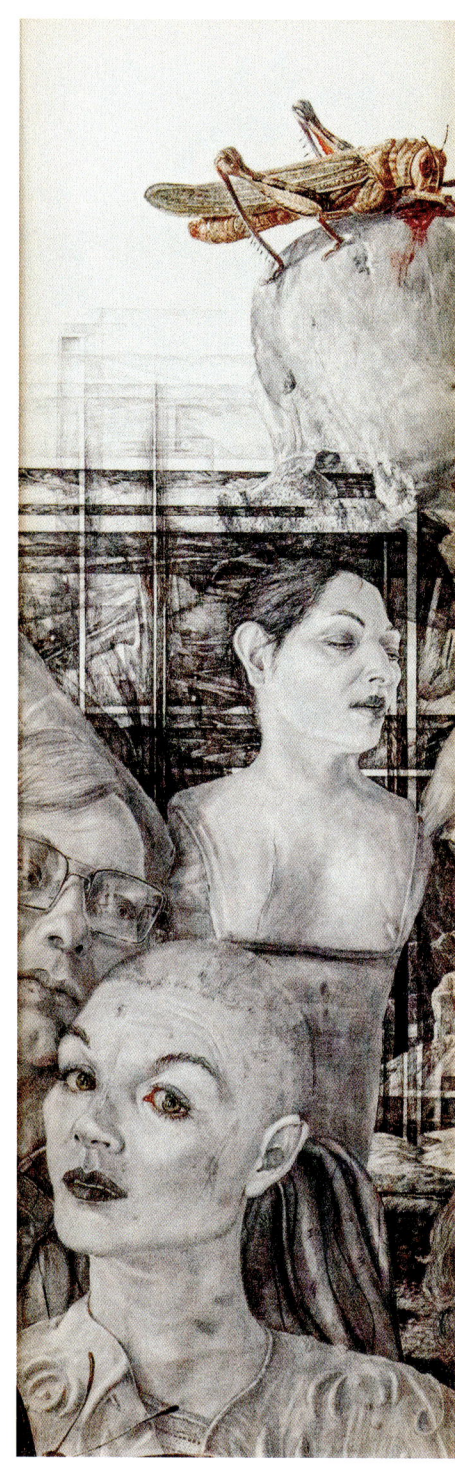

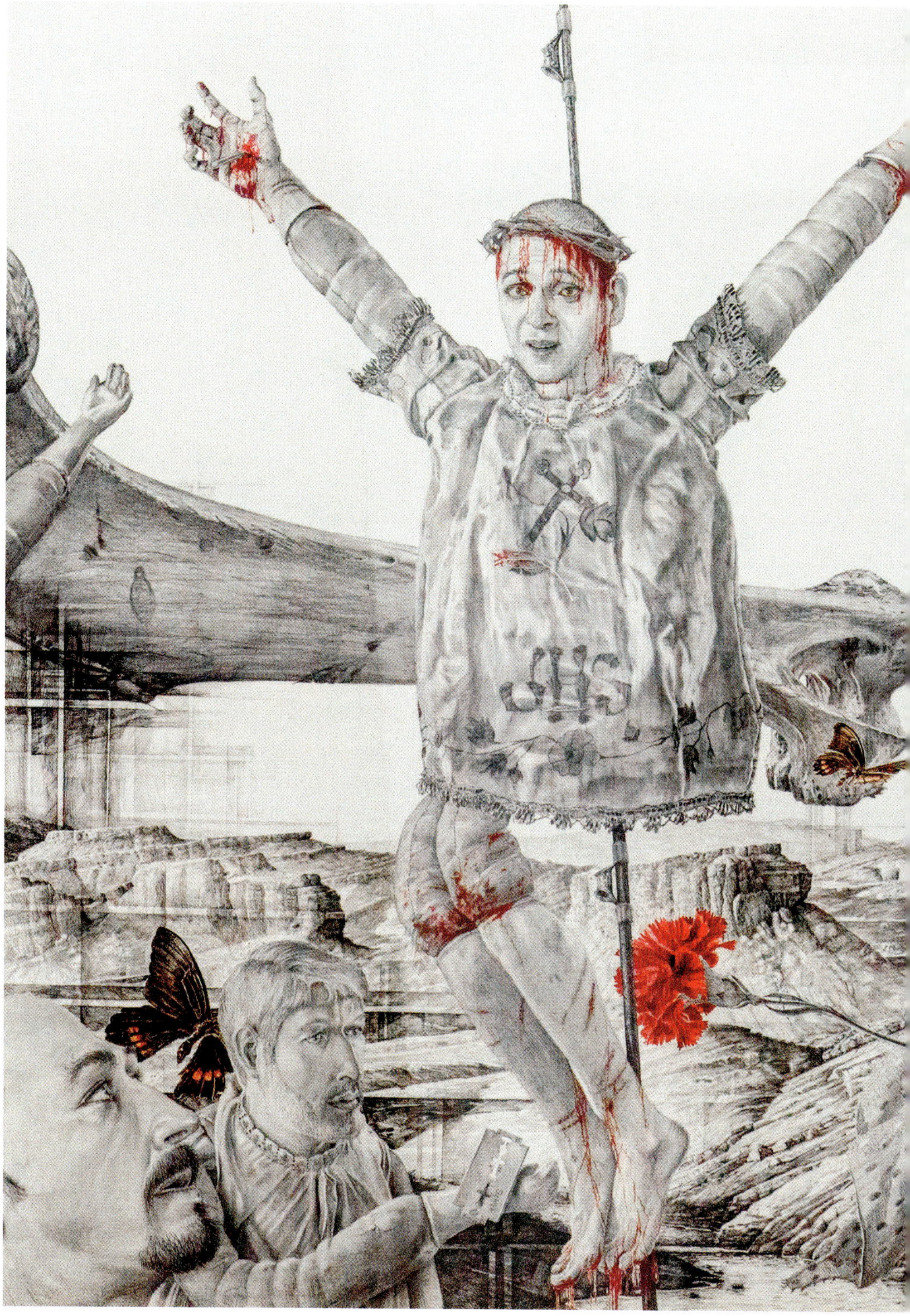

This crucifixion scene includes a self-portrait as the Christ figure, depicted crucified on a fishing pole, representing Jesus's work as a fisherman. The other figures in the piece are friends and associates, including fellow Alabama artist Bill Nance on the far left.

For several years, I regularly visited Algeria, traveling the countryside by hitchhiking and staying in Berber villages. Living alongside the Berbers, I saw firsthand the impact of oil drilling on those who called the desert home. The construction in the background of the piece evokes the exploitation of the desert by companies drilling for oil.

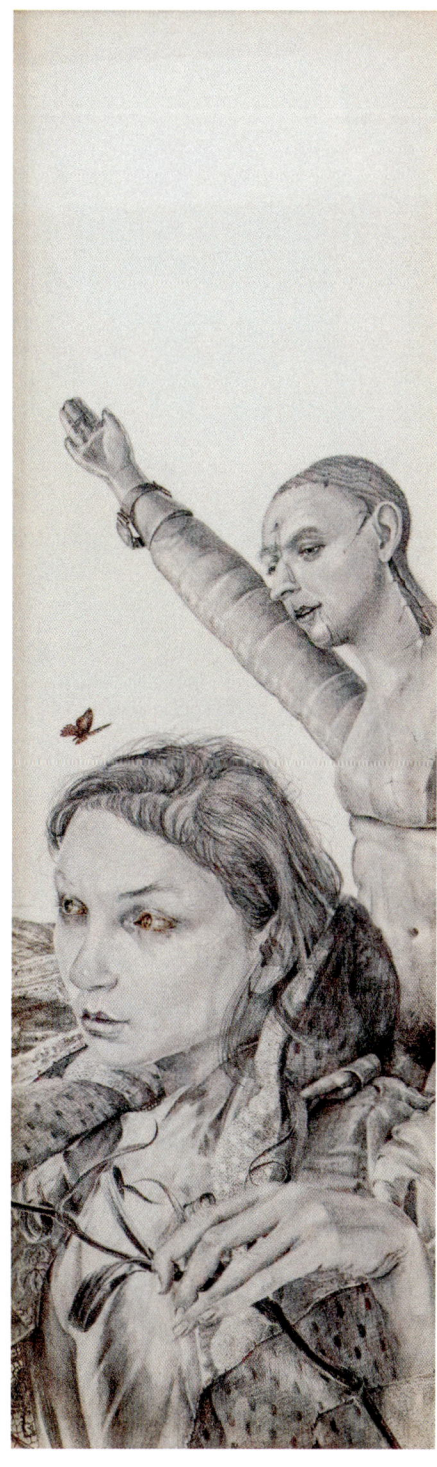

CRUCIFIXION
MIXED MEDIA
37" X 47"
1976–2016

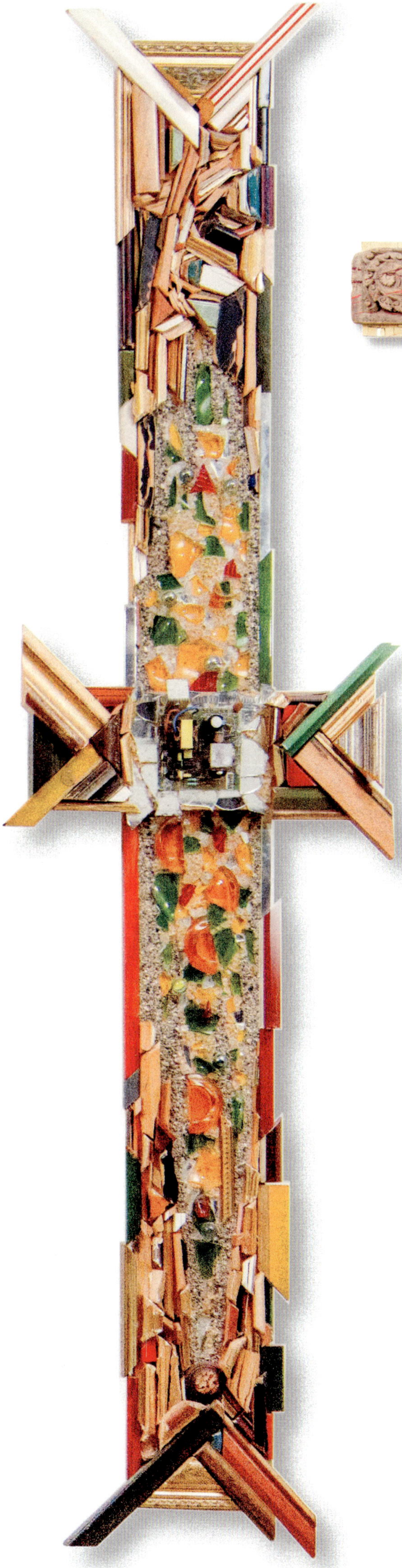

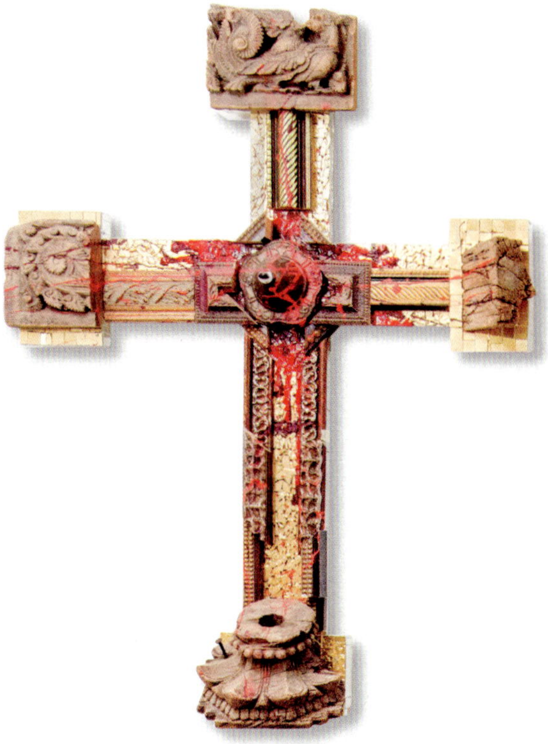

81

TOP:
ETHNIQUE CROSS
MIXED MEDIA
45" X 32"
2008

BOTTOM:
PALAIS DES PAPES CROSS
MIXED MEDIA
58" X 15"
1988

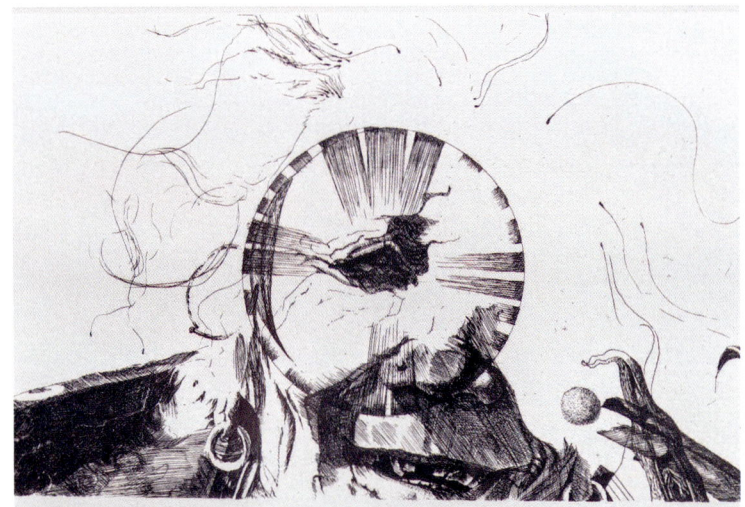

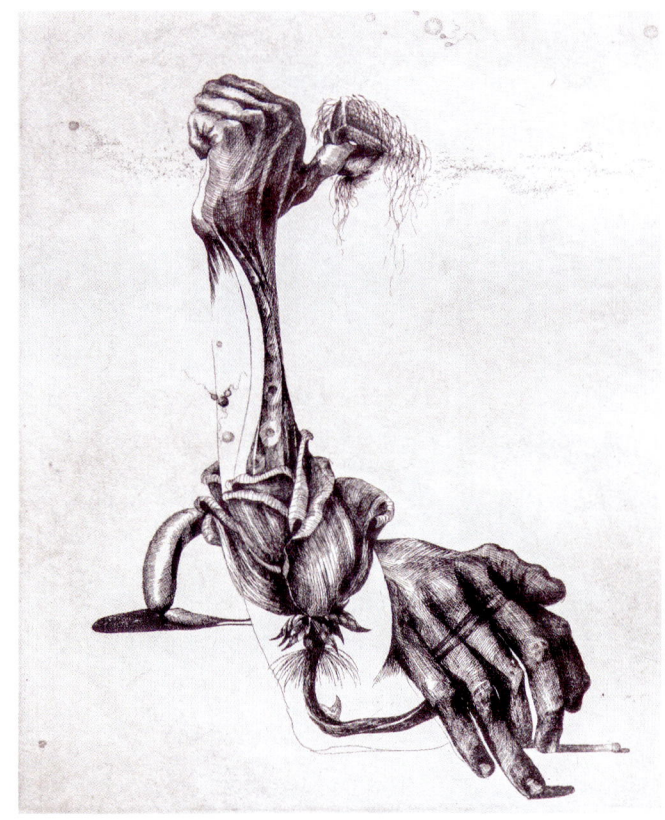

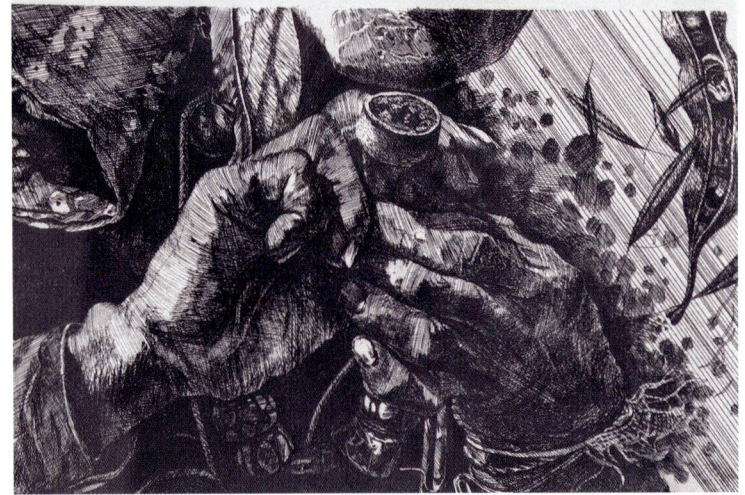

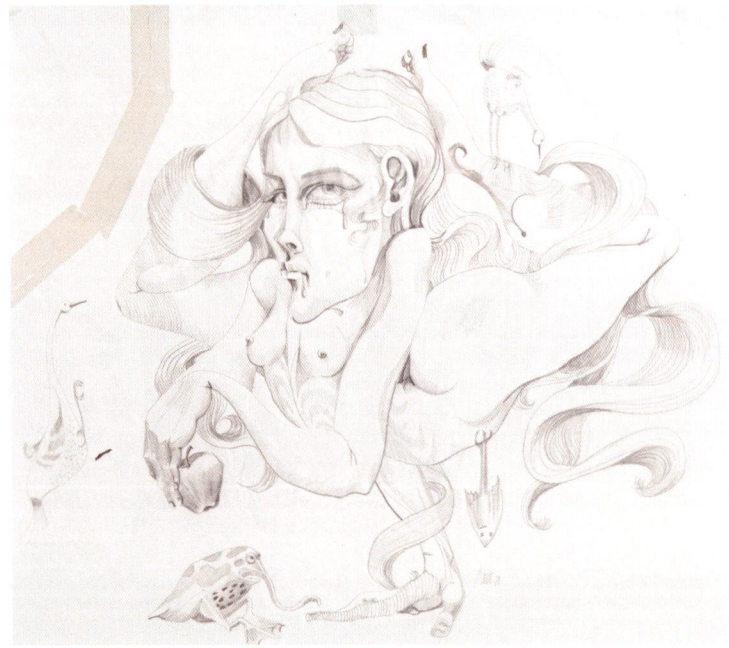

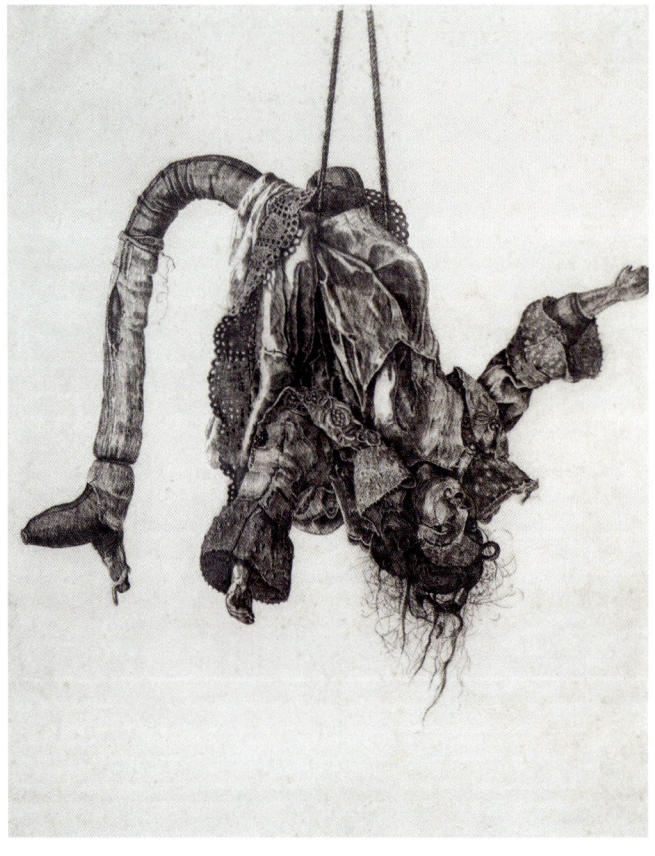

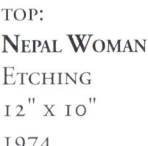

TOP:
NEPAL WOMAN
ETCHING
12" X 10"
1974

BOTTOM:
EYE WITH FROG
PENCIL
14" X 15"
1971

TOP:
MY STYLE
ETCHING
22" X 14.5"
1973

BOTTOM:
BALANCE
ETCHING
30.5" X 22"
1975

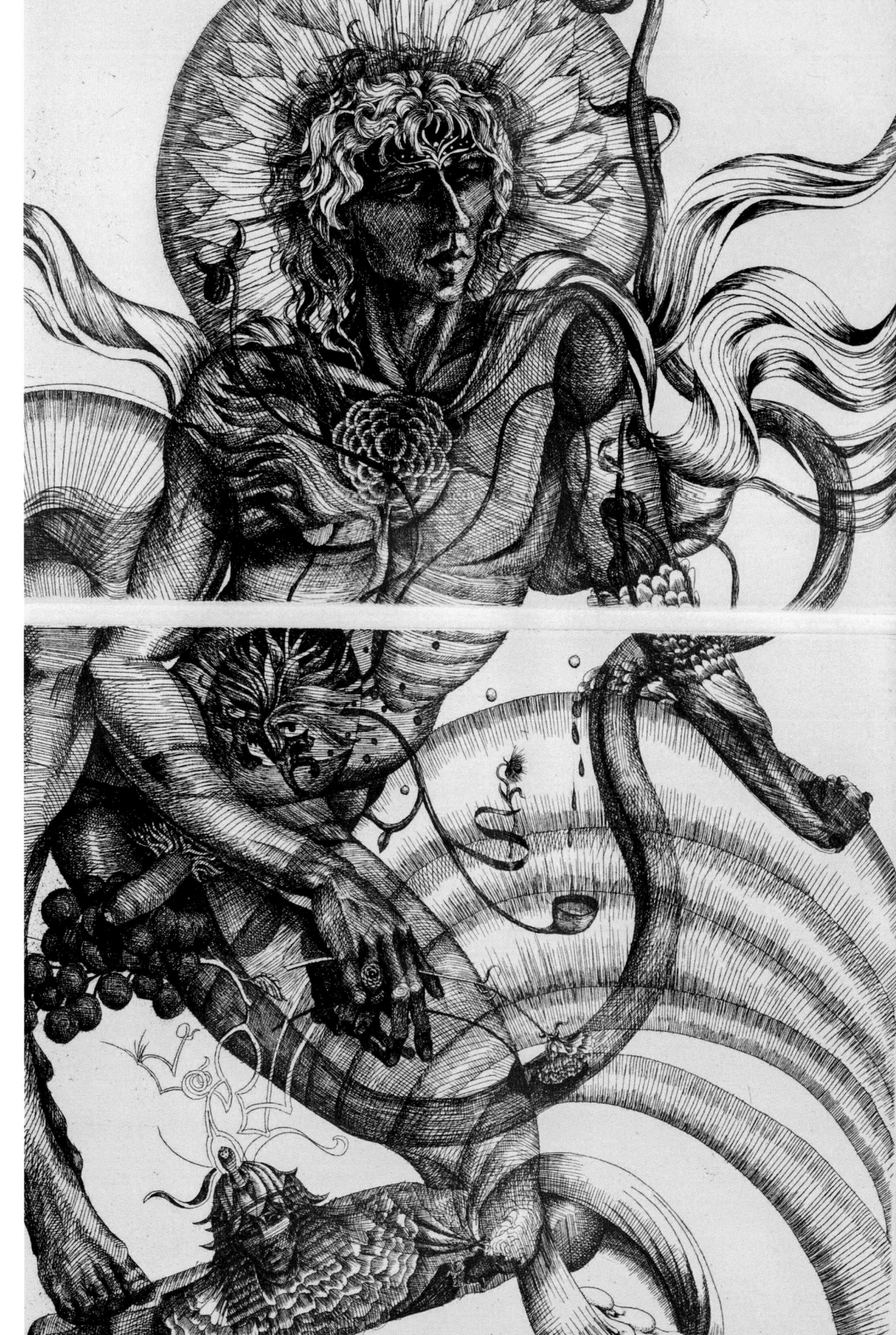

HADRIAN'S DREAM
ETCHING
24.5" X 17.5"
1972

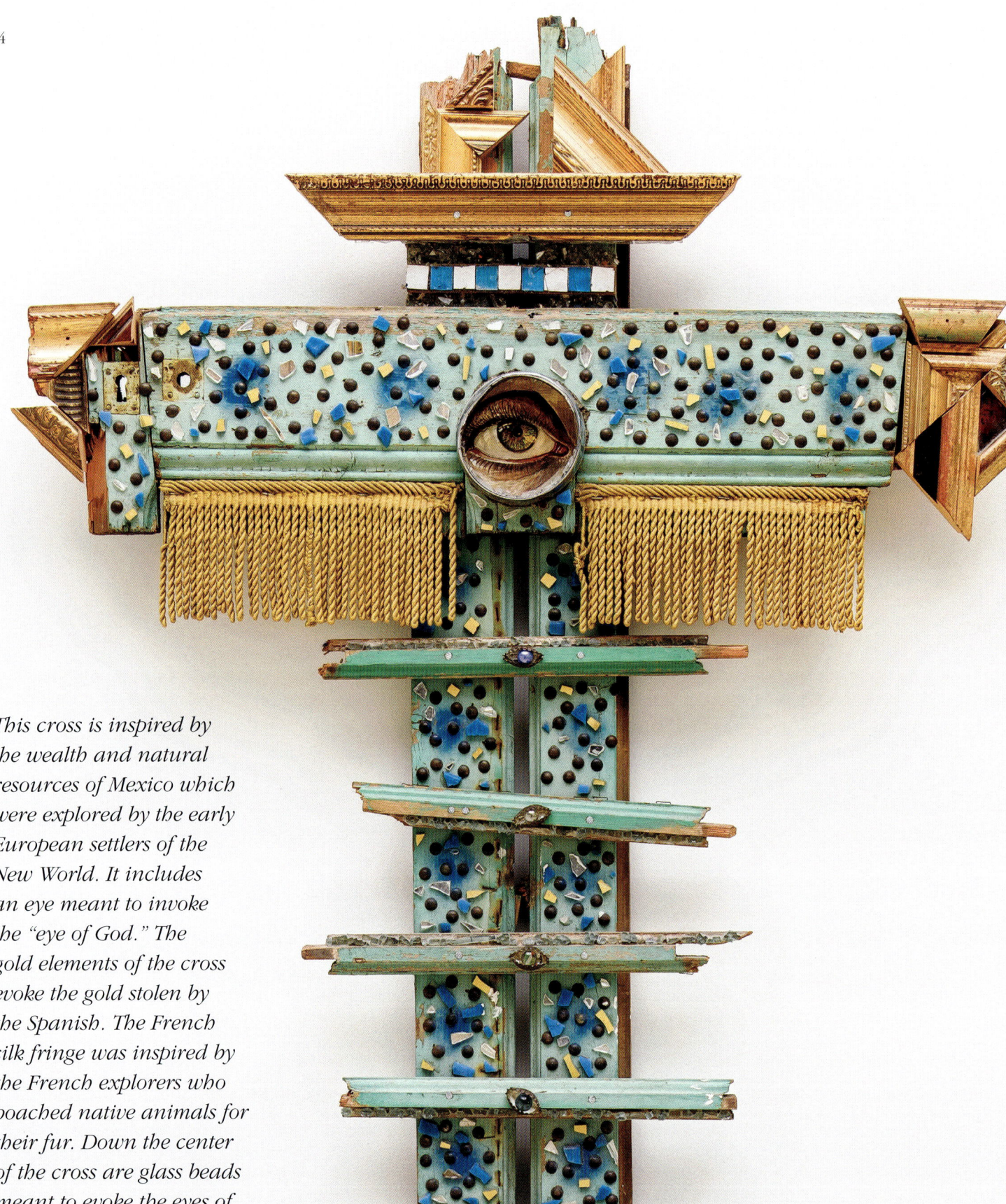

This cross is inspired by the wealth and natural resources of Mexico which were explored by the early European settlers of the New World. It includes an eye meant to invoke the "eye of God." The gold elements of the cross evoke the gold stolen by the Spanish. The French silk fringe was inspired by the French explorers who poached native animals for their fur. Down the center of the cross are glass beads meant to evoke the eyes of animals, which would glow in the darkened jungle as hunters shined their lights upon them.

MEXICAN ICON CROSS
MIXED MEDIA
51" X 33"
1989

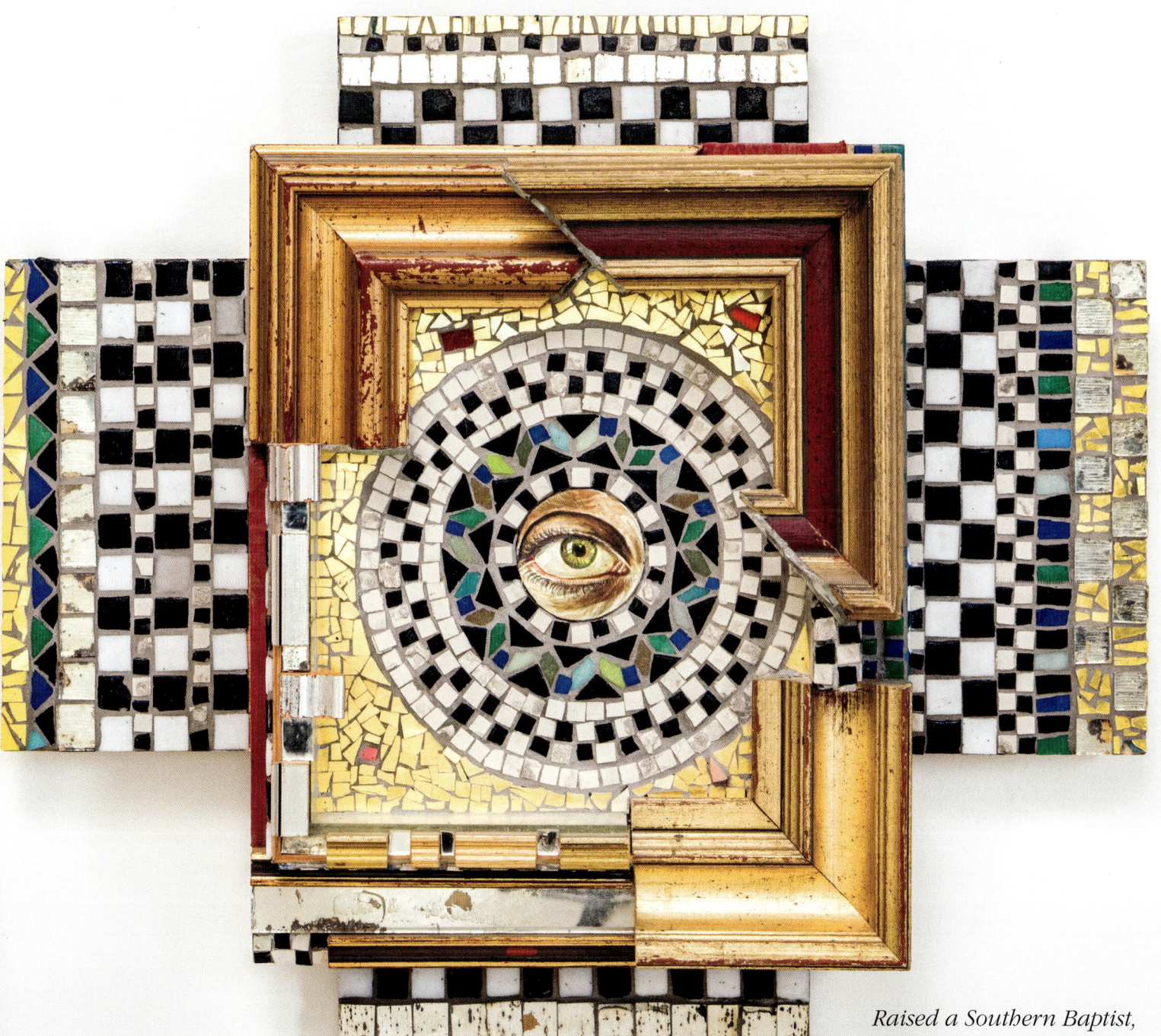

BYZANTINE CROSS
MIXED MEDIA
32" X 25"
1994

Raised a Southern Baptist, I long held a fascination with Christ, and crosses of varying styles and types are a frequent theme in my work. Here, I present a cross in the Byzantine style. The eye within a circle in its center evokes some of the earliest, prehistoric images associated with God and religious expression.

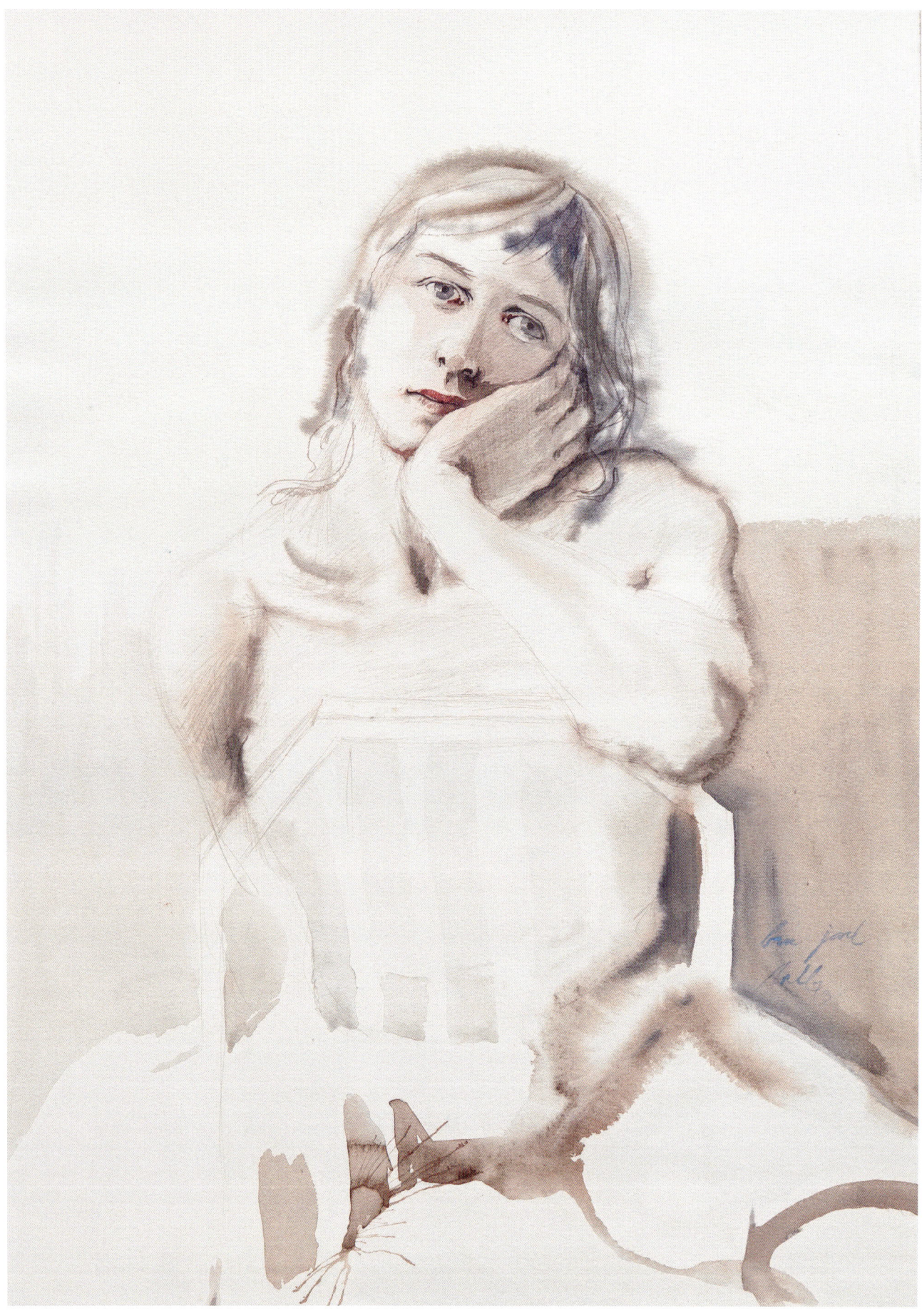

Yvon Croguennec
Watercolor
20" x 14"
1973

Ceiling Piece
Mixed Media
83" x 78"
1999

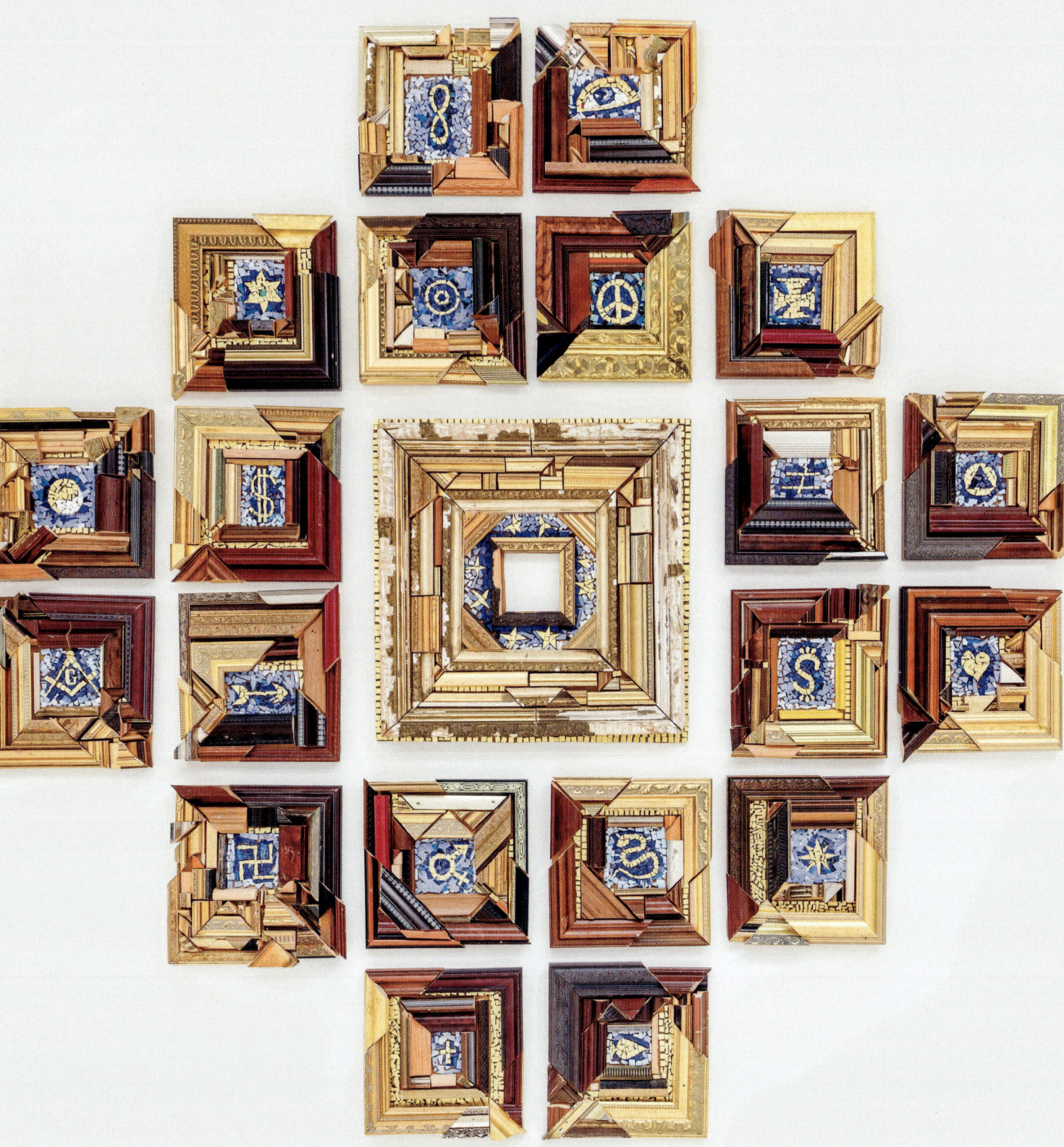

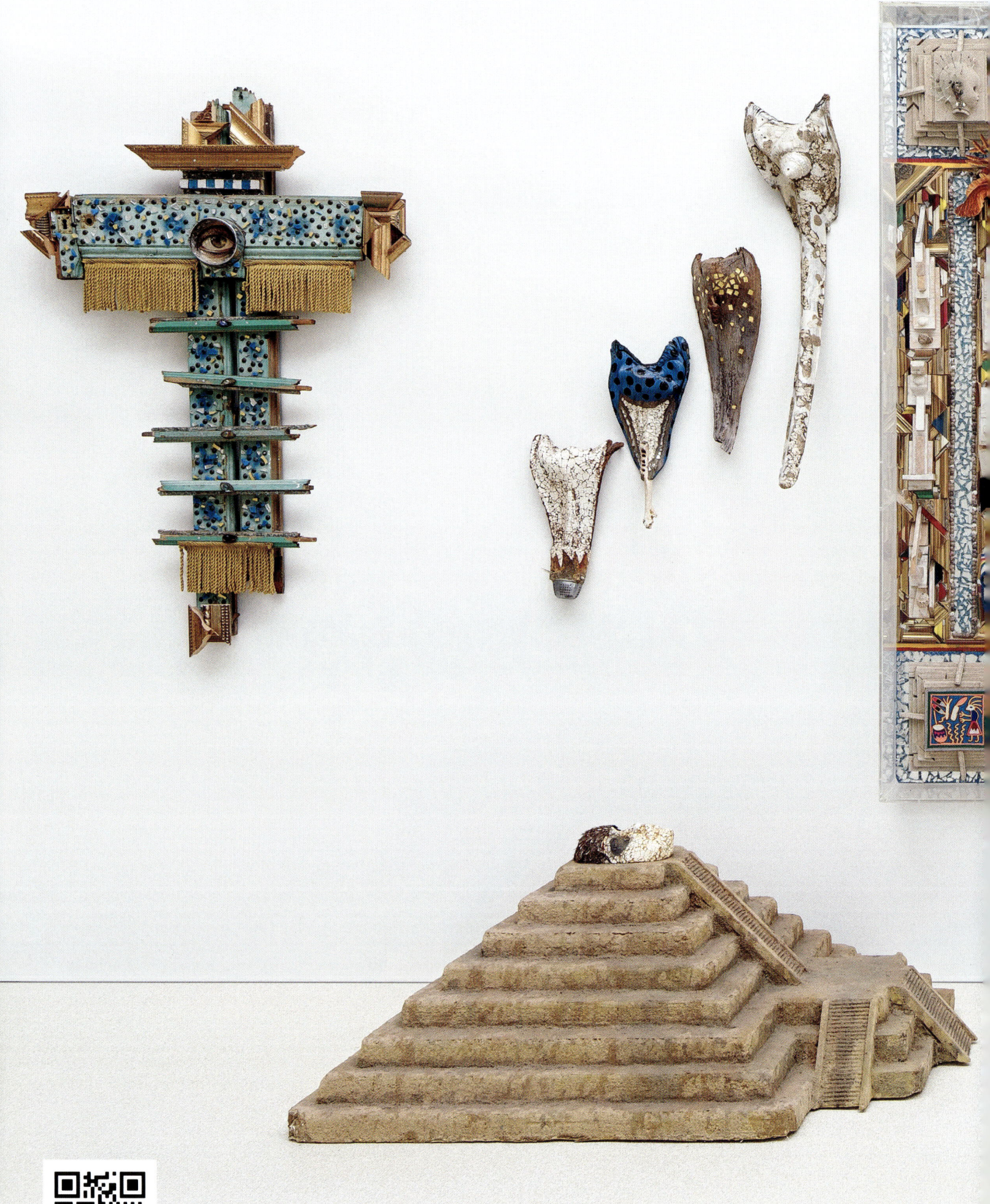

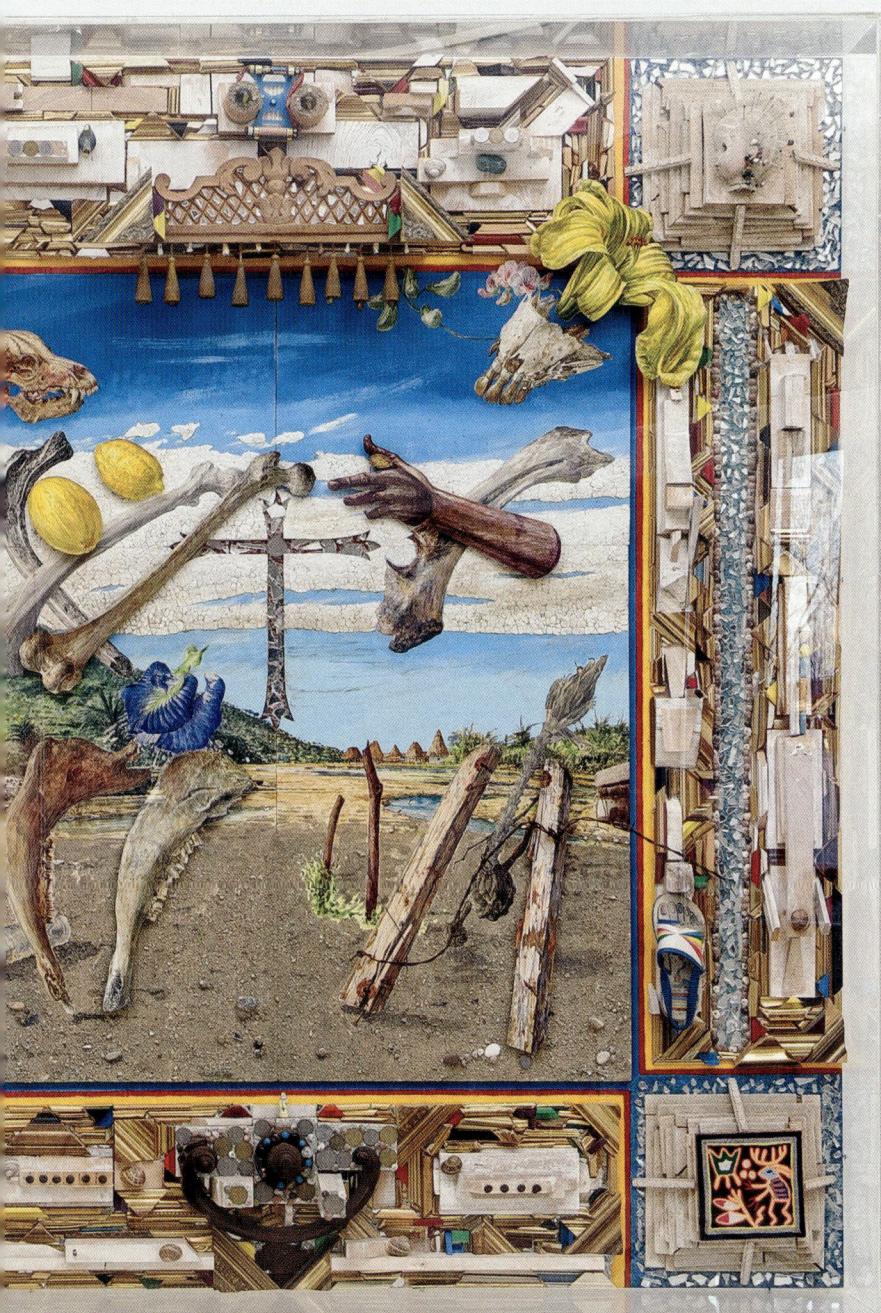

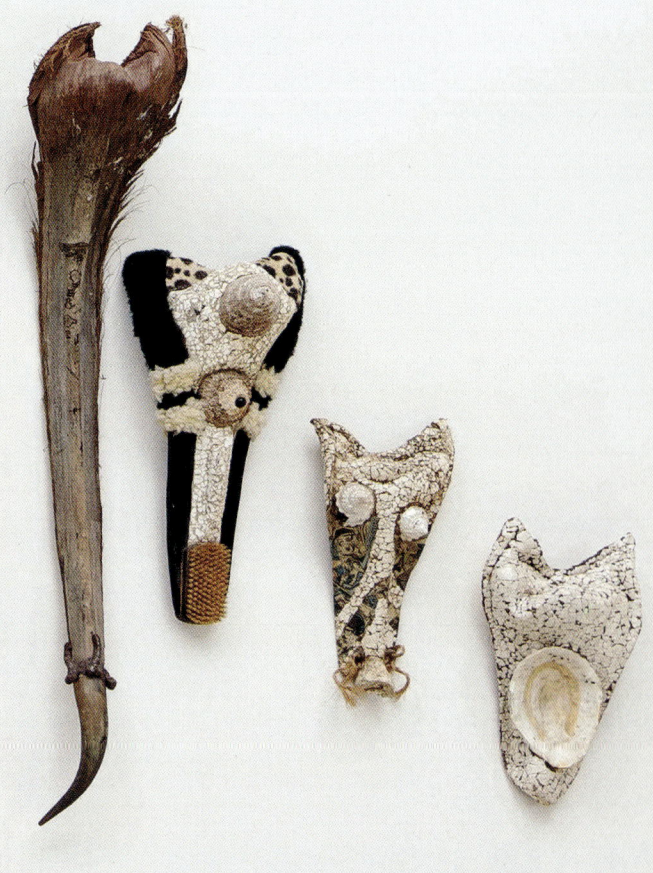

ADAM AND EVE IN YELAPA
MIXED MEDIA
64.5" X 70"
1989–2006

Inspired by my time spent in the secluded beach town of Yelapa on the west coast of Mexico, this painting depicts a lagoon drained of water, revealing a variety of objects reminiscent of the things I would find washed ashore while walking along the beach. I considered the beach my "office," and many of these found objects would be incorporated into my art. The masks hanging to the left and right of this piece are some of the works I made from found natural items and are inspired by masks made by the indigenous peoples of the region. The skulls and bones in the painting evoke the dust to dust energy of living in the jungle between sunrise and sunset. Positioned in front of the painting are the Pyramids of the Sun and Moon, made with assistance from fellow Alabama artist Bruce Larsen, a frequent collaborator.

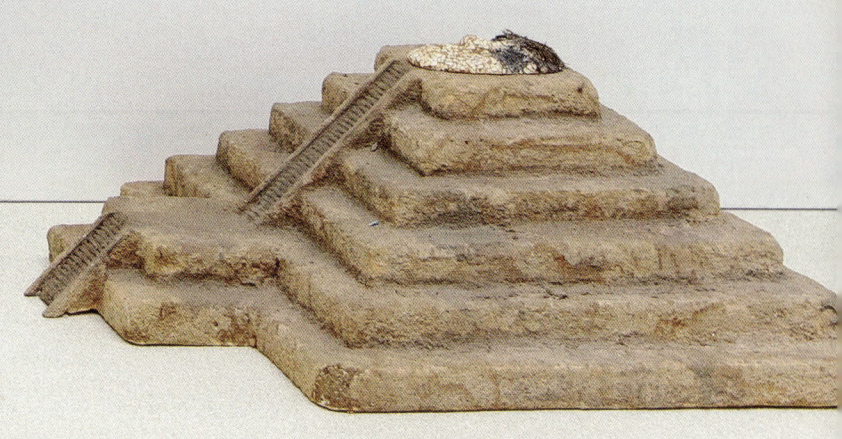

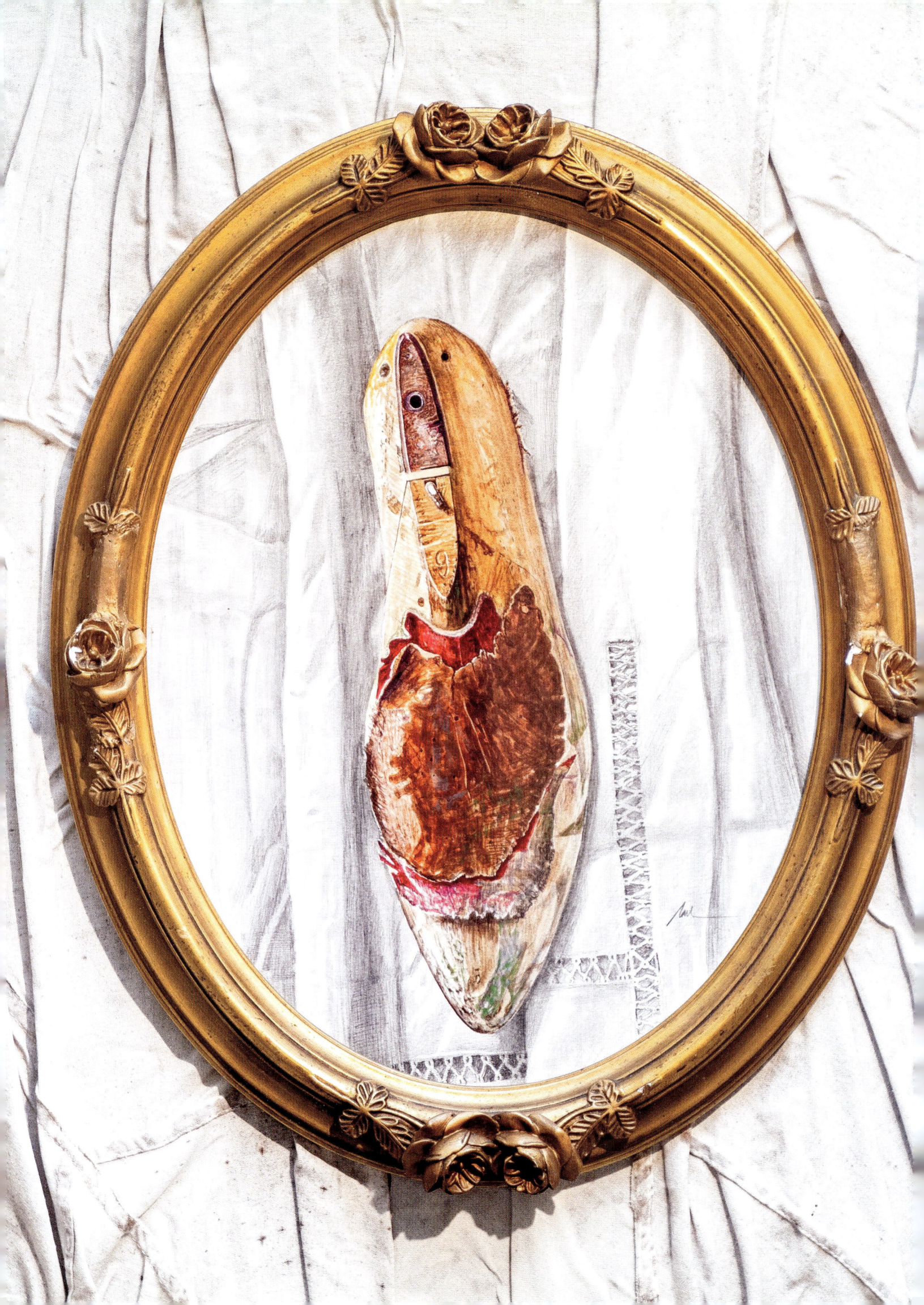

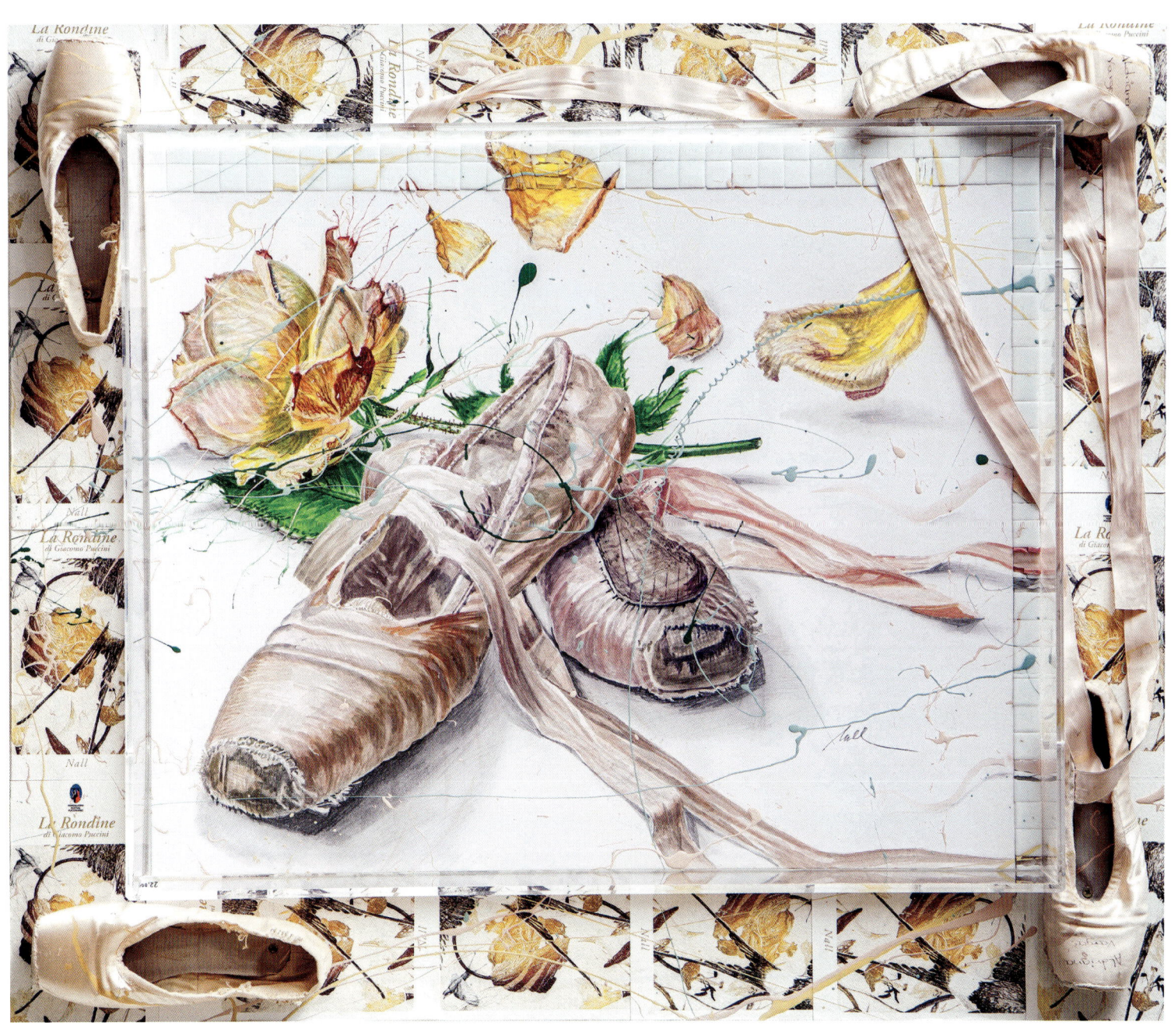

BALLET SHOES – OUT OF THE BOX
MIXED MEDIA
29" X 34.5"
2008

SHOE LAST
MIXED MEDIA
39" X 32"
2001

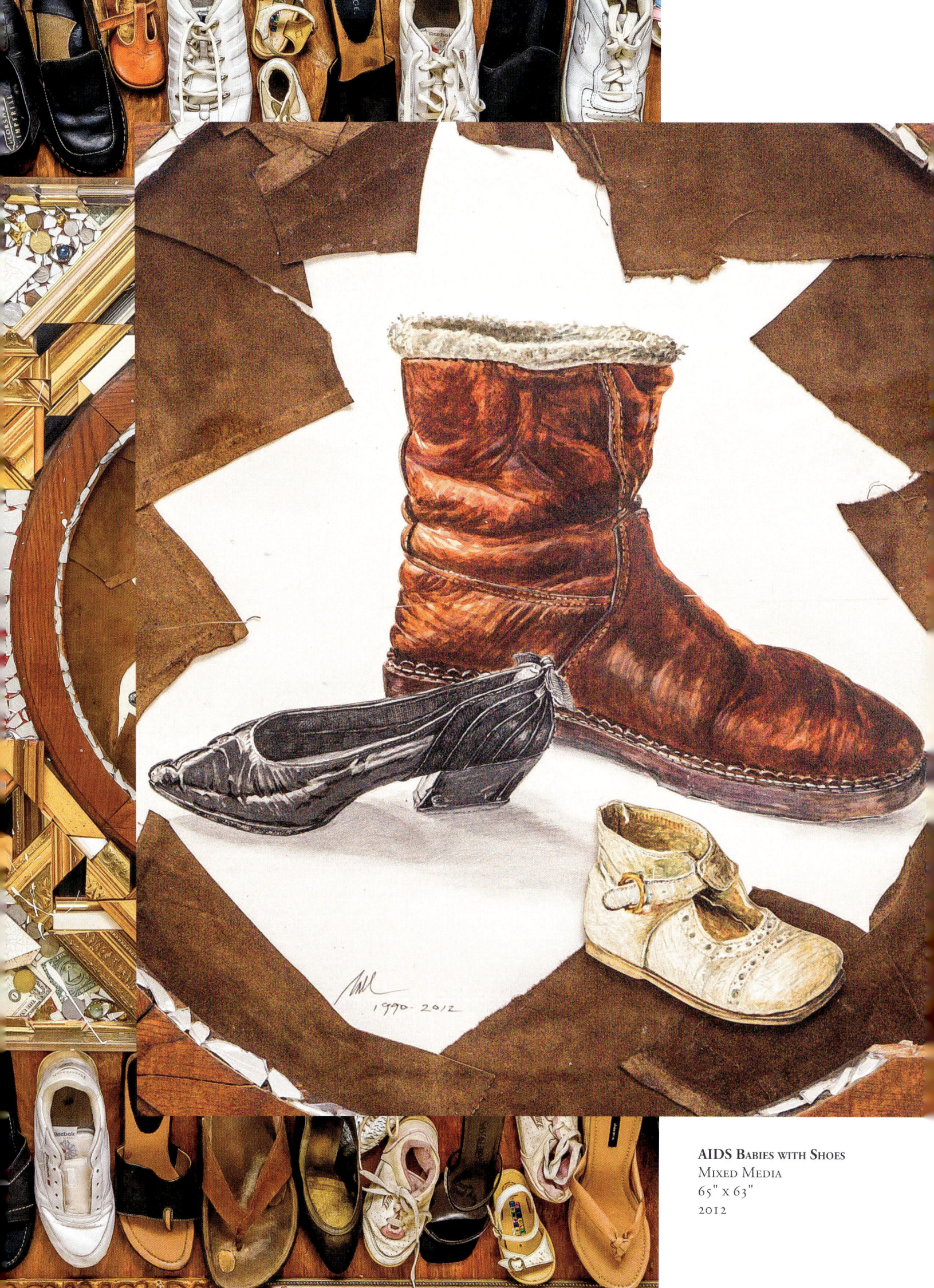

AIDS Babies with Shoes
Mixed Media
65" x 63"
2012

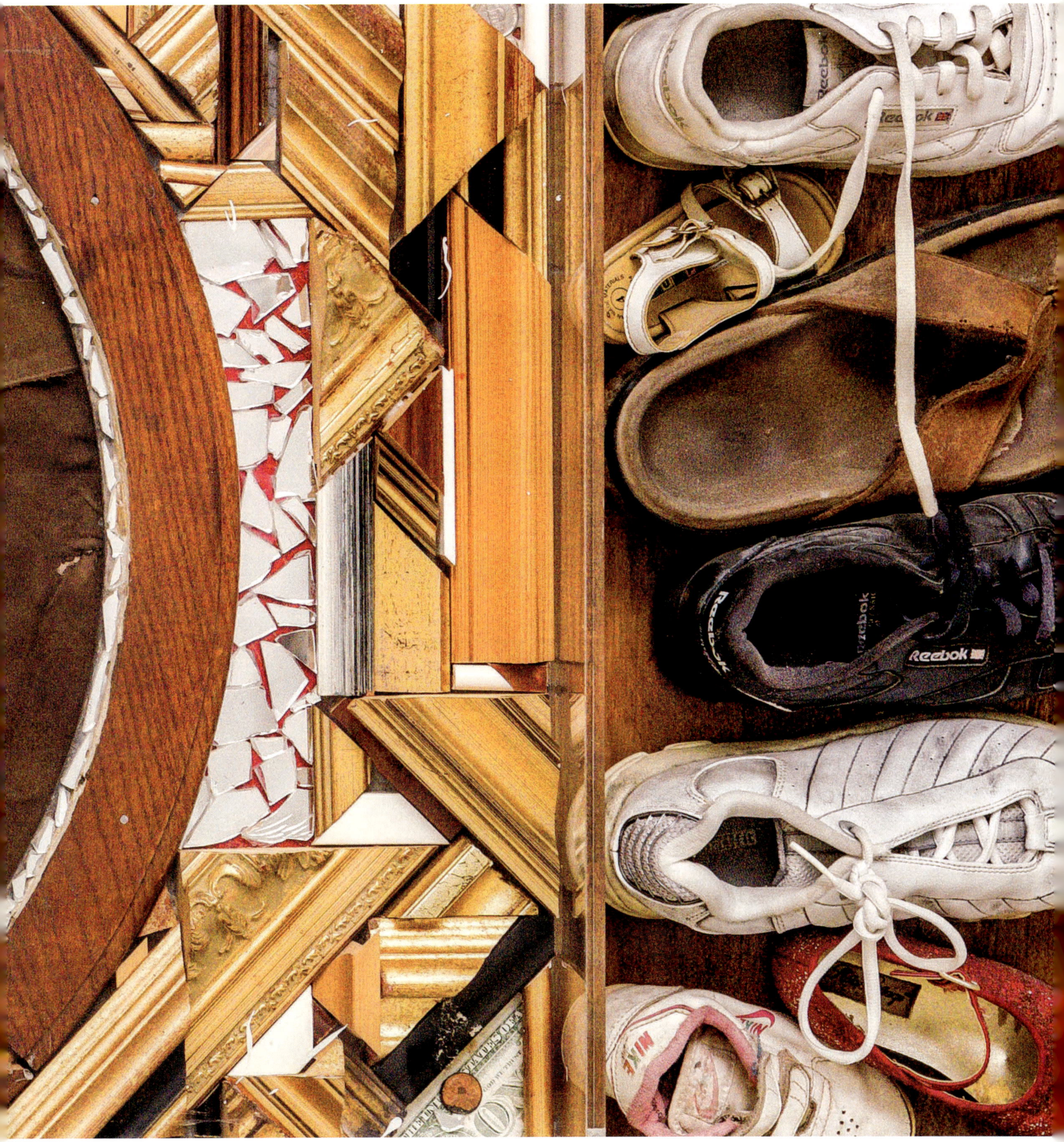

Moved by the growing AIDS crisis and concerned over the then-widespread misconception that only certain types of people could get AIDS, I created this piece as a reminder that the disease affects people from all walks of life. The various shoes, in differing styles and sizes, illustrate that AIDS can afflict anyone regardless of their background or sexual orientation.

VIDEO

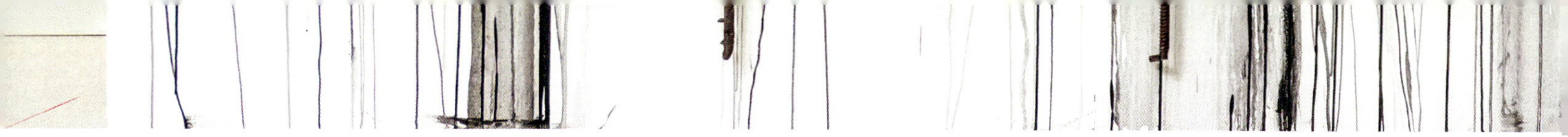

AL QAEDA TIC-TAC-TOE
Mixed Media
88" x 195"
2006

VIDEO

In this piece, I explore the intersection of war, politics, and oil. Having grown up with a grandfather who owned gas stations and distributed petroleum throughout the southeast, and later having lived and traveled throughout the Middle East, I felt a personal connection to the global war on terrorism which took place amidst the backdrop of many oil-producing nations. In Al Qaeda Tic-Tac-Toe, I symbolized the ineffectiveness of violence as a way to solve global problems by contrasting two very different

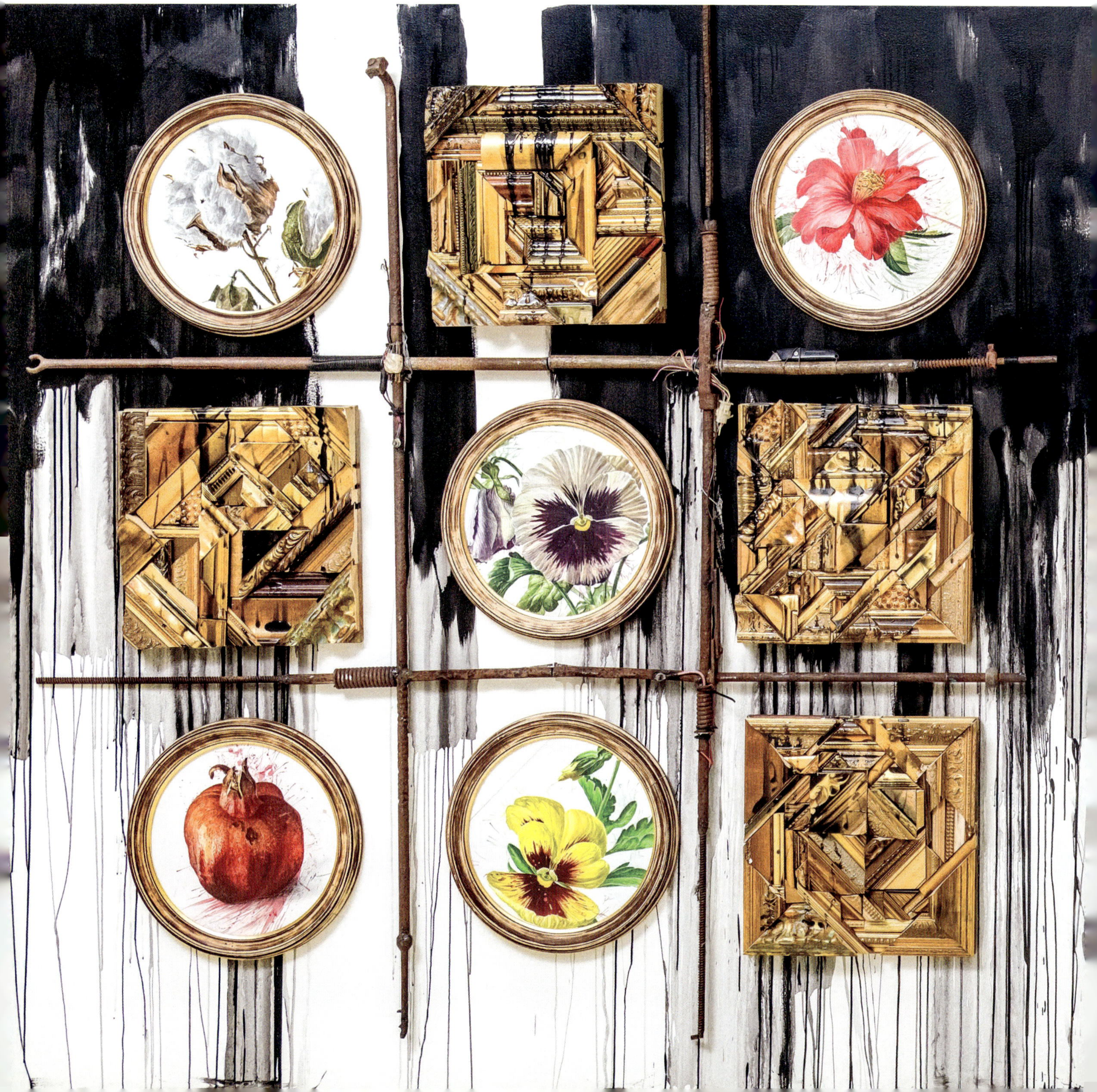

games of tic-tac-toe. On the right, war is depicted in the form of several portraits that have been shot with a gun. I took the portraits to a shooting range and fired on them myself. The gold panels are meant to depict oil, which I describe as the "new gold." In this contest between violence and oil, there is no winner. On the left, the violence is replaced by paintings of flowers, symbols of peace and joy. In this game, peace is victorious. We can't win with war; we can't win with hatred.

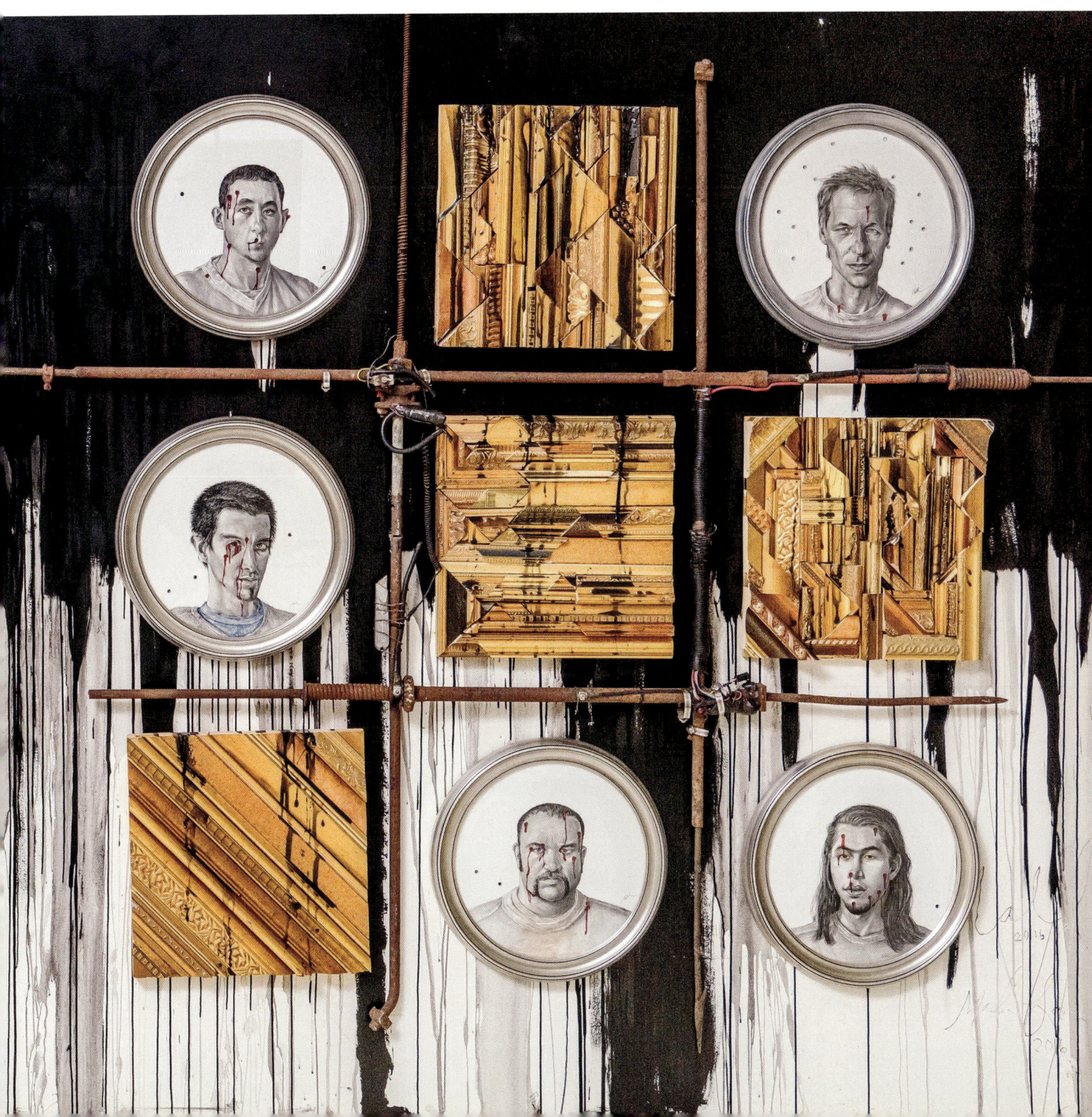

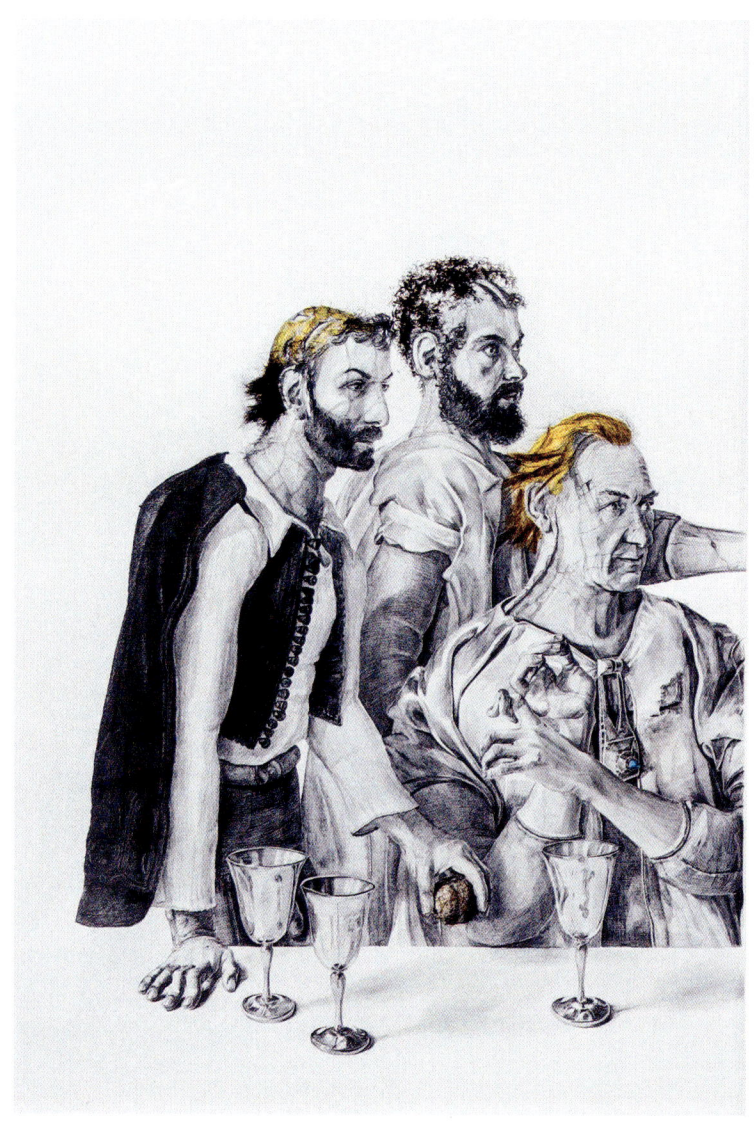
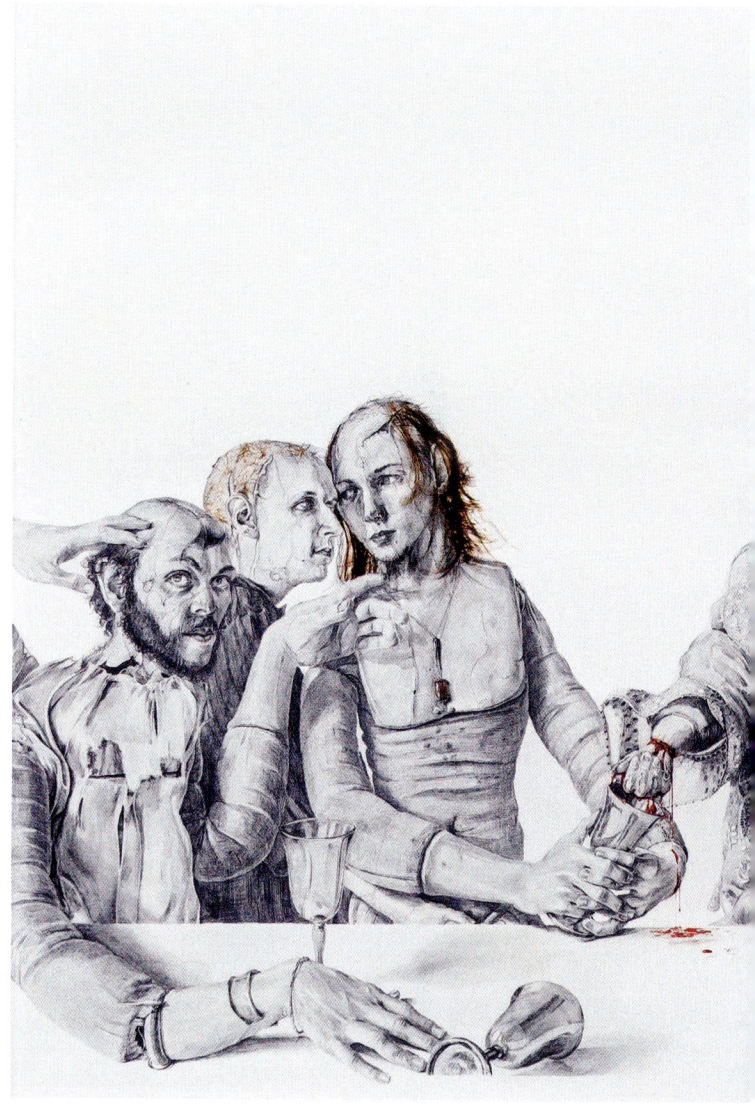

THE LAST SUPPER
PAINTED GICLEE
84" x 30"
1975

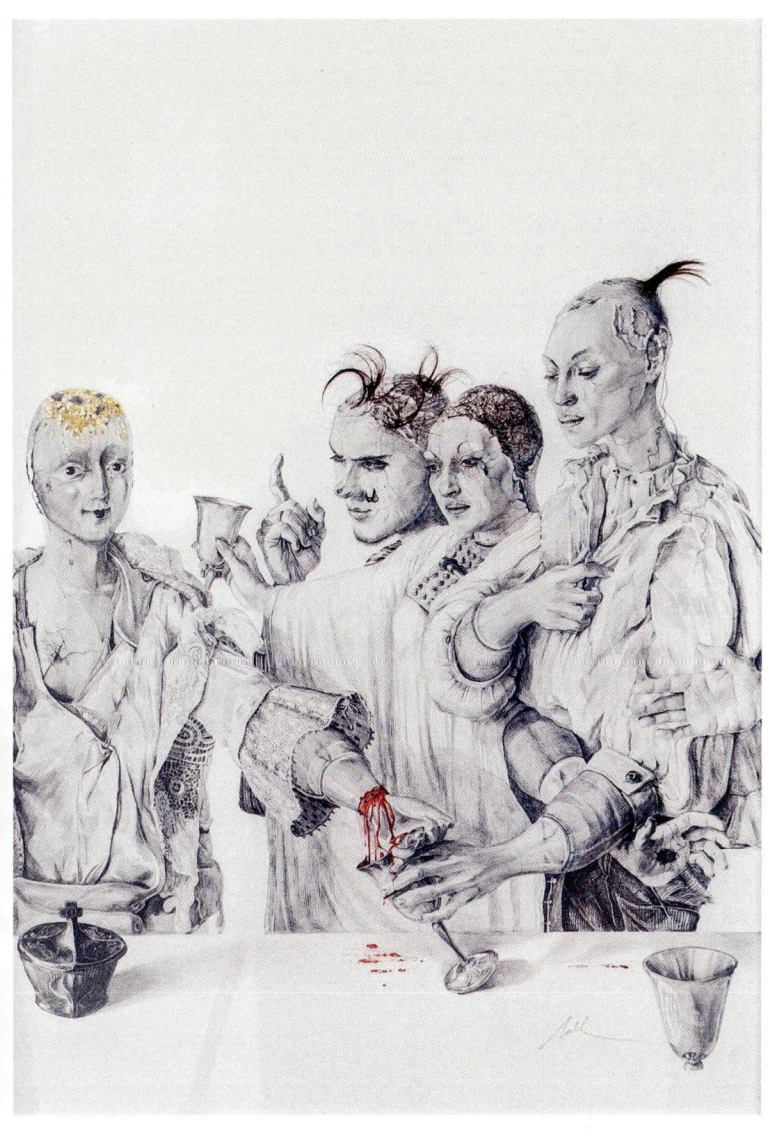
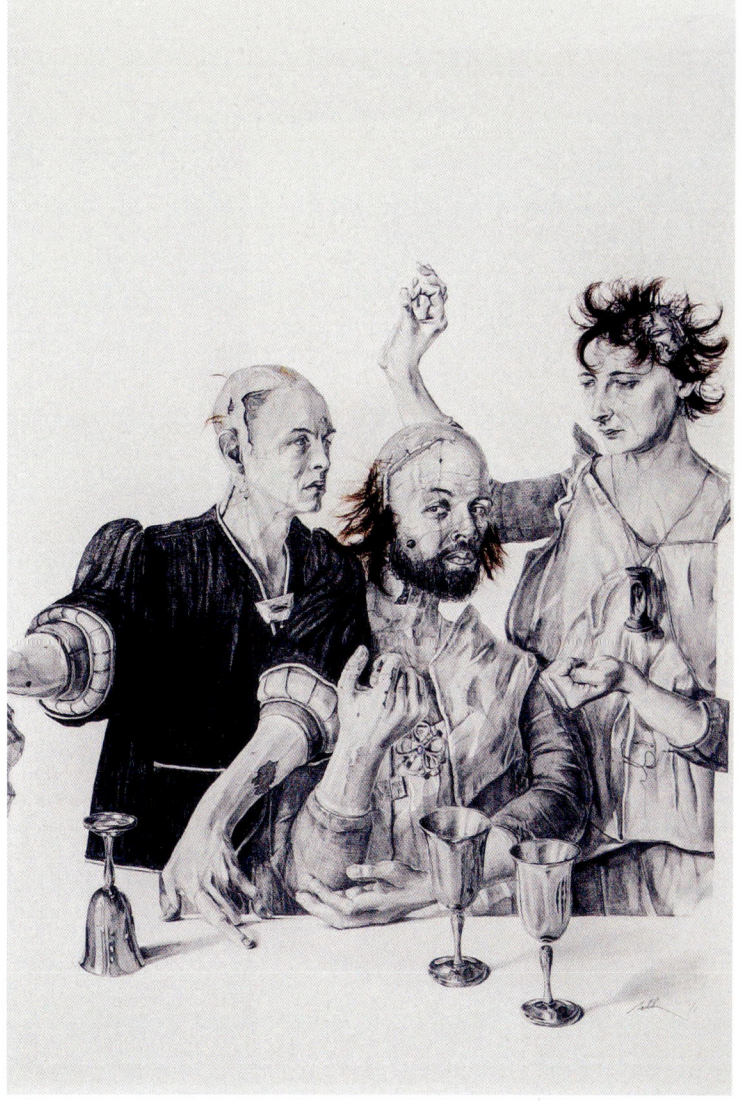

My version of "The Last Supper" takes da Vinci's familiar composition and populates it with friends and fellow artists. I admit I did not research who each figure was supposed to represent in da Vinci's original mural and, without realizing it, I placed myself in the position traditionally ascribed to be that of Judas. This piece was another produced during my "doll period" and here Christ is depicted as a doll, which is my commentary on man's attempts to create God in his own image. Here, Christ's sacrifice is depicted as literal blood being poured into the disciples' goblets. I was active in making jewelry during this time, and some of my jewelry designs adorn the figures.

VIDEO

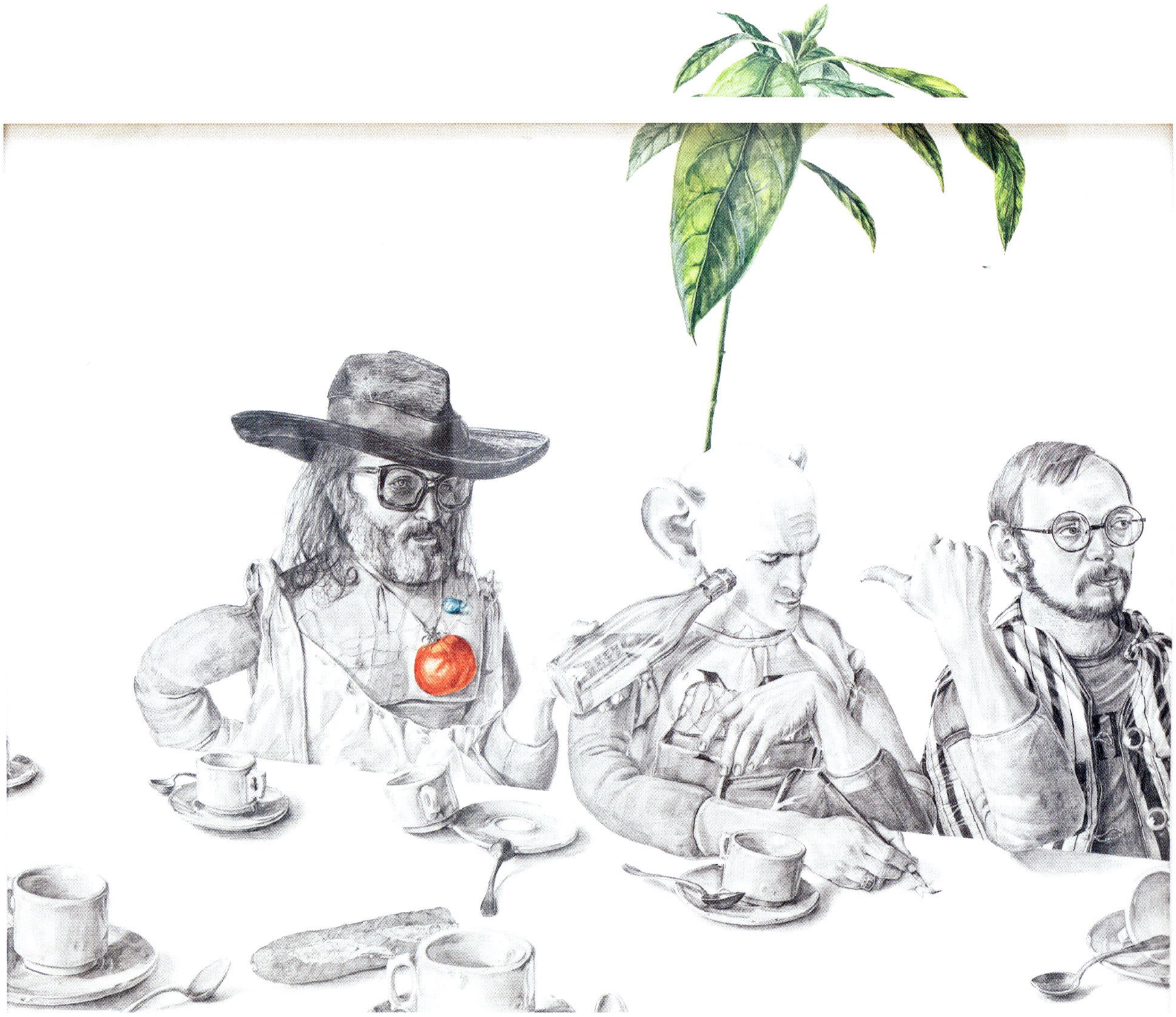

VIDEO

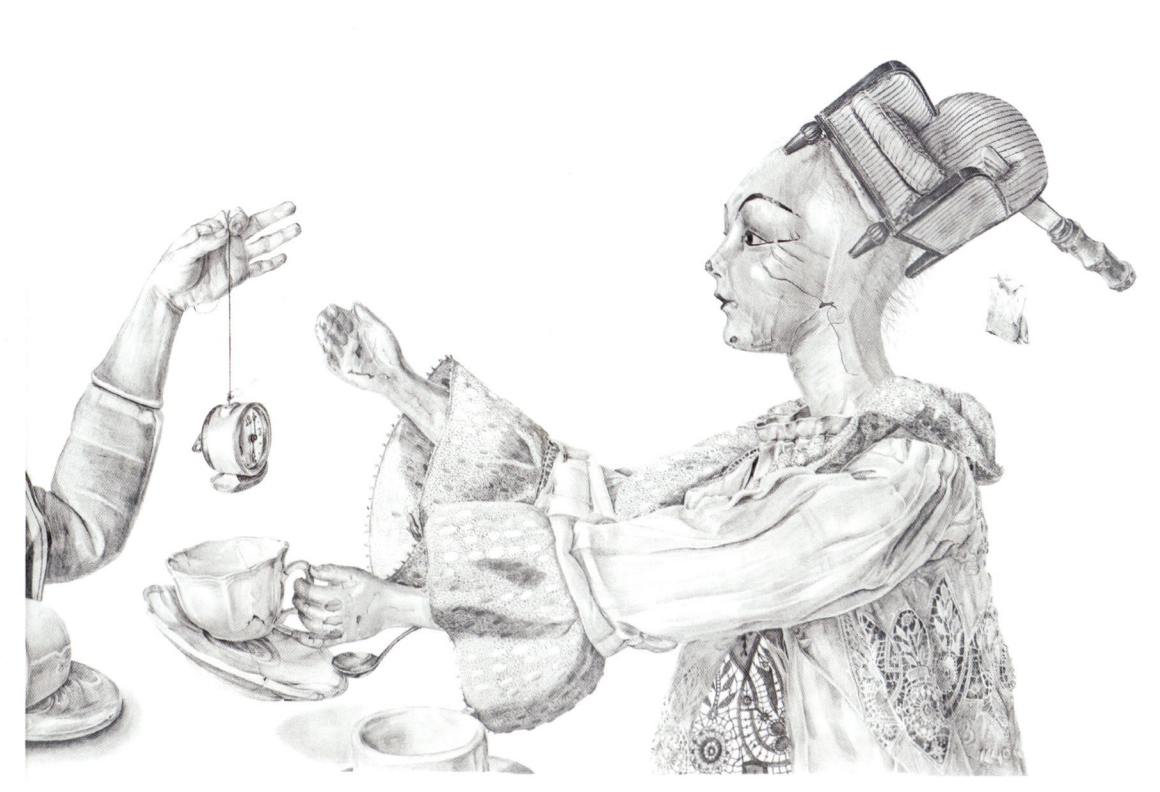

TEA PARTY
PENCIL & WATERCOLOR
63" x 35.5"
1977–1979

BELOW:
**WHITE QUEEN PRICKS
HER FINGER**
PENCIL & WATERCOLOR
31" X 23.5"
1979

OPPOSITE PAGE:
ALICE AND THE BILL LIZARD
PENCIL & WATERCOLOR
39.5" X 25.5"
1979

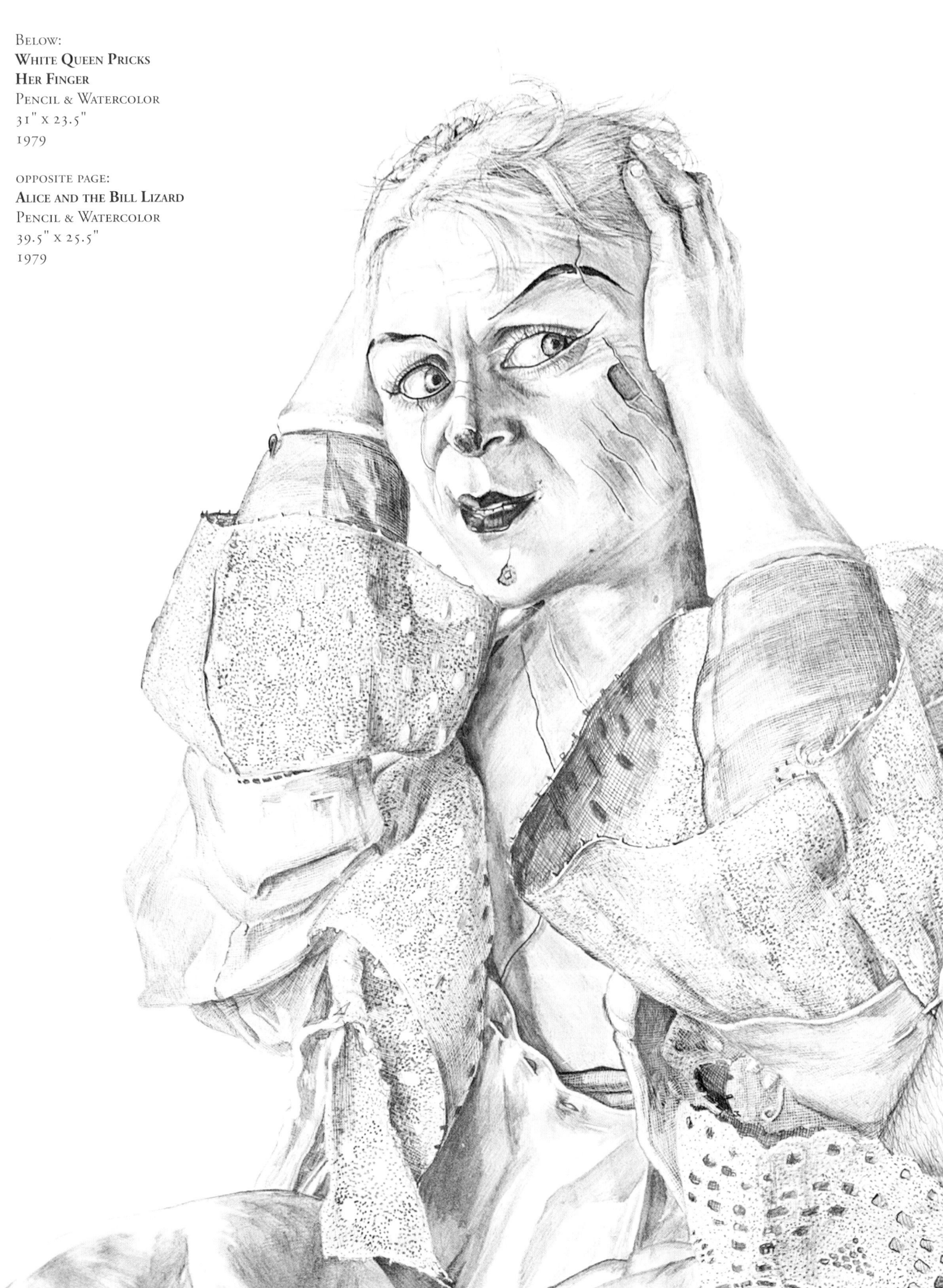

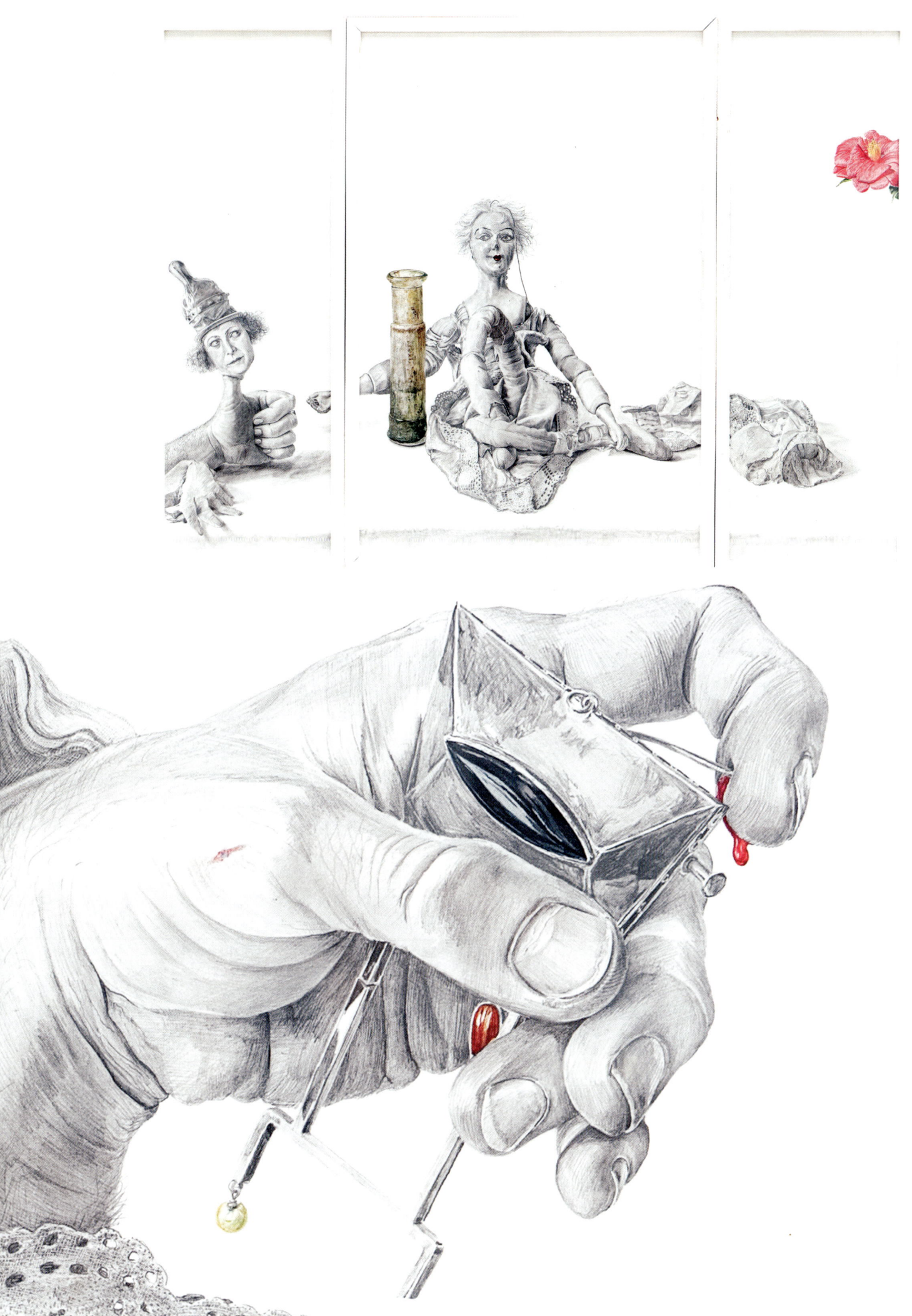

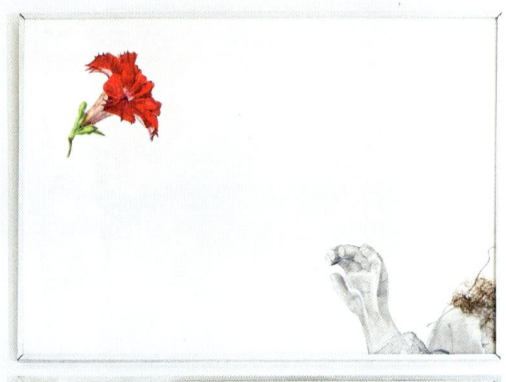
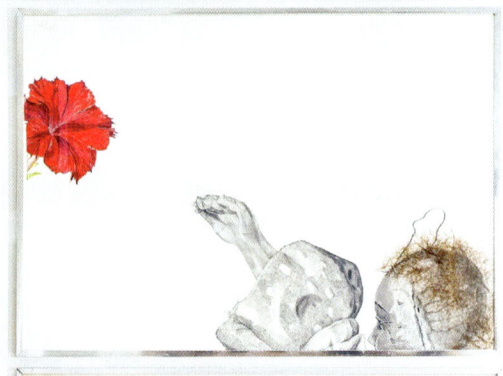
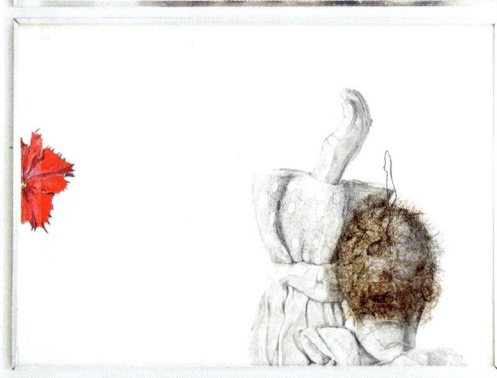
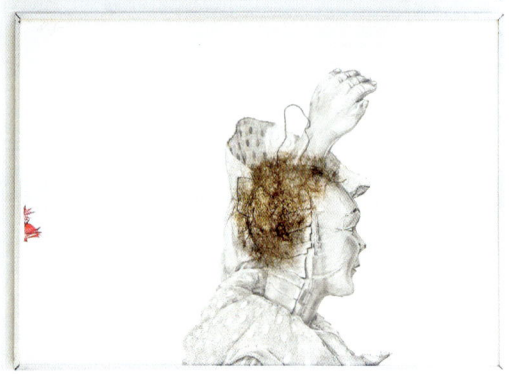

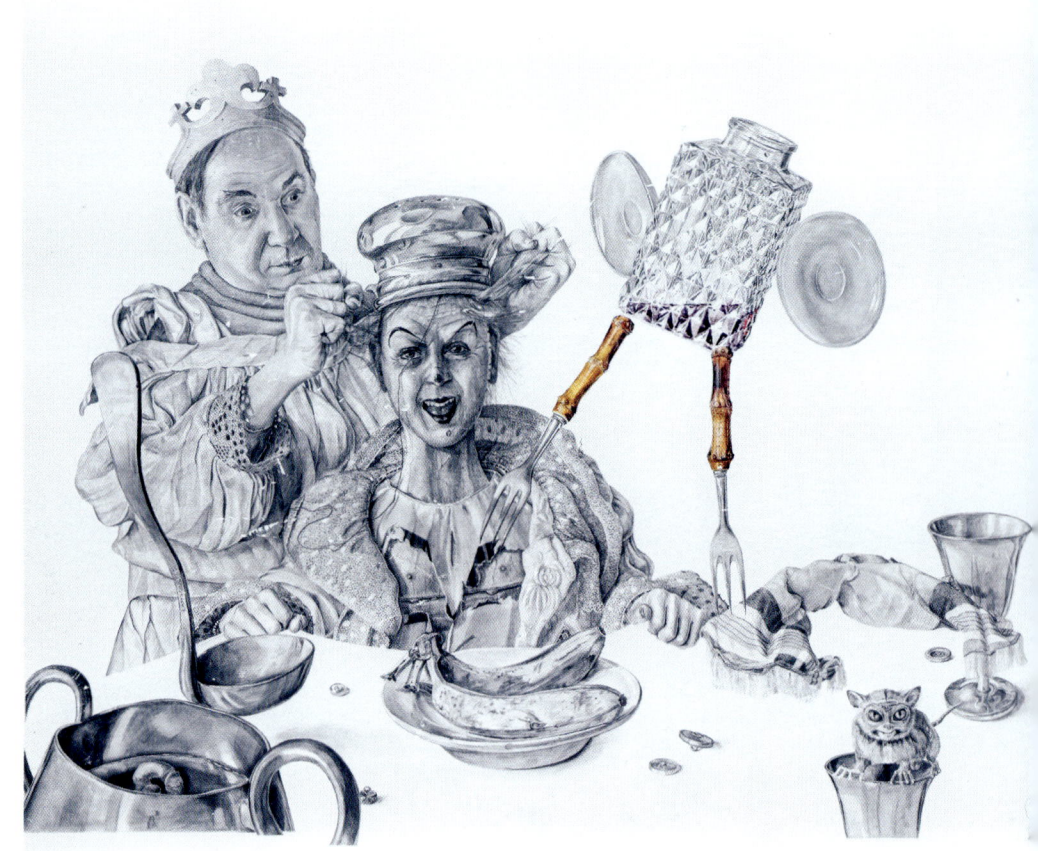

ABOVE:
ANIMATED PIROUETTE
MIXED MEDIA
25.5" X 19.5"
1976

BOTTOM RIGHT:
ANIMATED PIROUETTE
DETAIL

TOP RIGHT:
ALICE CROWNED QUEEN
PENCIL & WATERCOLOR
39" X 25.5"
1977–1979

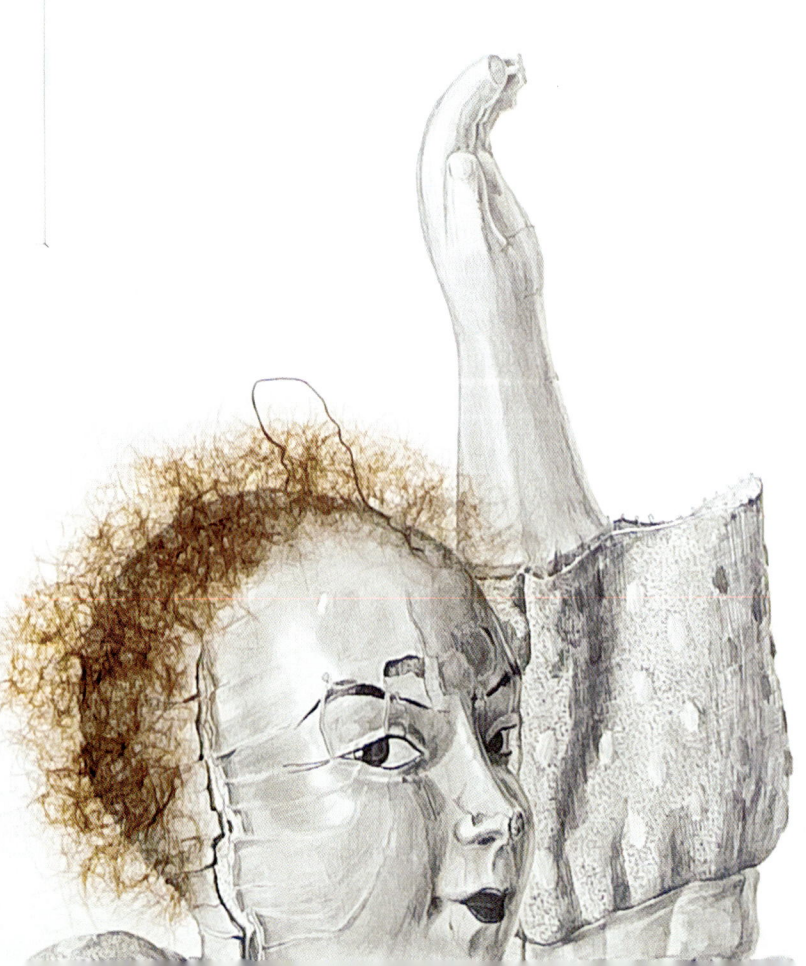

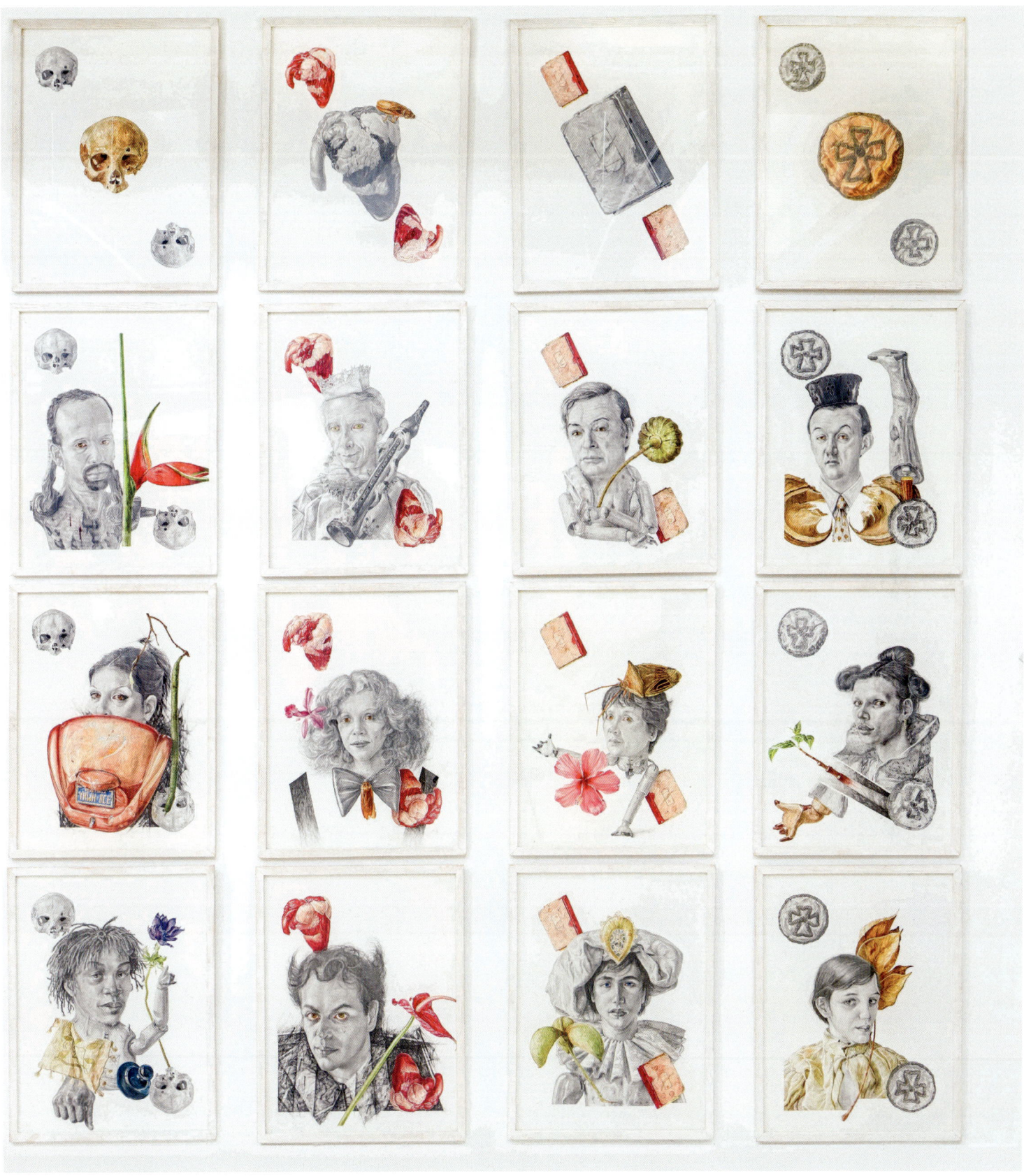

"ALICE IN WONDERLAND"
PLAYING CARDS
PENCIL & WATERCOLOR
24.5" X 19" EACH
1977–1979

My continued fascination with "Alice in Wonderland" and the life of Lewis Carroll led to this series of portraits done in the style of playing cards. The subjects are friends and fellow artists from my years in France, and each "card" incorporates imagery from tarot cards and astrology, from which modern playing cards are derived.

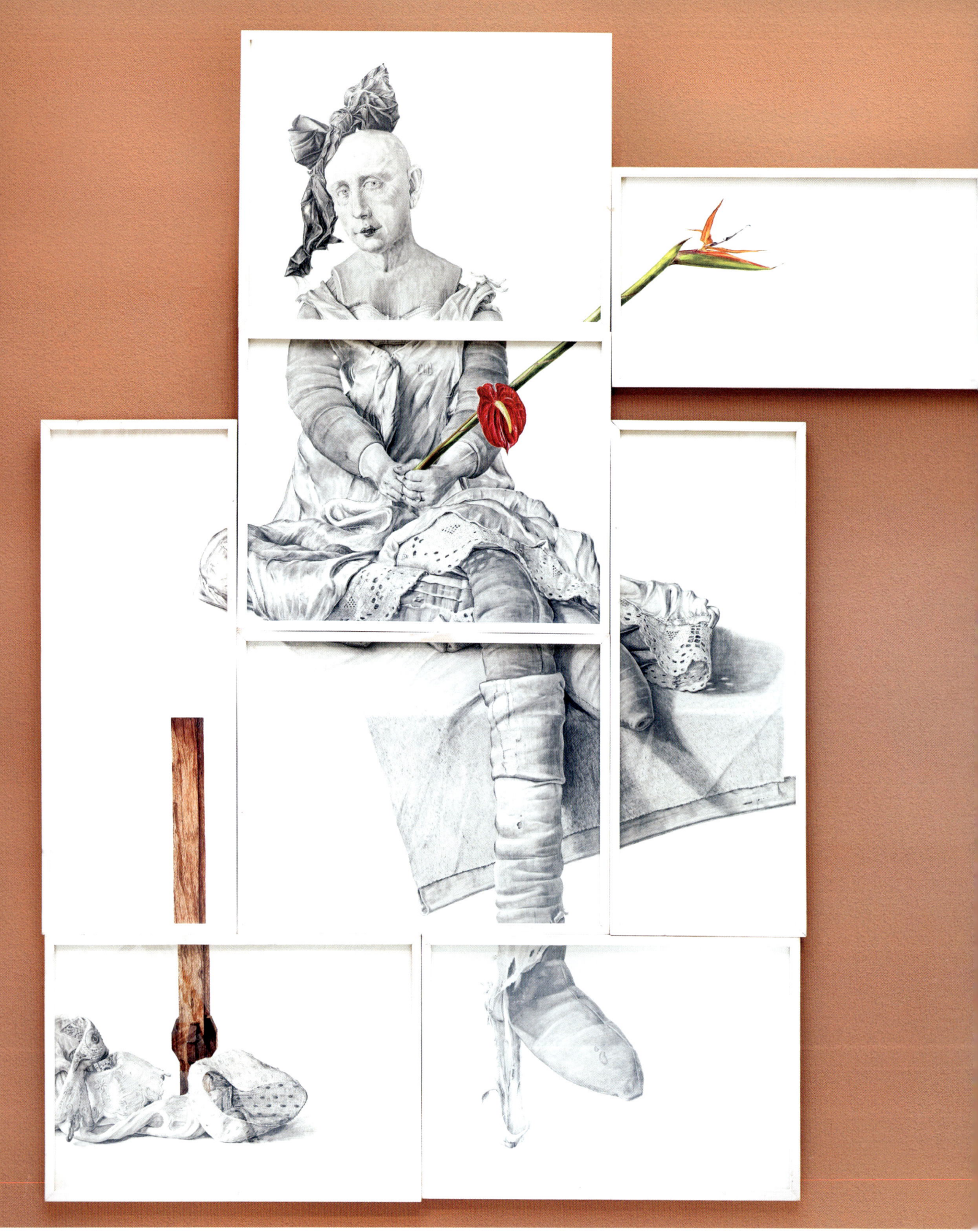

ABOVE:

LEWIS CARROLL AS ALICE
PENCIL & WATERCOLOR
88.5" X 114"
1977–1979

OPPOSITE PAGE TOP LEFT:

THE COOK
PENCIL, PEN AND INK, AND
WATERCOLOR
25.5" X 19.5"
1977

OPPOSITE PAGE TOP RIGHT:

**WHITE KNIGHT, HORSE,
AND AGED MAN**
PENCIL & WATERCOLOR
47" X 31"
1977–1979

OPPOSITE PAGE BOTTOM:

FOOTMEN
PENCIL & WATERCOLOR
19.5" X 25.5"
1979

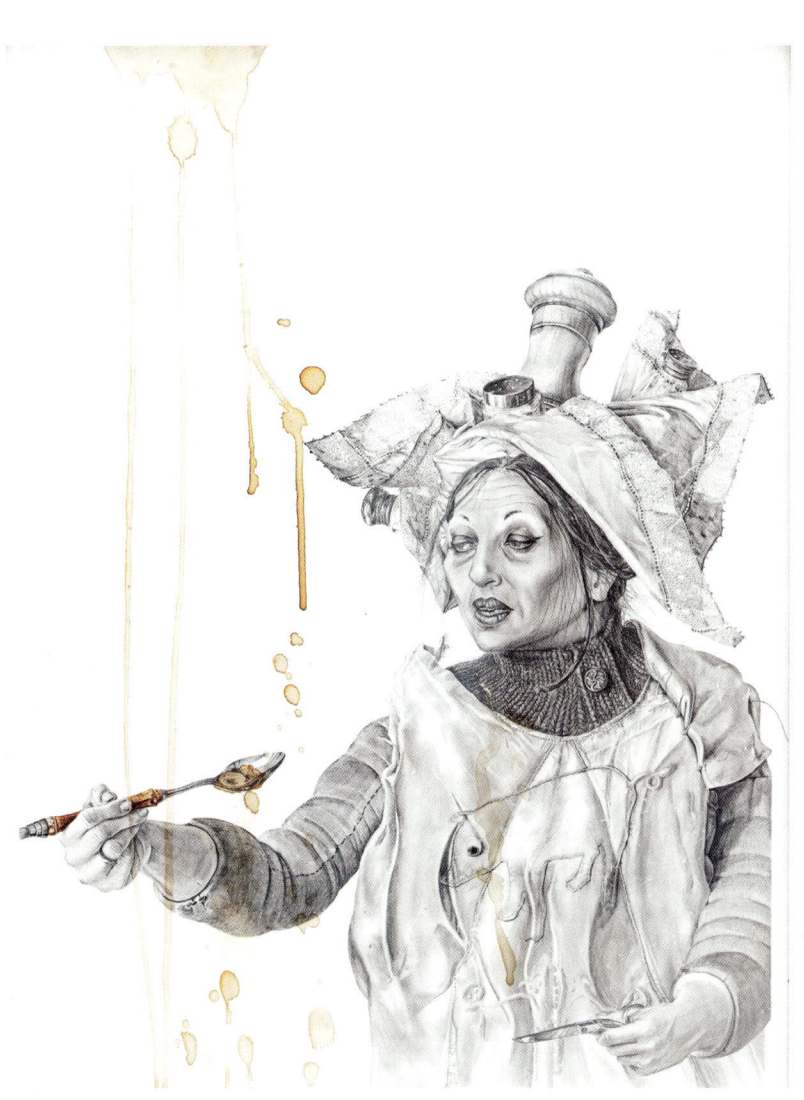

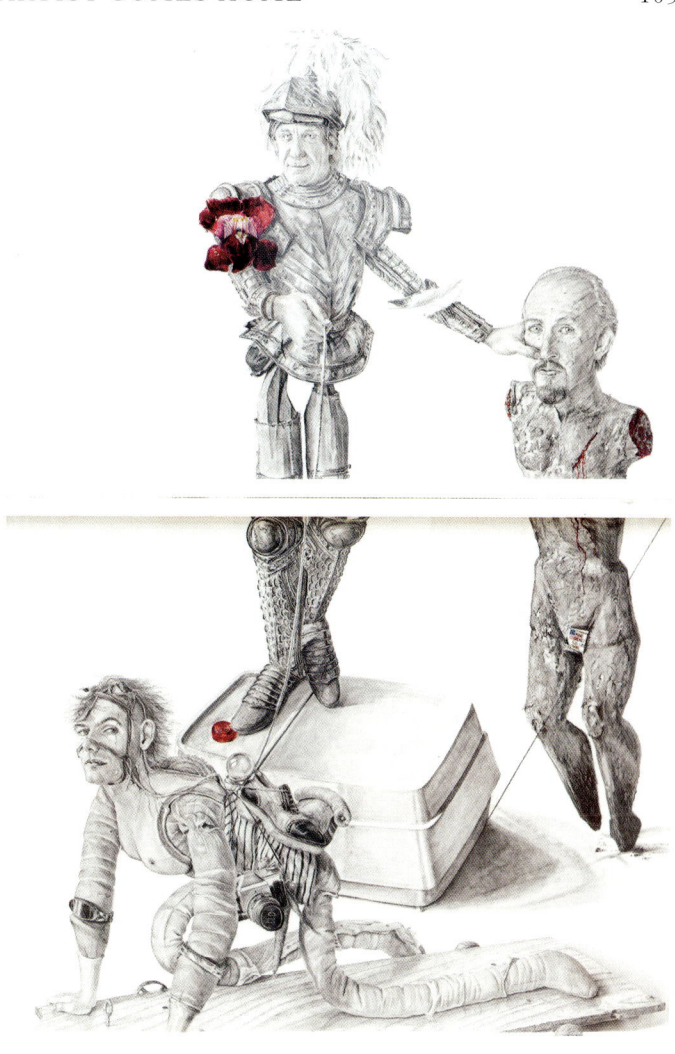

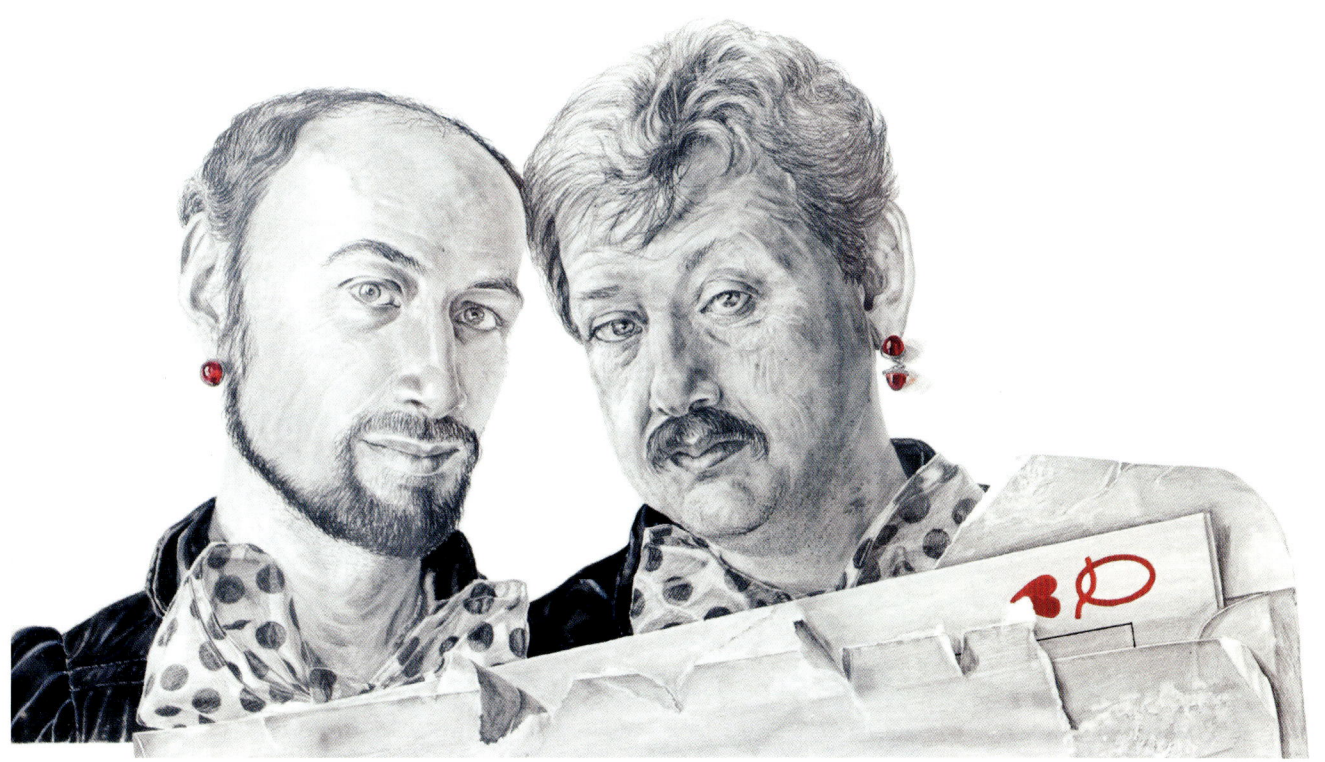

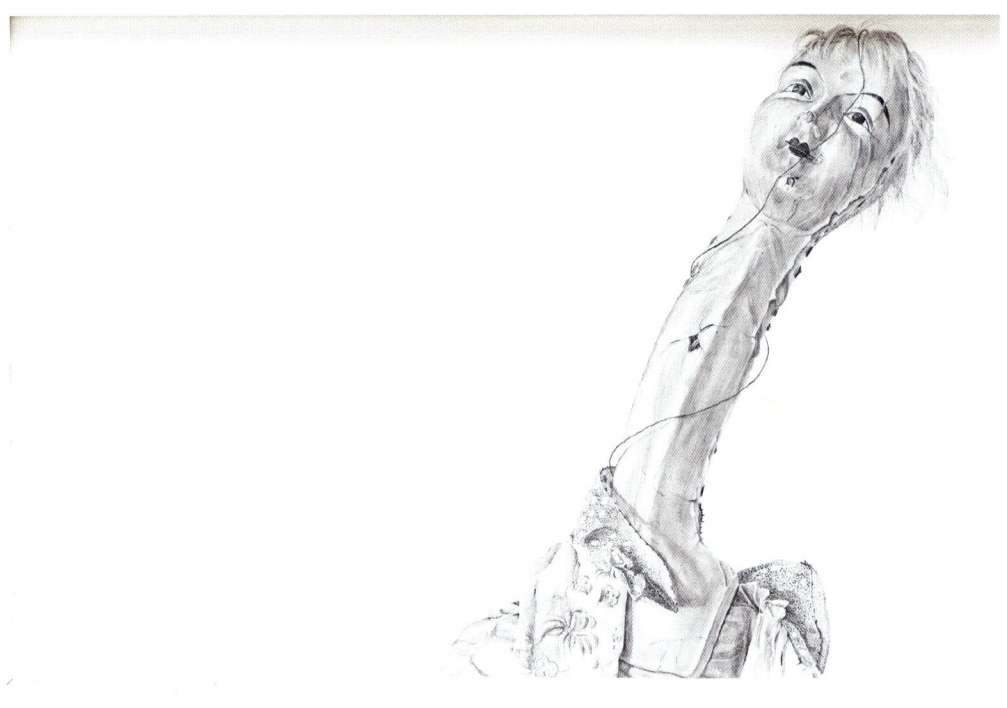

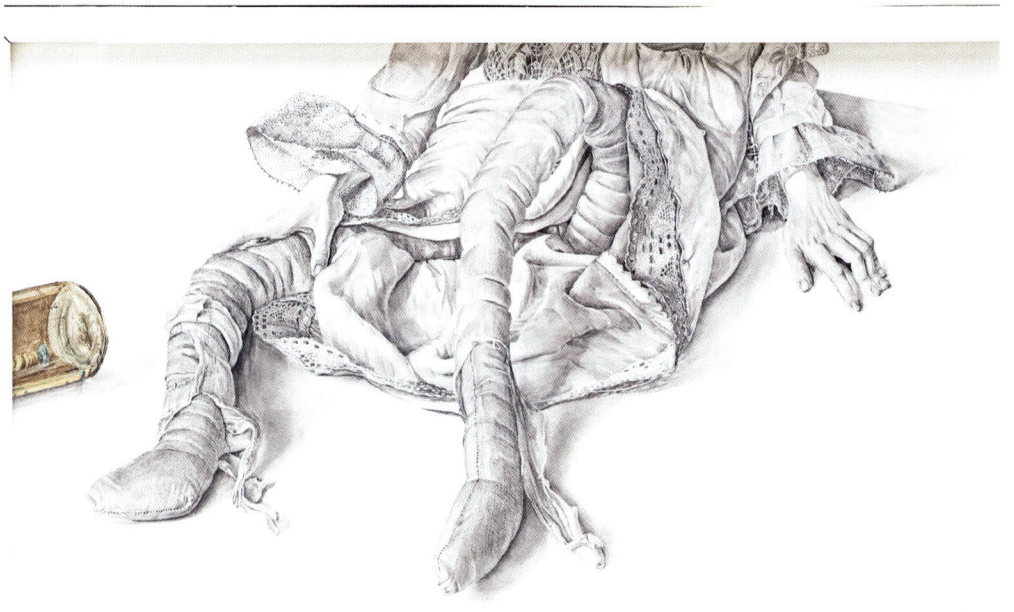

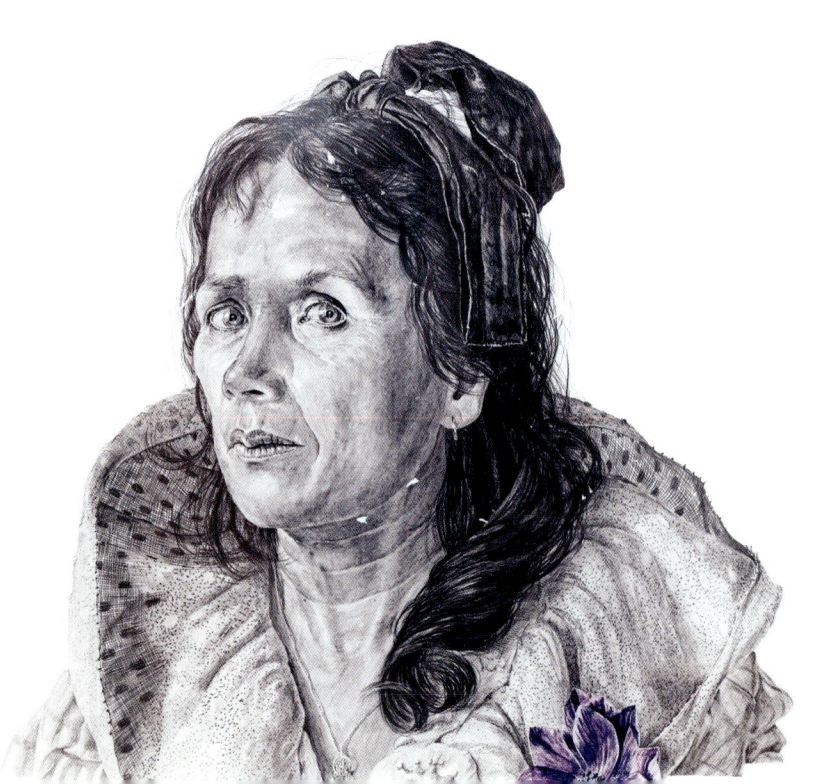

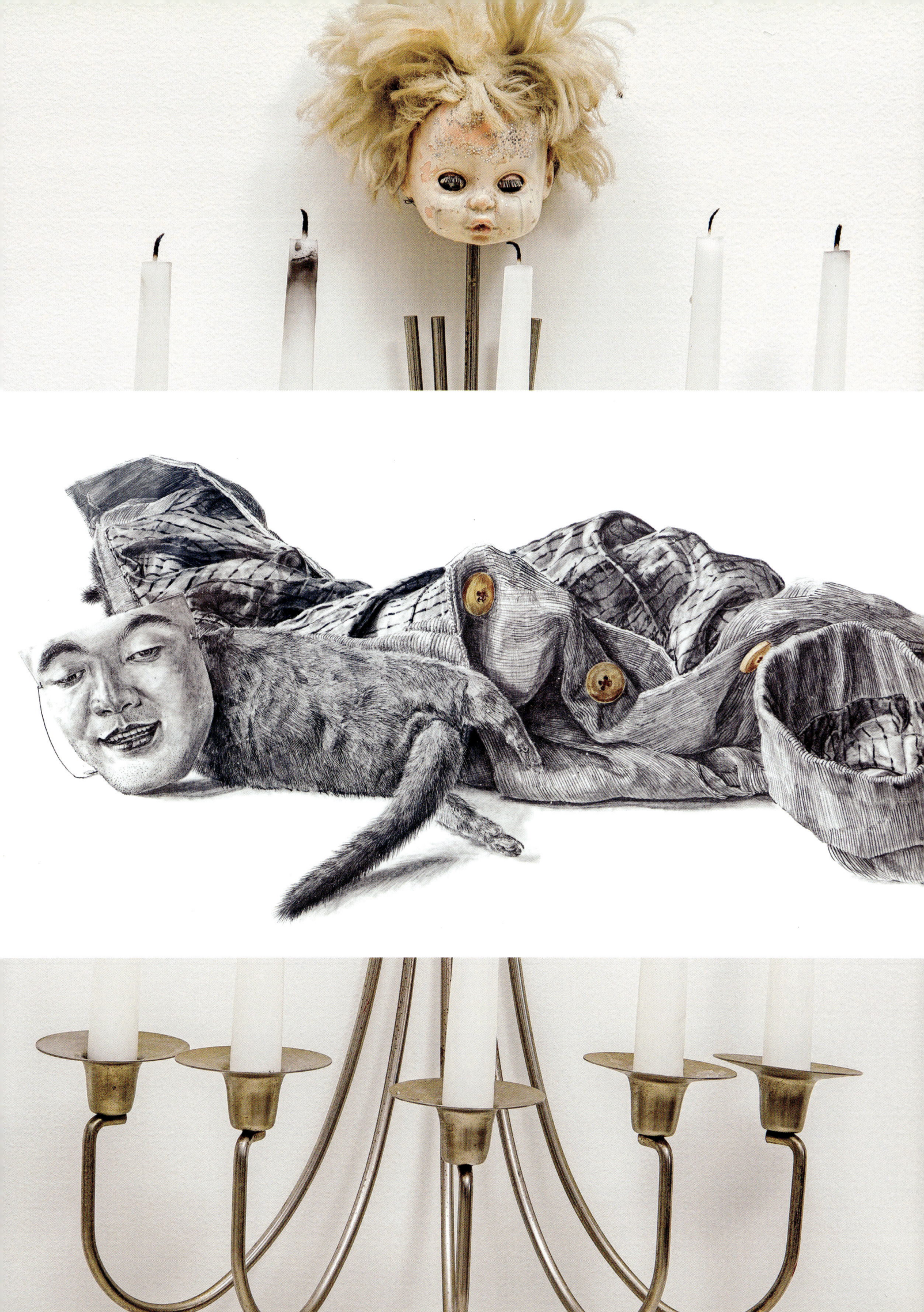

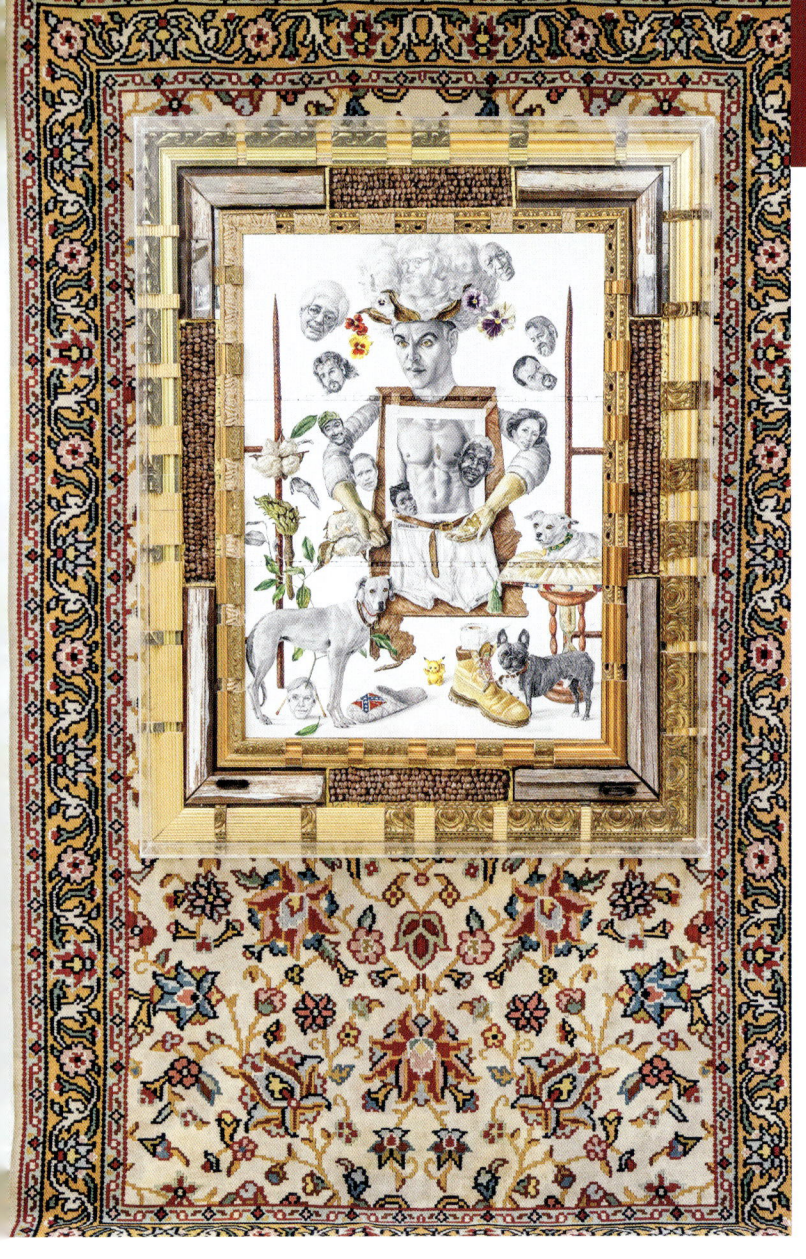

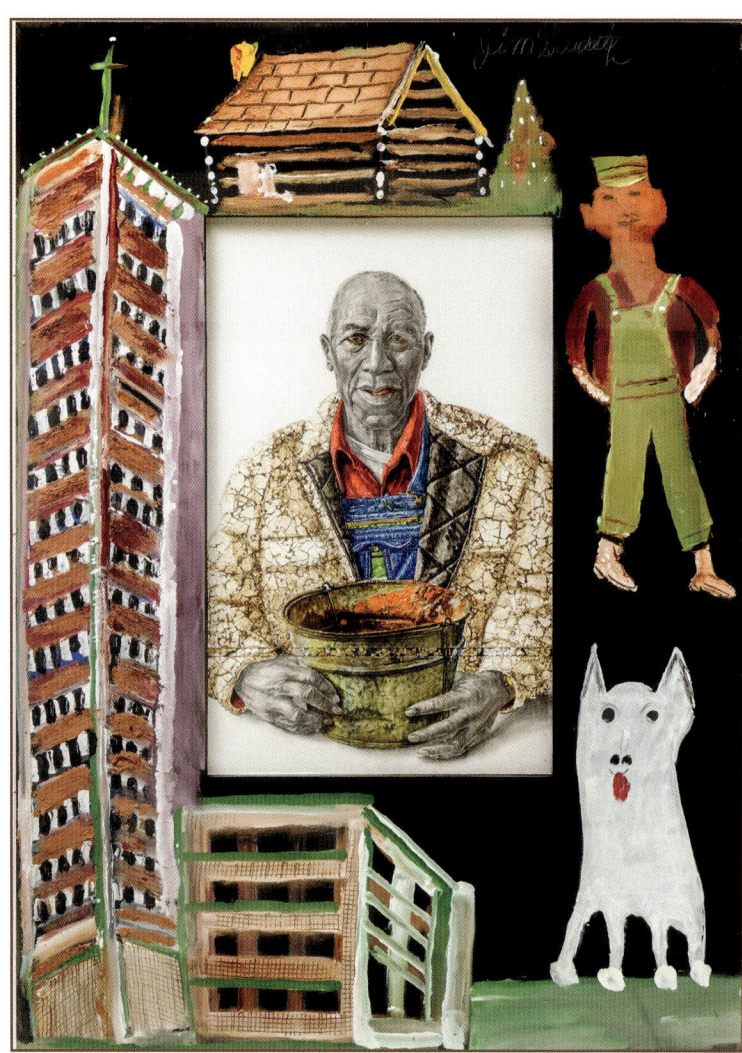

**NALL SELF-PORTRAIT
JUGGLING ALABAMA ARTISTS**
MIXED MEDIA
57" x 46"
2000

JIMMY LEE SUDDUTH
MIXED MEDIA
48" x 35"
1999

This painting and the accompanying series of portraits celebrate Nall's fellow Alabama artists, including Mose T, Betty Sue Matthews, and Jimmy Lee Sudduth, among others. It was completed in 2000–2001 while Nall was artist-in-residence at Troy University. Nall has long been a collector and supporter of Alabama artists,

citing their unique artistic visions and shared backgrounds as a source of inspiration.

These portraits and related works made up the content of the "Alabama Art" exhibition that opened in Alabama and was also showcased in the south of France in 2000.

VIDEO

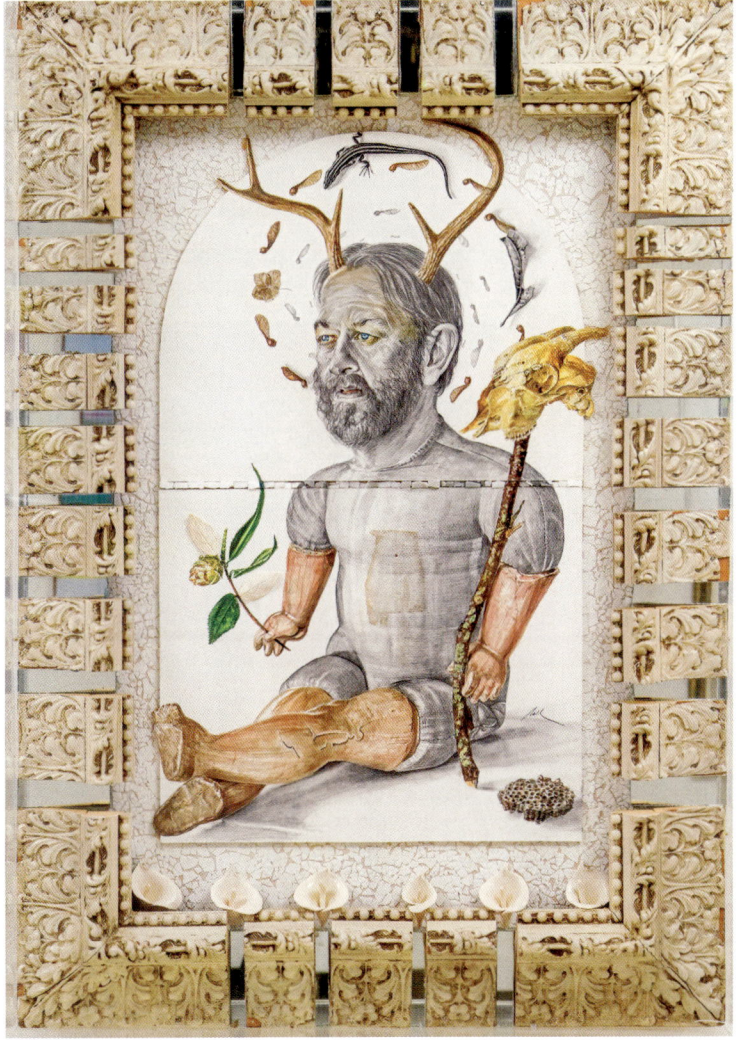

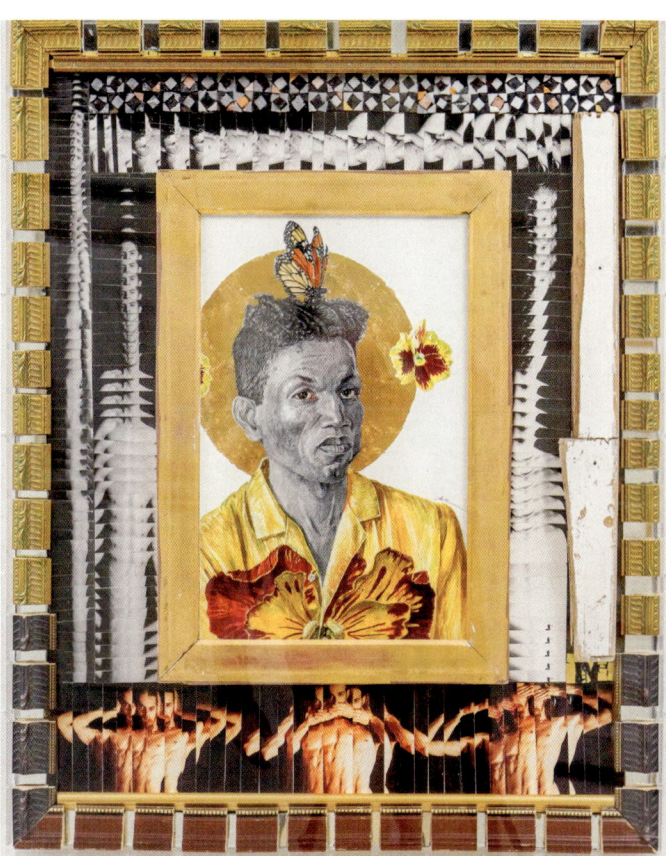

FLEMMING TYLER WILSON
MIXED MEDIA
35" X 28"
1999

FRANK FLEMING
MIXED MEDIA
42" X 30"
1999

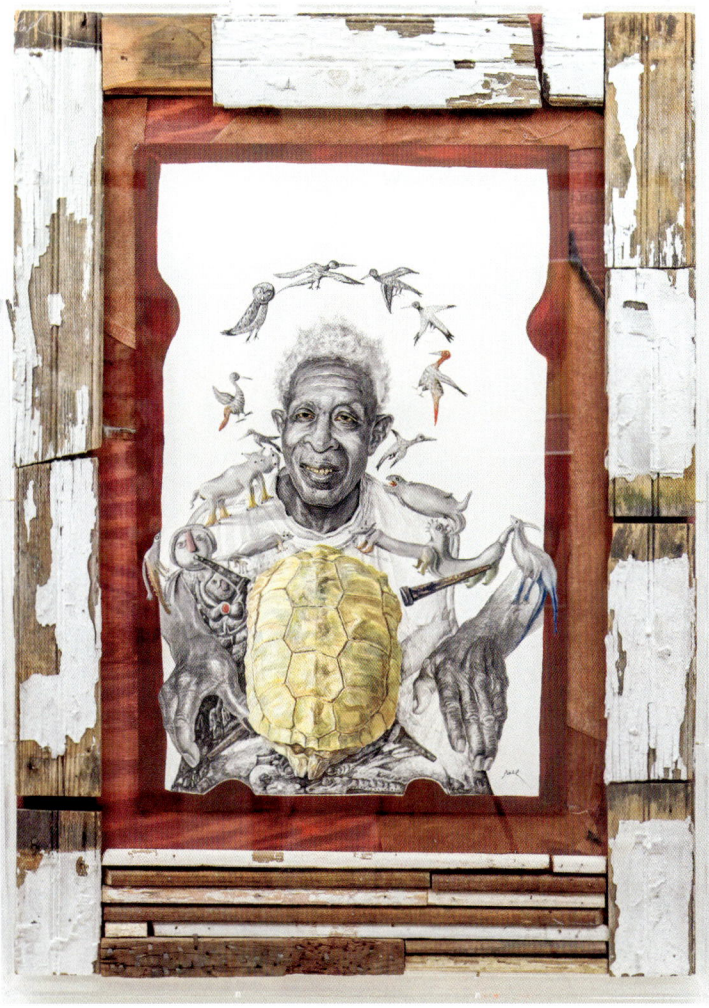

MOSE T
MIXED MEDIA
44" X 33"
1999

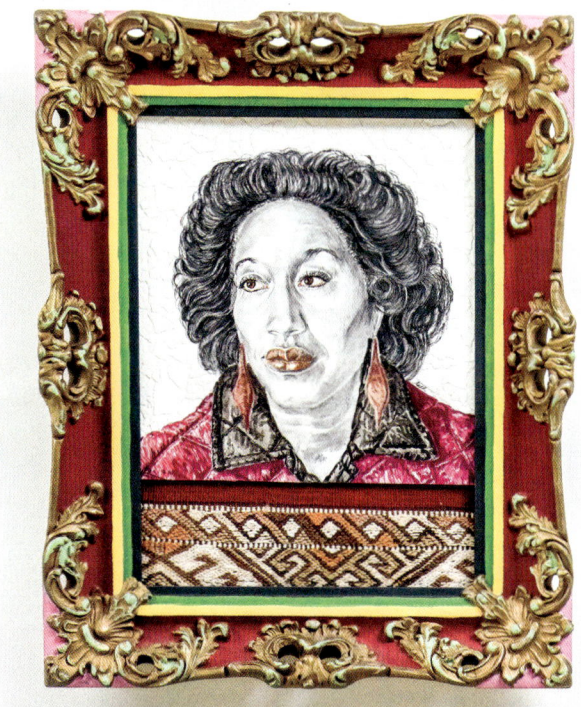

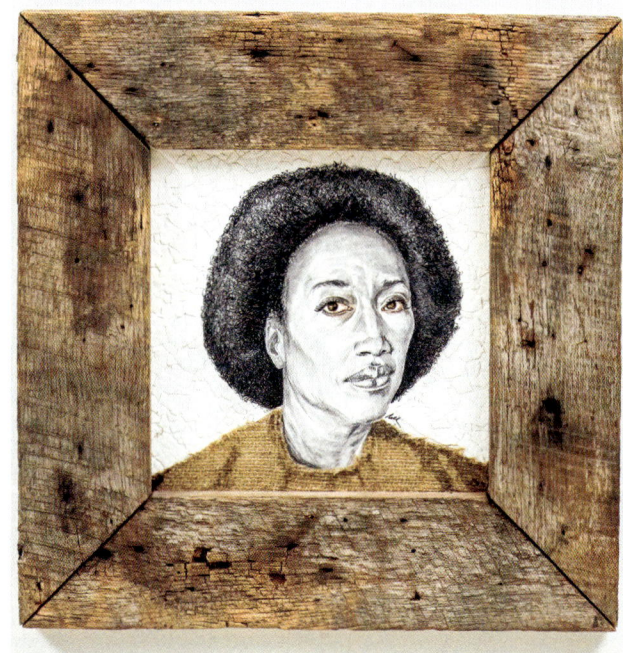

YVONNE WELLS
MIXED MEDIA
TOP: 13" X 6"
BOTTOM: 15" X 15"
1999

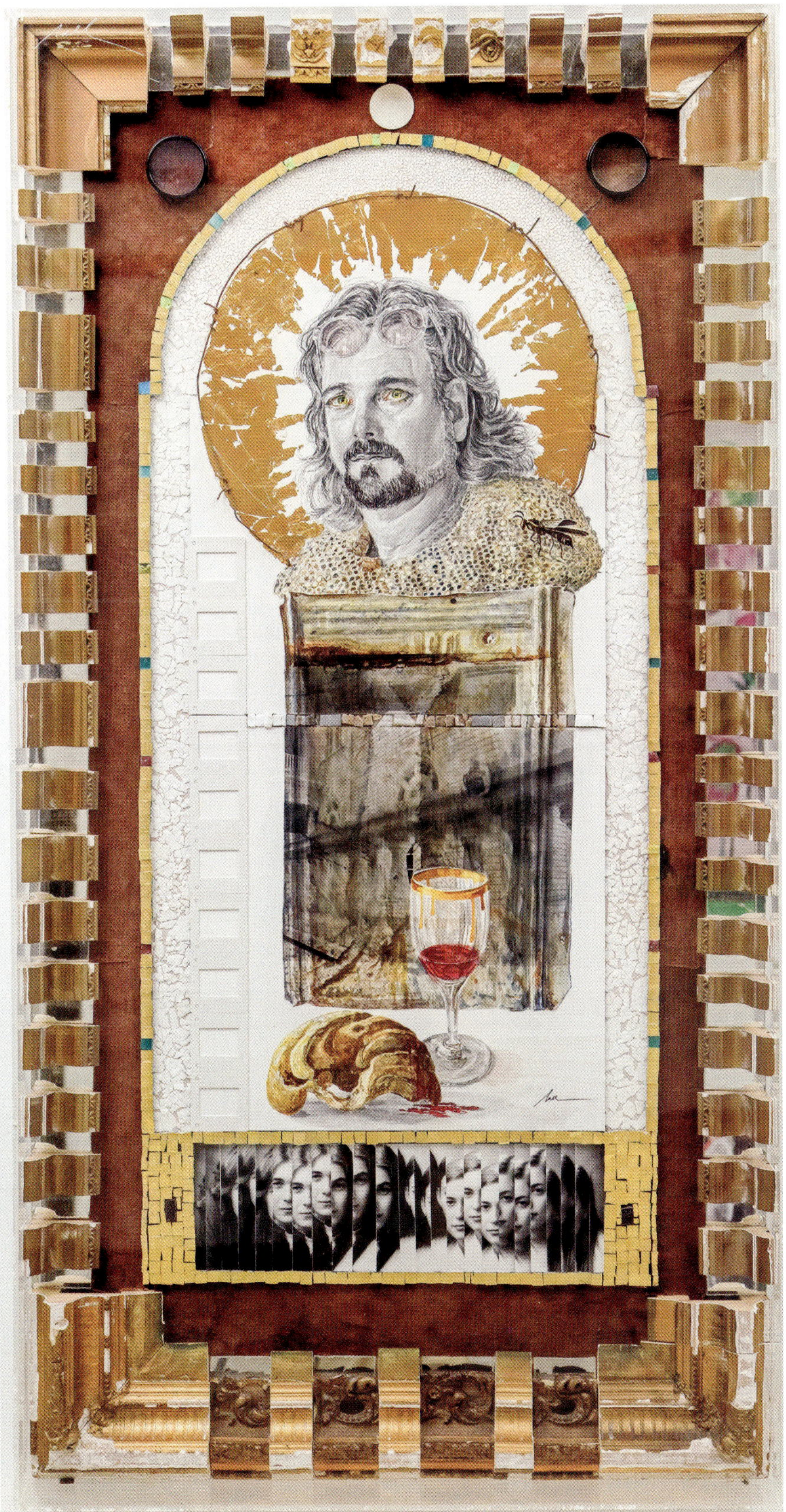

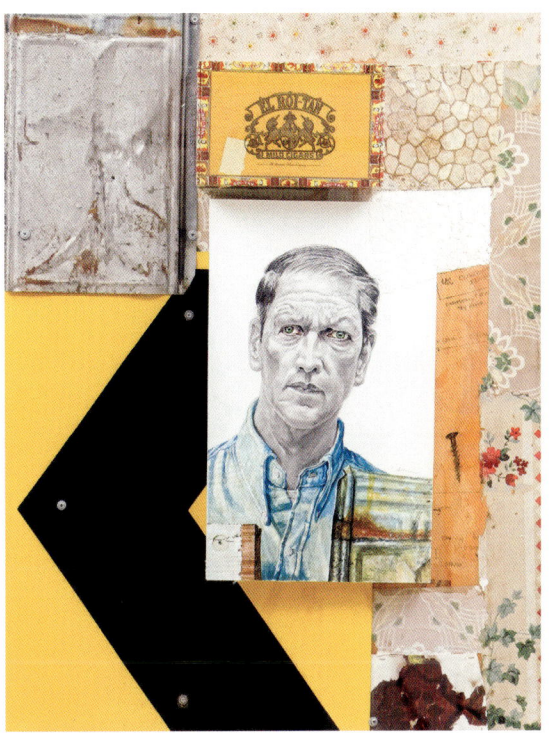

WILLIAM CHRISTENBERRY
MIXED MEDIA
37" X 31"
1999

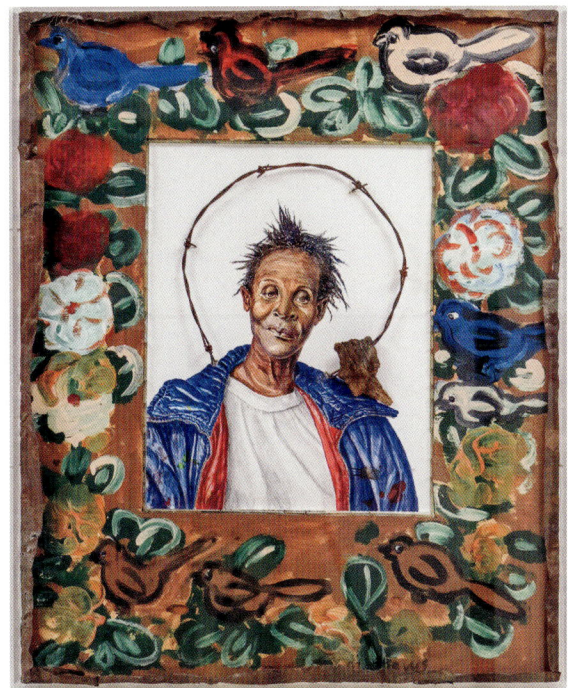

CHIP COOPER
MIXED MEDIA
48" X 25"
1999

BETTY SUE MATTHEWS
MIXED MEDIA
37" X 31"
2000

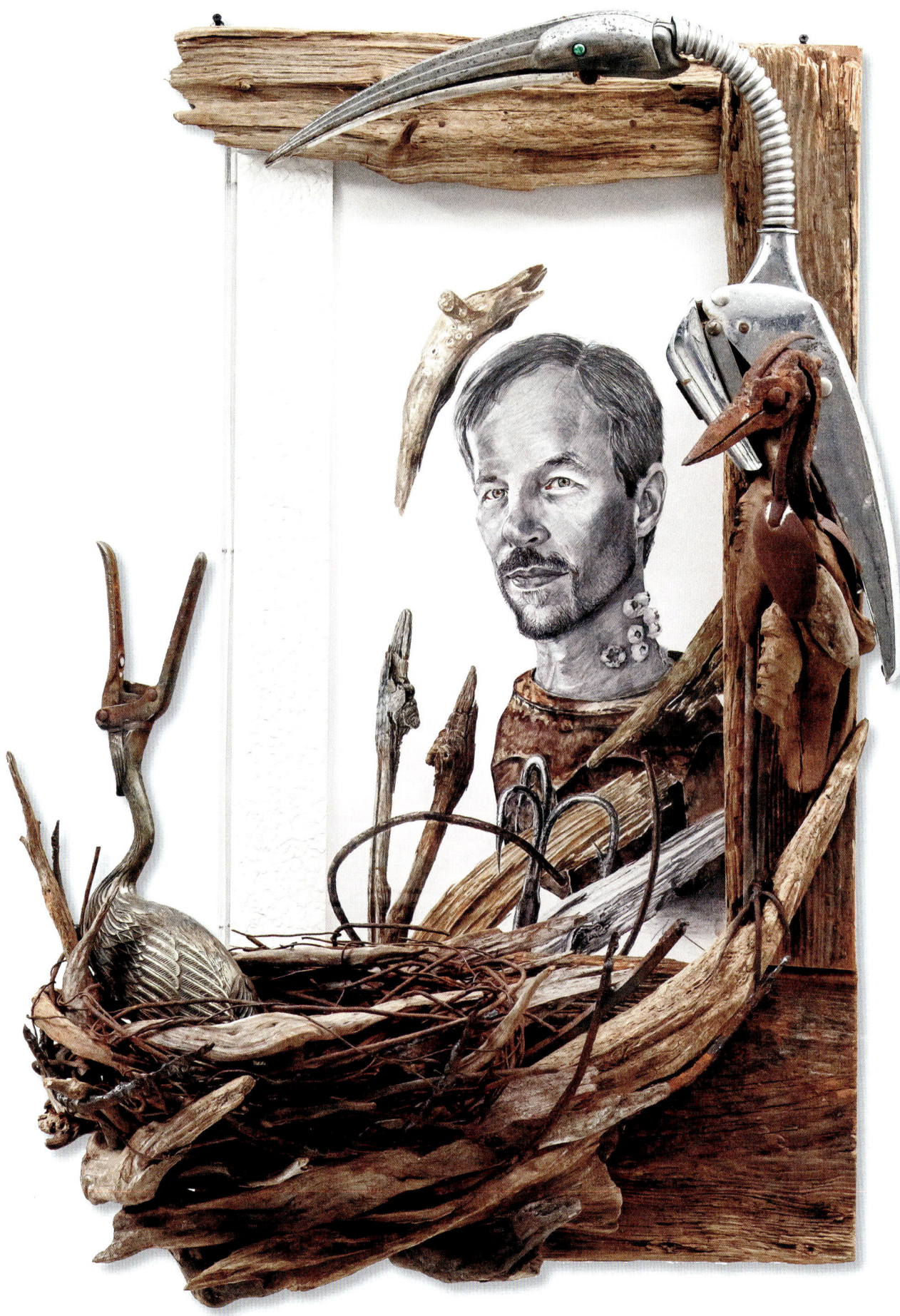

BRUCE LARSEN
MIXED MEDIA
38" X 24"
2000

CLIFTON PEARSON
MIXED MEDIA
50" X 27"
1999

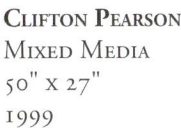

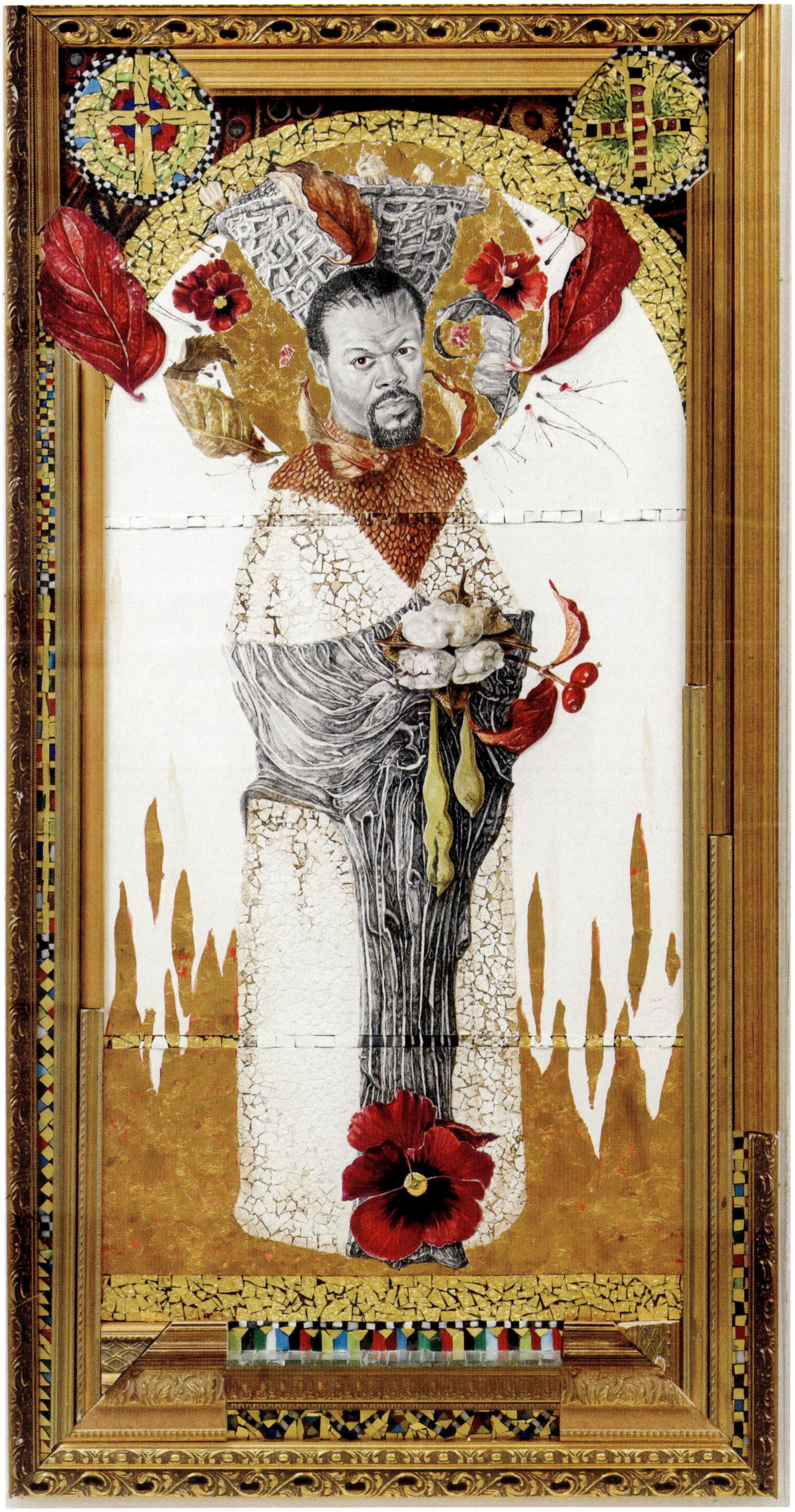

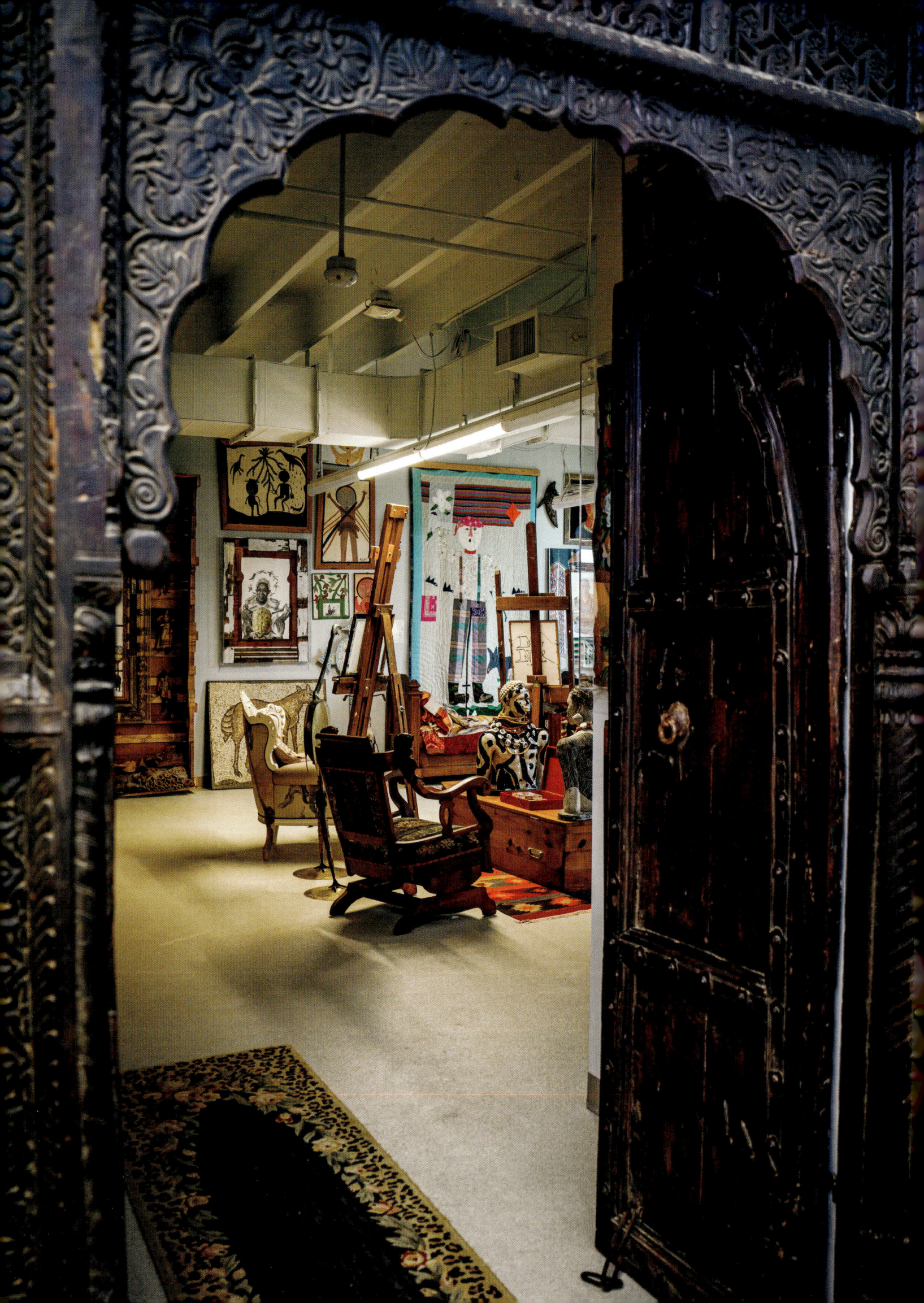

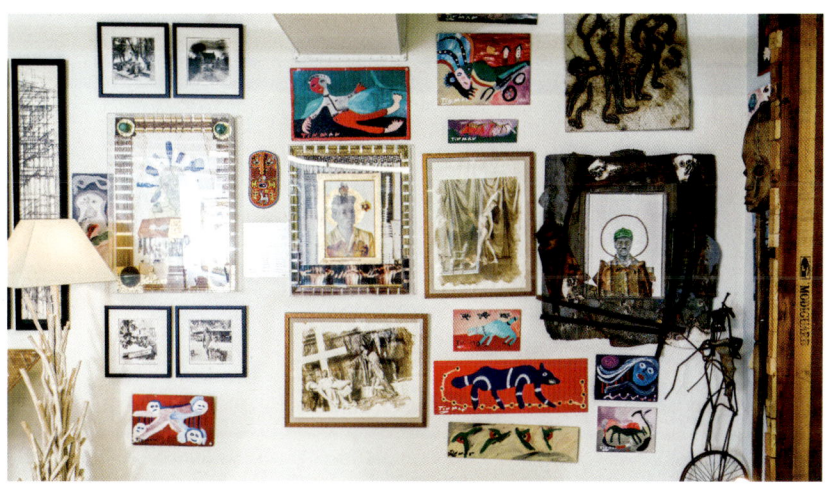

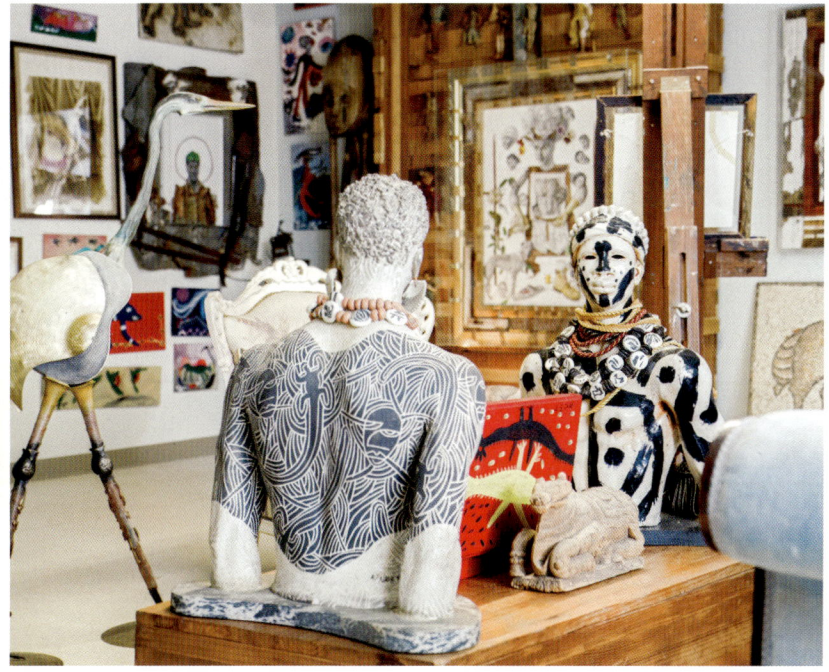

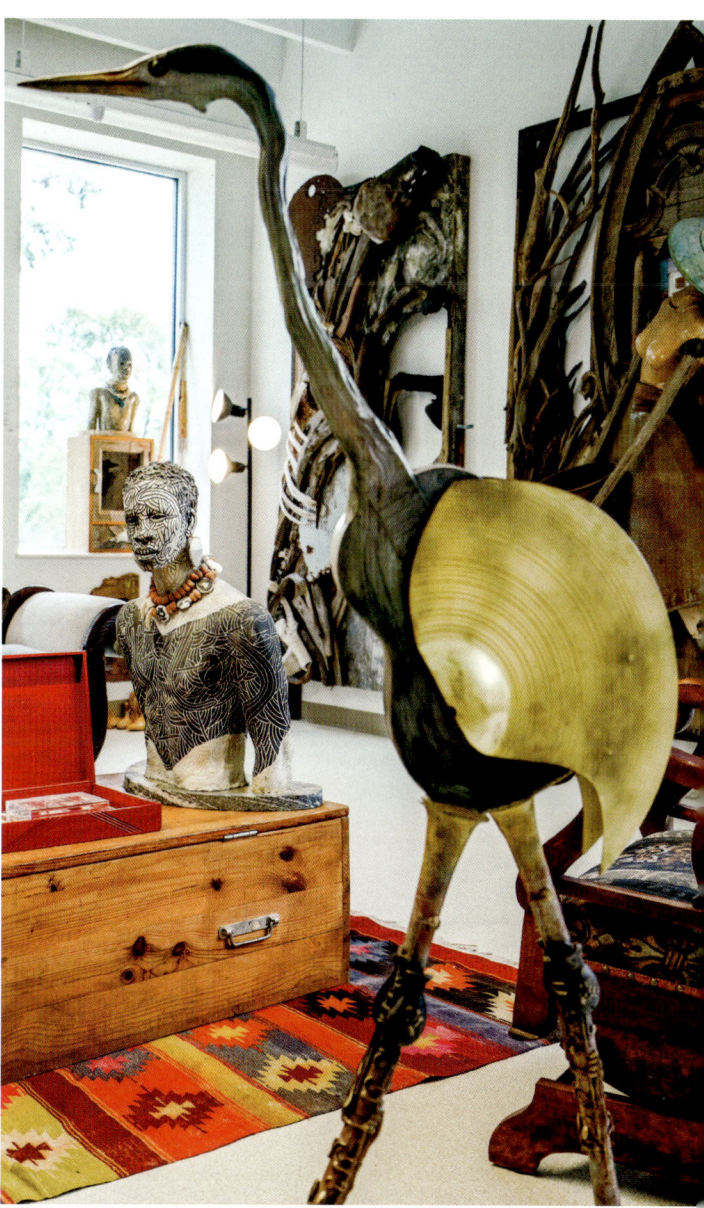

Nall's studio recreated in the Nall Museum as part of the International Arts Center. The studio includes the "Alabama Art" collection, Nall's work, and collected art of other artists over five decades.

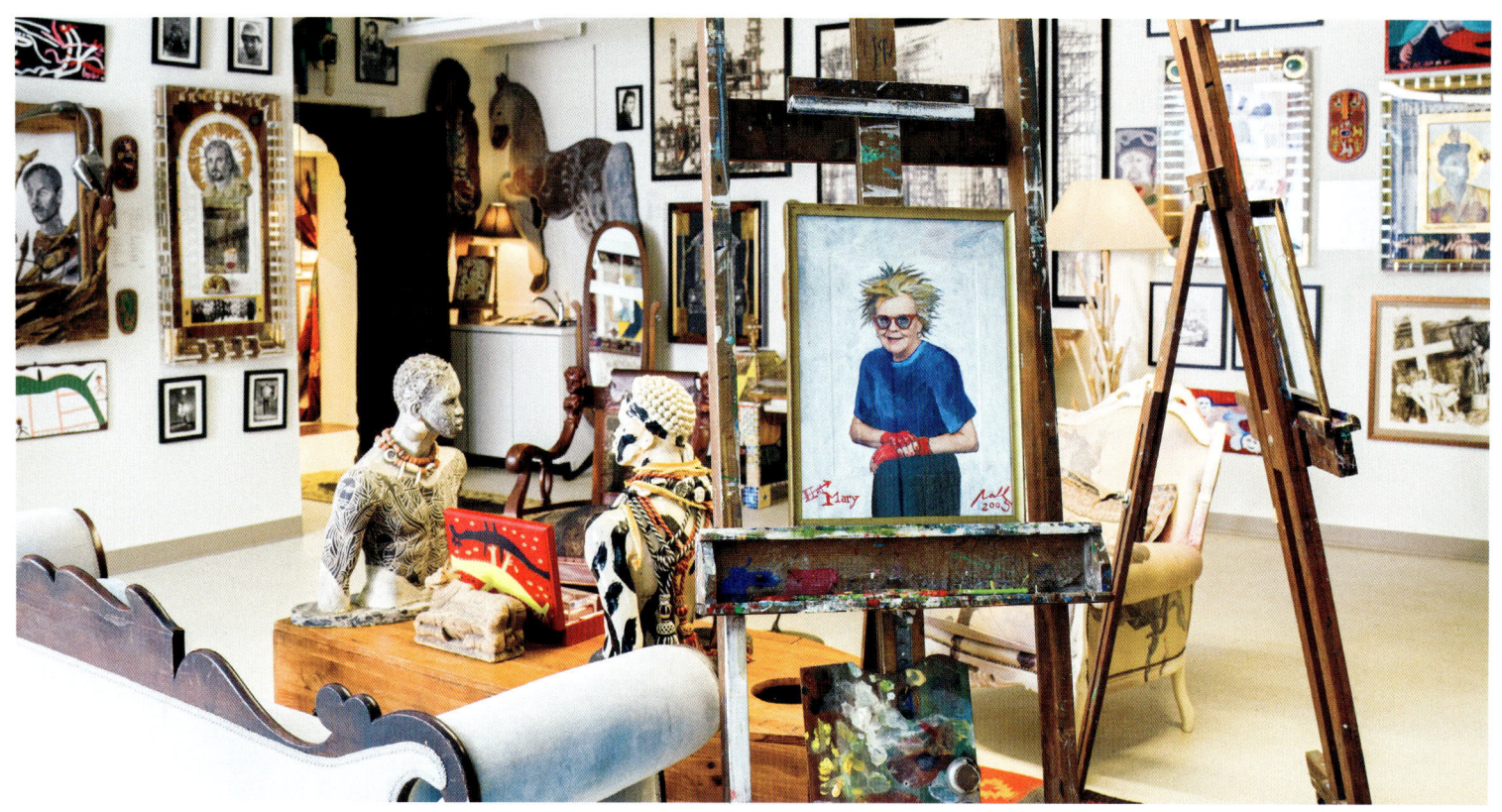

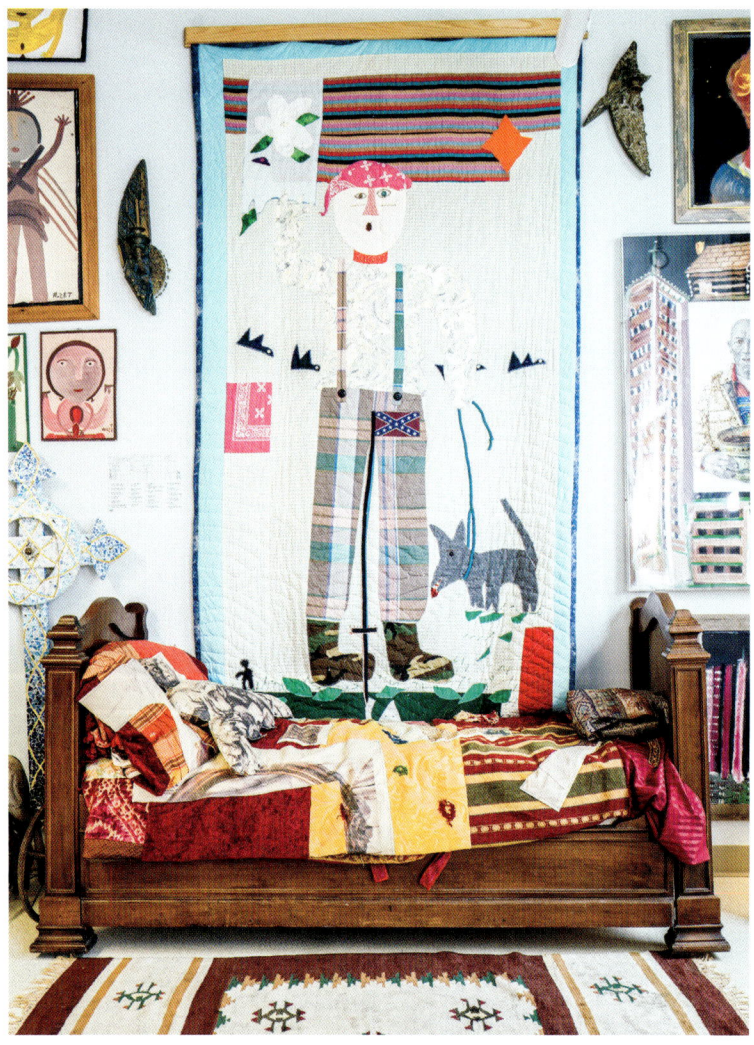

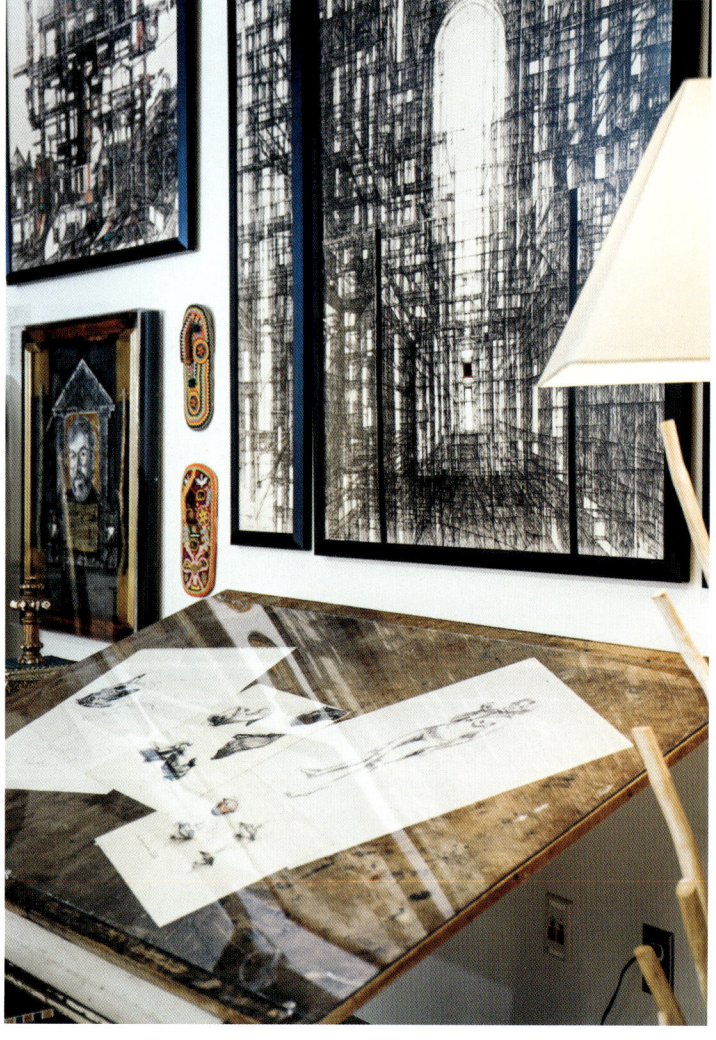

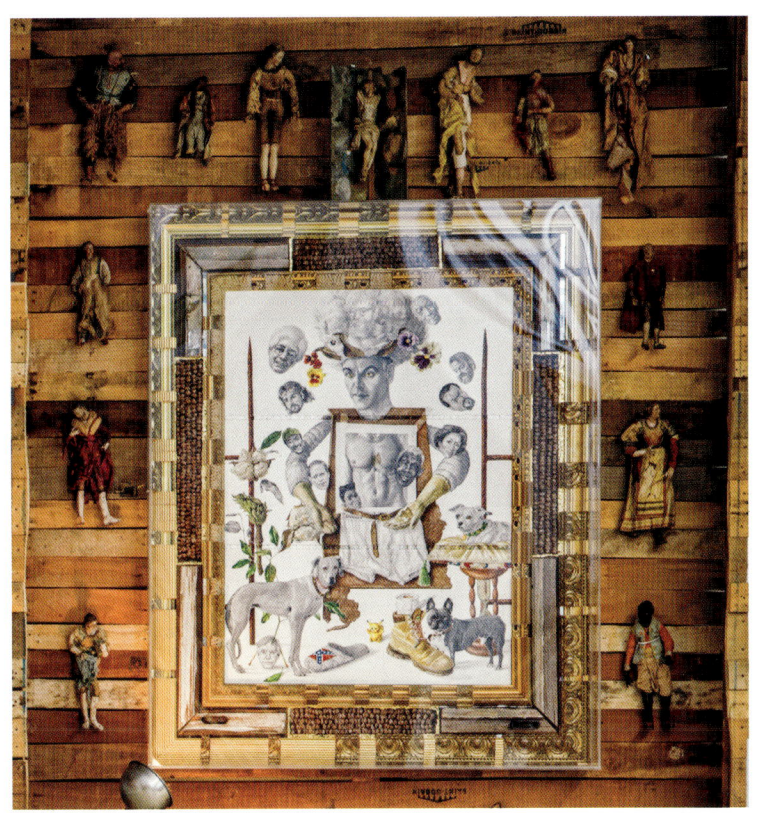

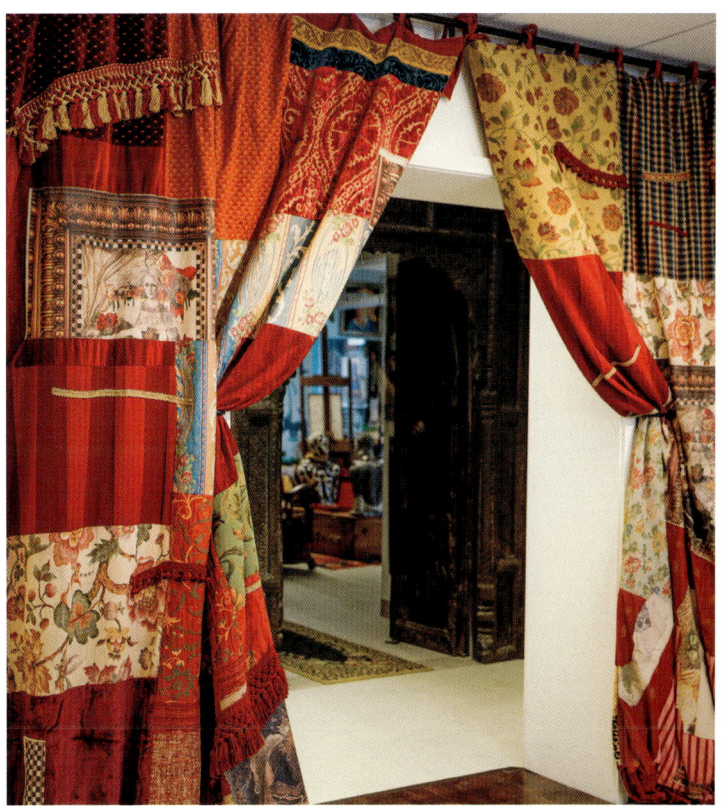

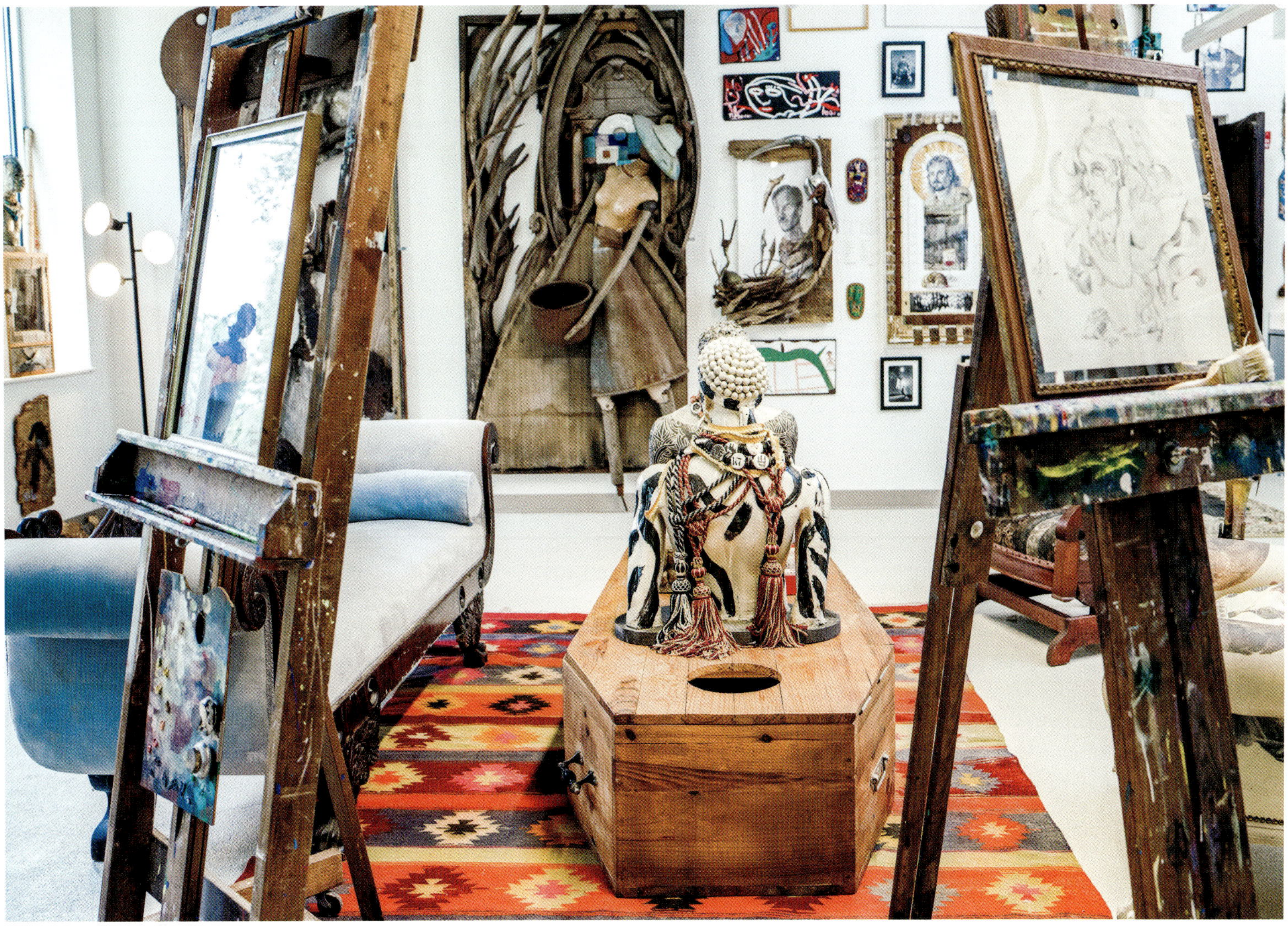

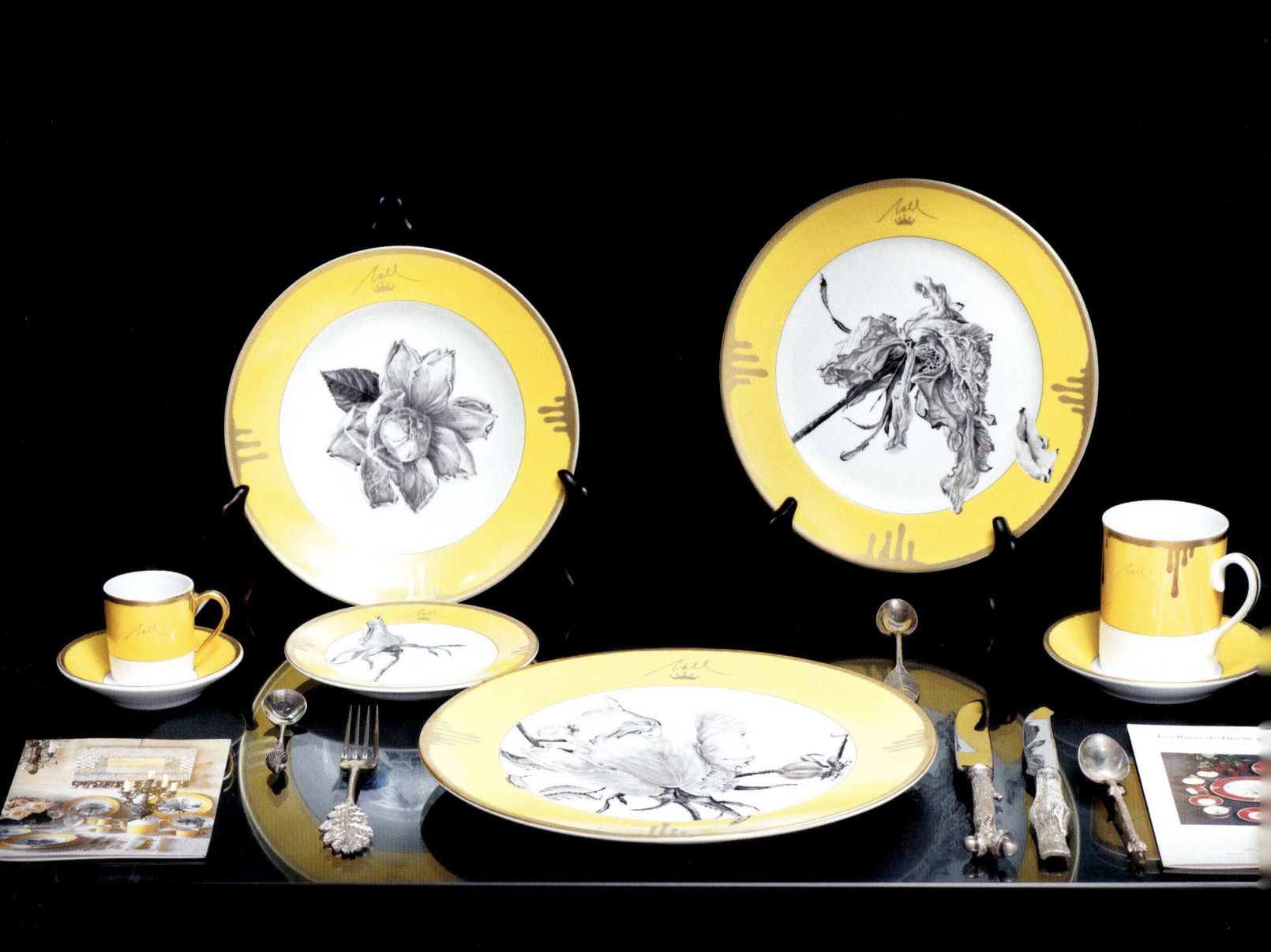

Dinnerware Place Settings
Porcelain
R. Haviland and C. Parlon
Left: Tuscia's Roses
ca. 1984

Right: Mediterranean Gold Pansy
ca. 1990

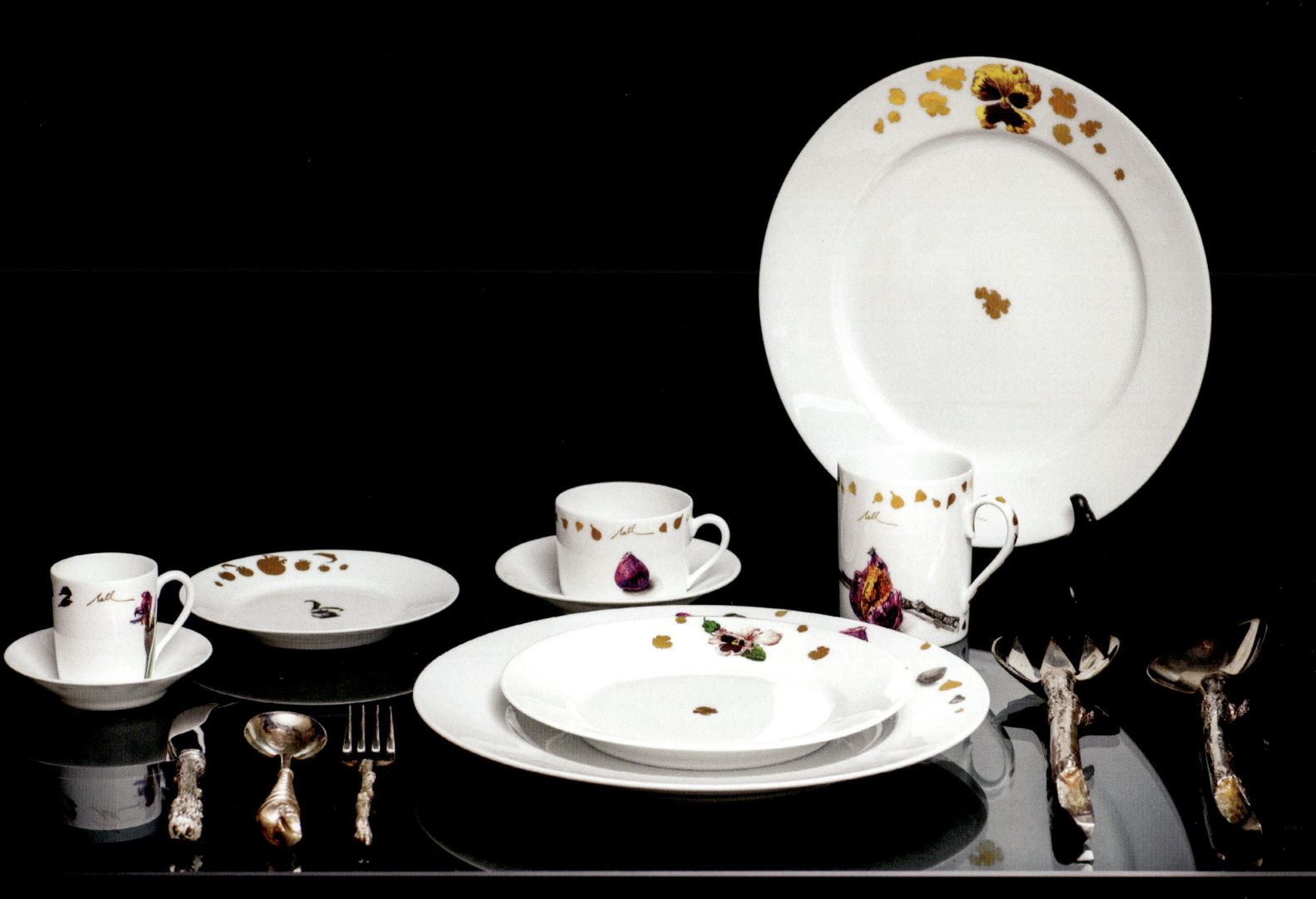

Glass work designed and hand-blown in Murano, Italy

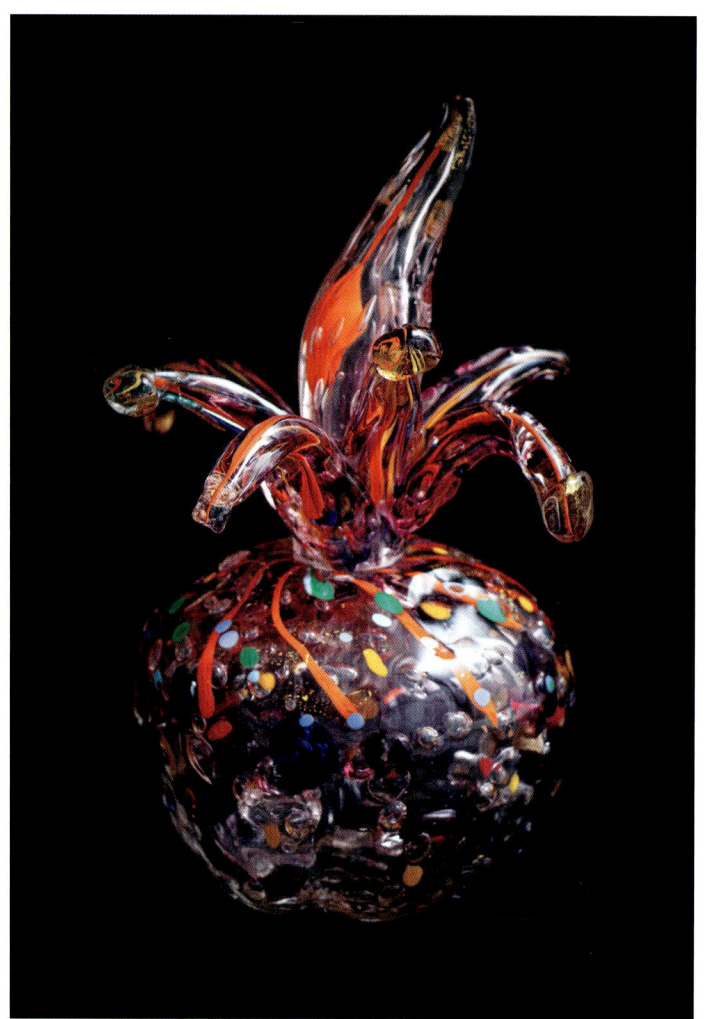
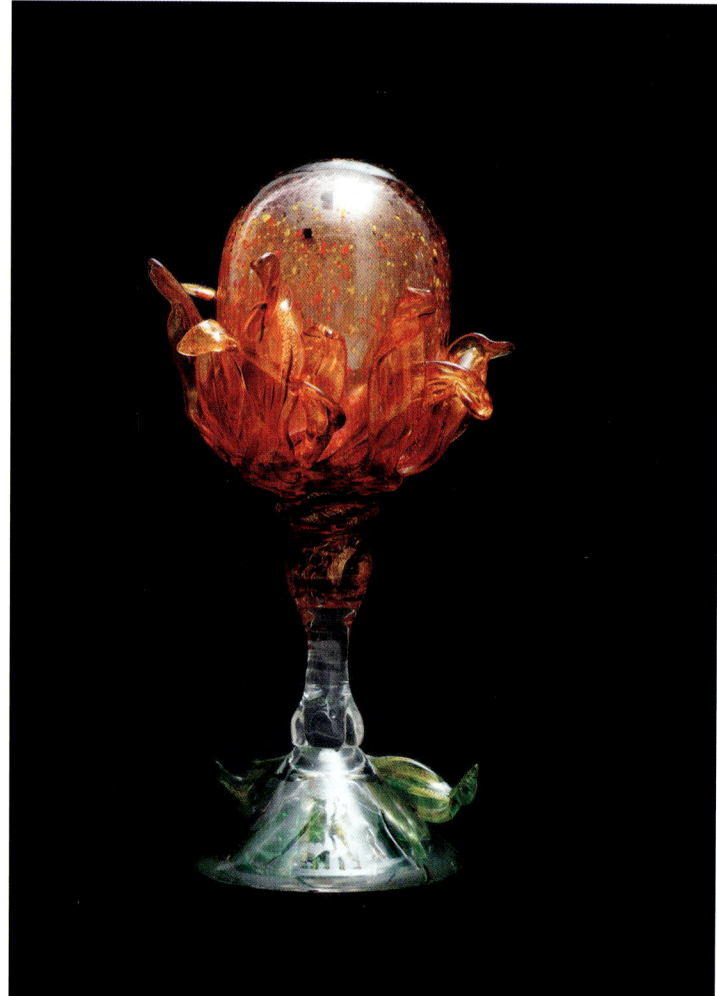
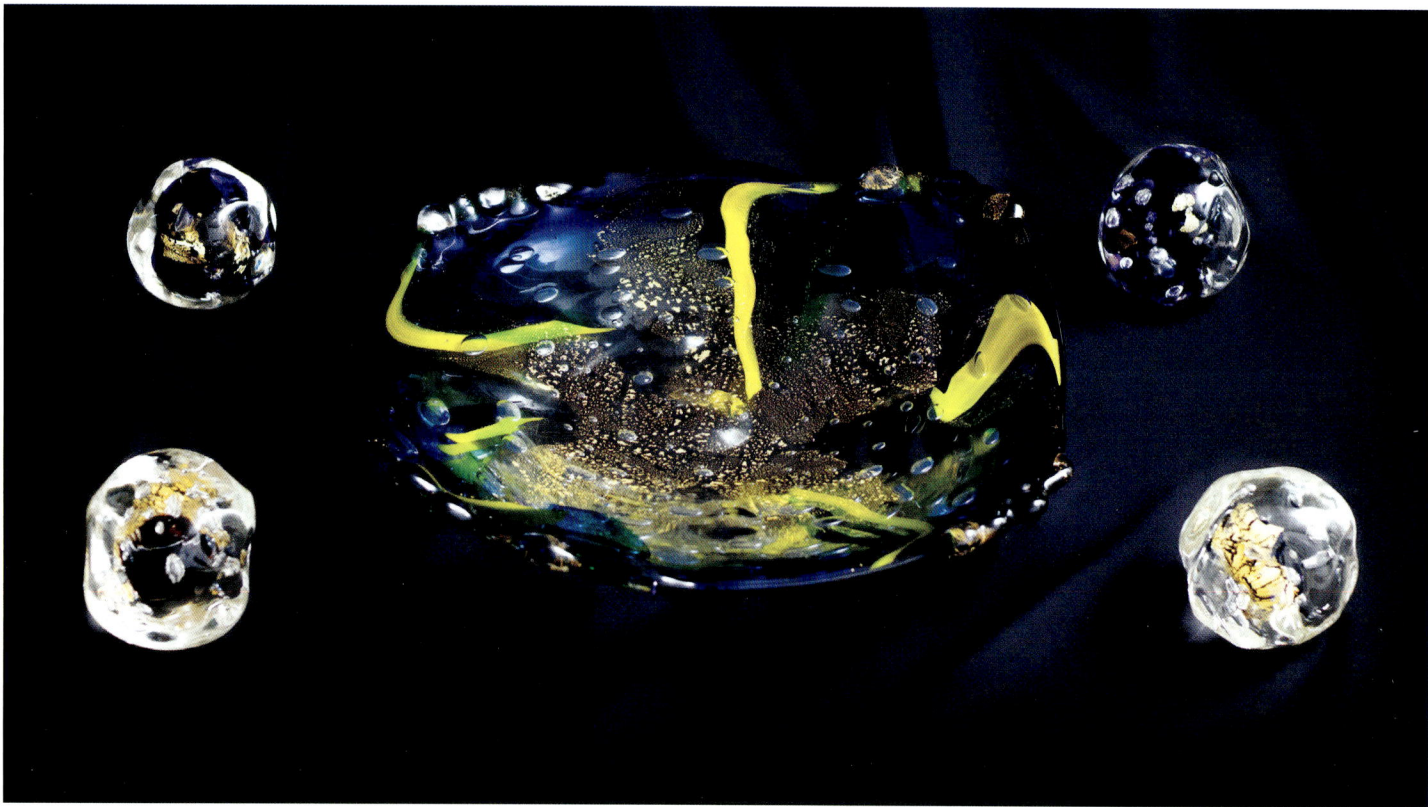

Glass work designed and hand-blown in Murano, Italy

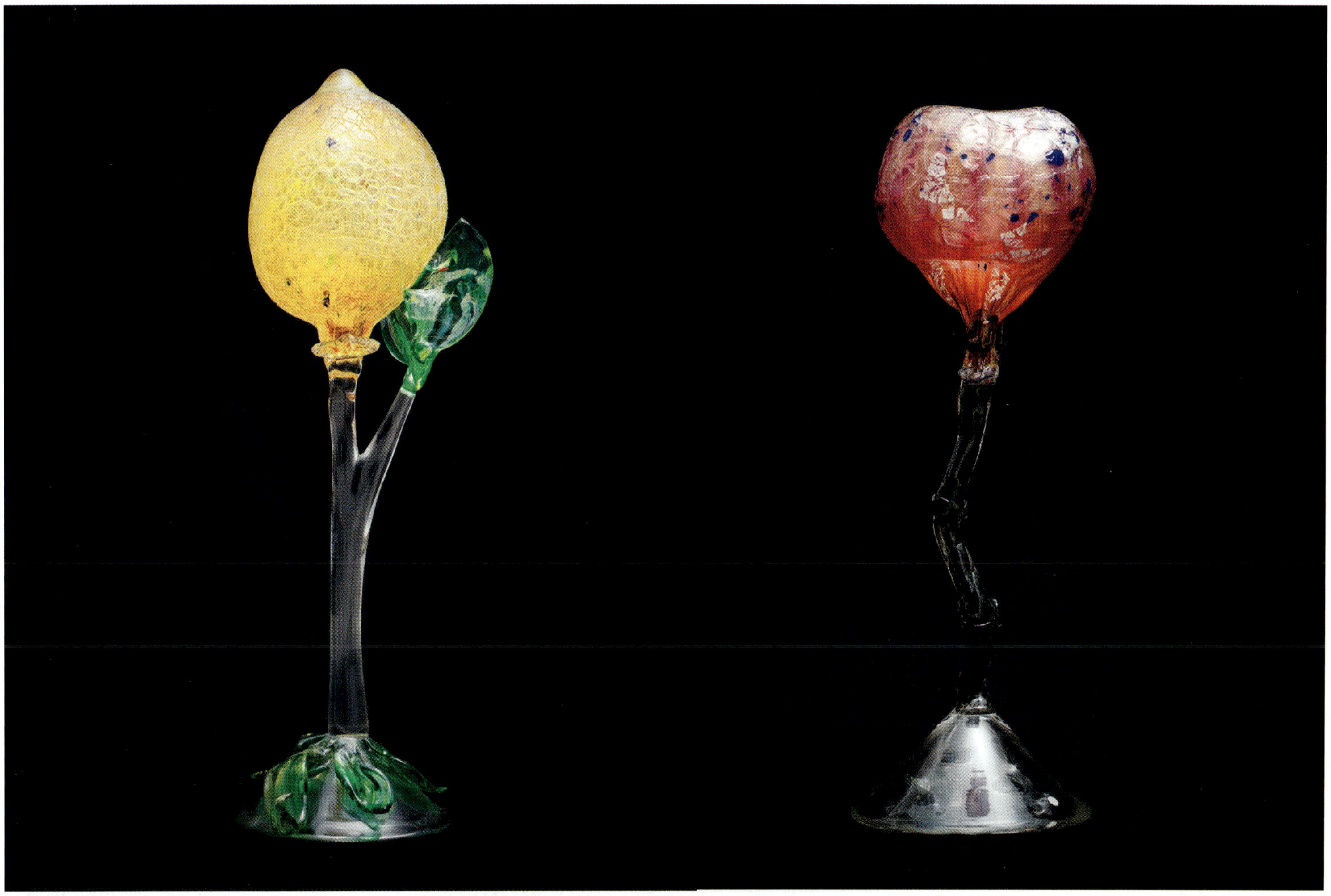

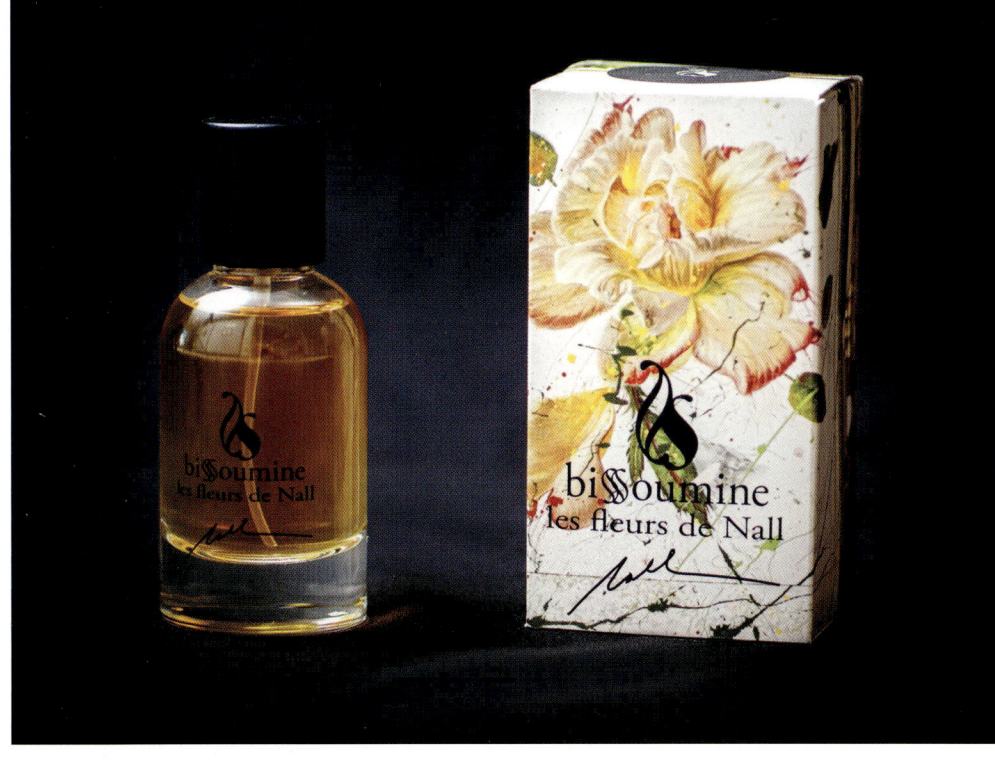

OPPOSITE PAGE LEFT:
HAND-BLOWN GLASS POMEGRANATE
18" x 8.5"
ca. 2000

OPPOSITE PAGE RIGHT:
HAND-BLOWN GLASS PASSION FRUIT
17" x 7"
ca. 2000

OPPOSITE PAGE BOTTOM:
HAND-BLOWN GLASS BOWL WITH FEET
BOWL: 16" x 6"
FEET: 3.5" X 3.5"
ca. 2000

TOP LEFT:
HAND-BLOWN GLASS LEMON
23" x 6"
ca. 2000

TOP RIGHT:
HAND-BLOWN GLASS FIG
18" x 6"
ca. 2000

BOTTOM LEFT:
BISSOMINE GRASSE, FRANCE LES FLEURS DE NALL
4" X 2"
ca. 1990

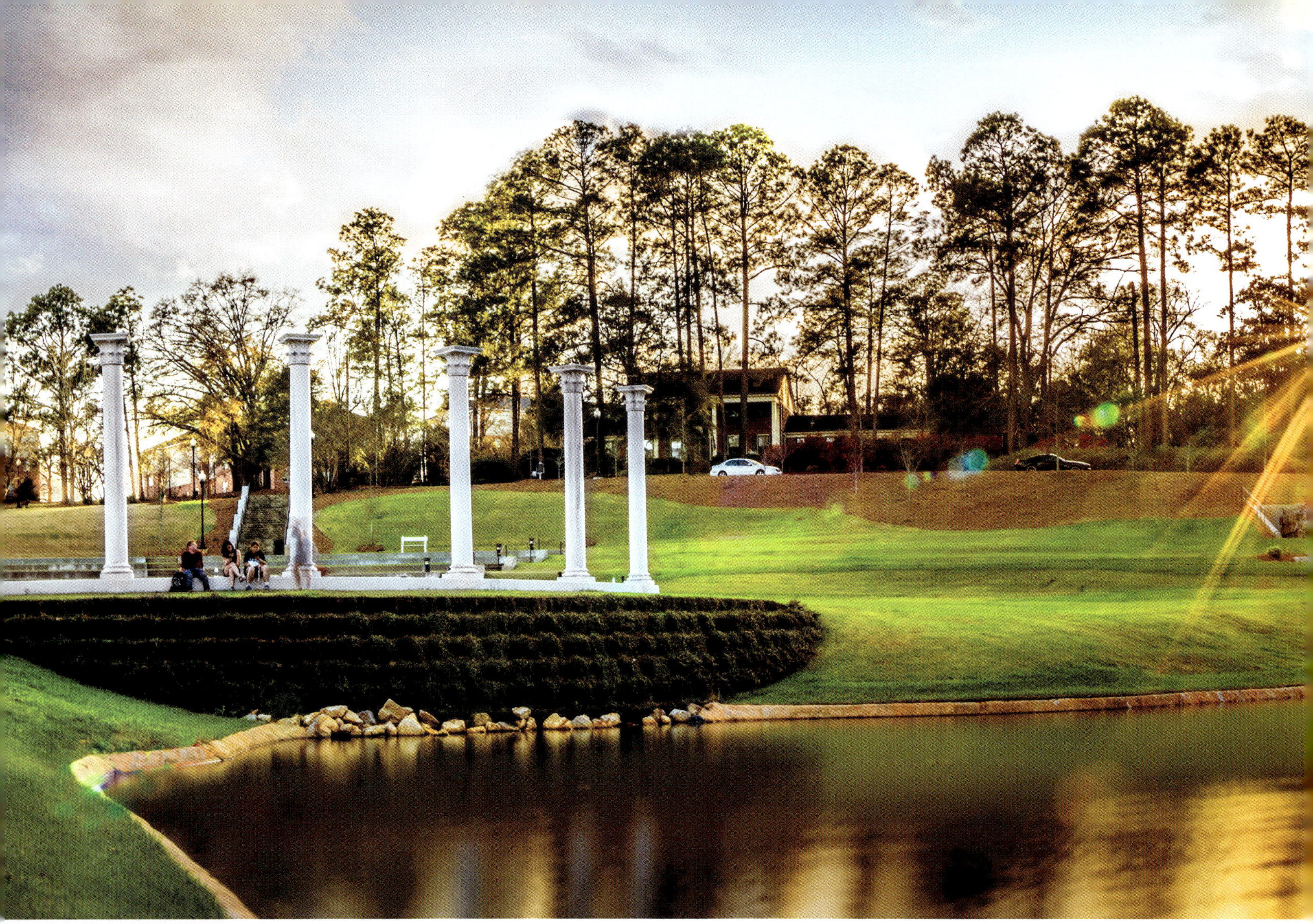

VISIT THE INTERNATIONAL
ARTS CENTER

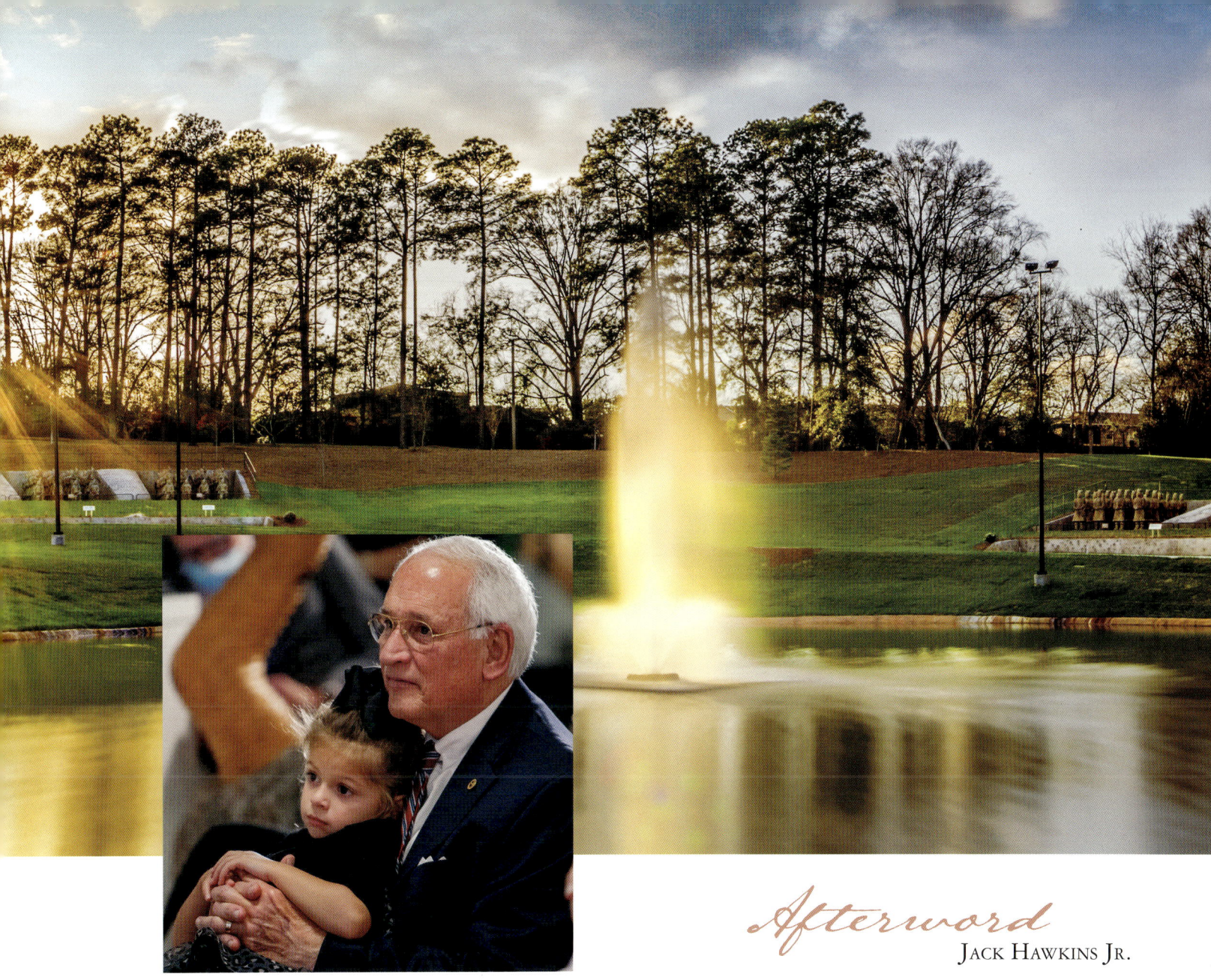

NALL AT TROY: AN INTERNATIONALLY REGARDED ALABAMA ARTIST COMES HOME shines a well-deserved spotlight on the artistic genius of Nall Hollis. I am certain readers will take away a new appreciation of this Alabama treasure. For all his considerable talent, however, Nall's impact on Troy University far exceeds the artwork he has entrusted to us to preserve for future generations.

To give full context to Nall's contributions to Troy, we must invoke the late Dr. Clayton Christensen, formerly of Harvard University. Dr. Christensen was the foremost advocate of disruption theory as a force for good in higher education. He saw the value in "disrupters" sweeping into institutions suffering from "hardening of the categories" to shake up the status quo and point us down different—and more productive—paths.

Nall Hollis is the textbook definition of a "disrupter," and in that role he reshaped forever the fine arts at Troy University. Nall introduced the idea that students earning art degrees should be able to produce work that is both critically well received and commercially viable. Art for art's sake has its place, but Nall saw a greater point of focus, namely that creativity and financial success are not necessarily mutually exclusive. Nall tossed a figurative hand grenade

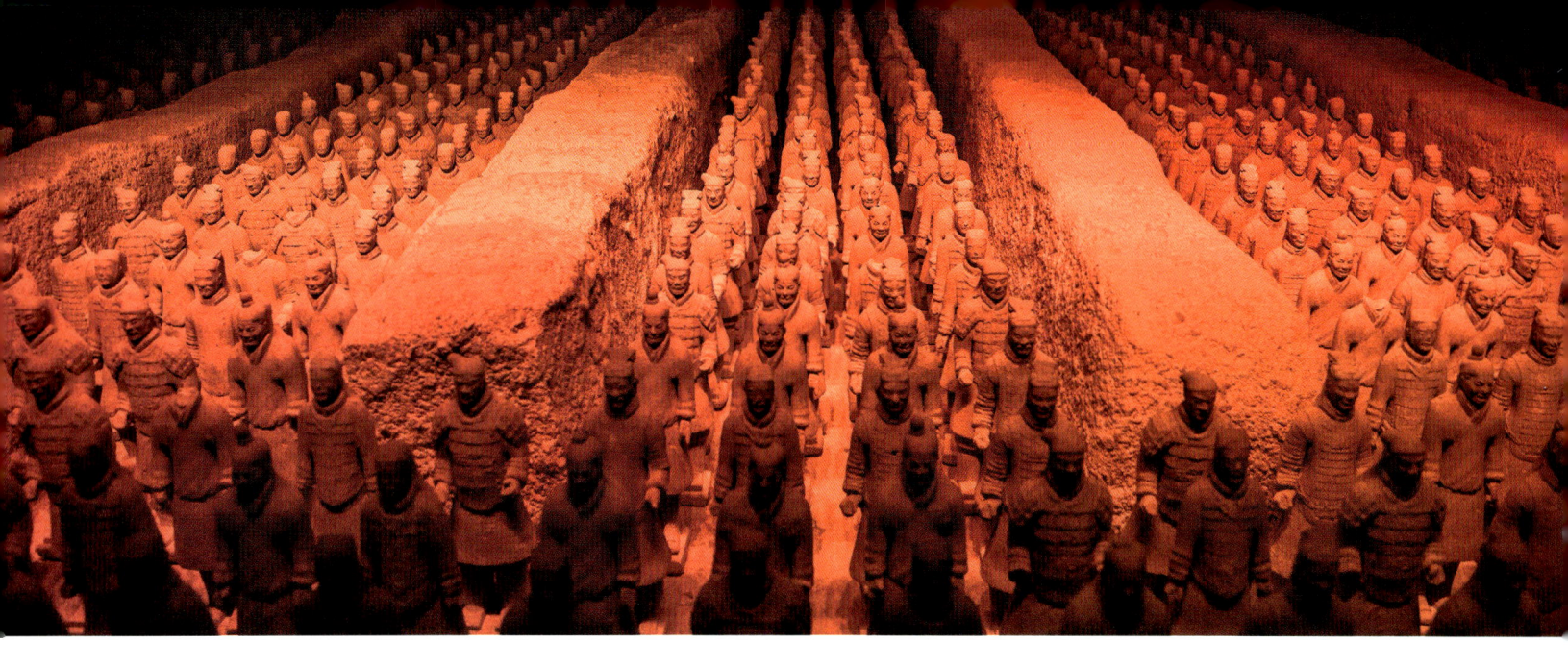

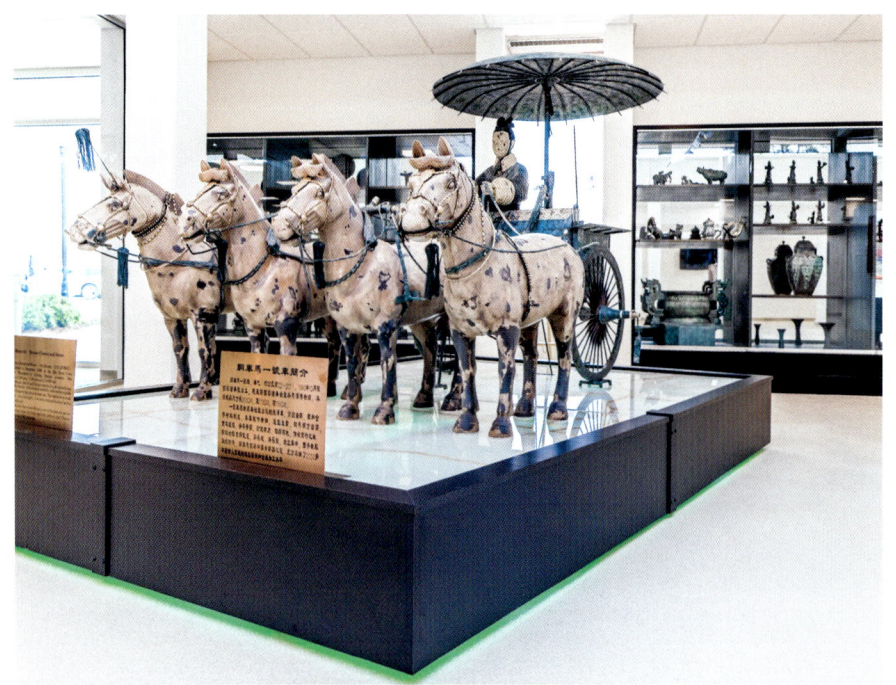

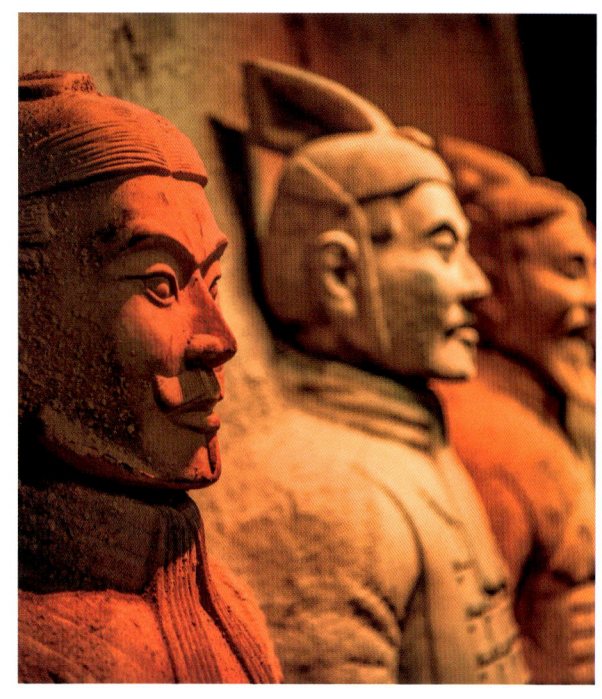

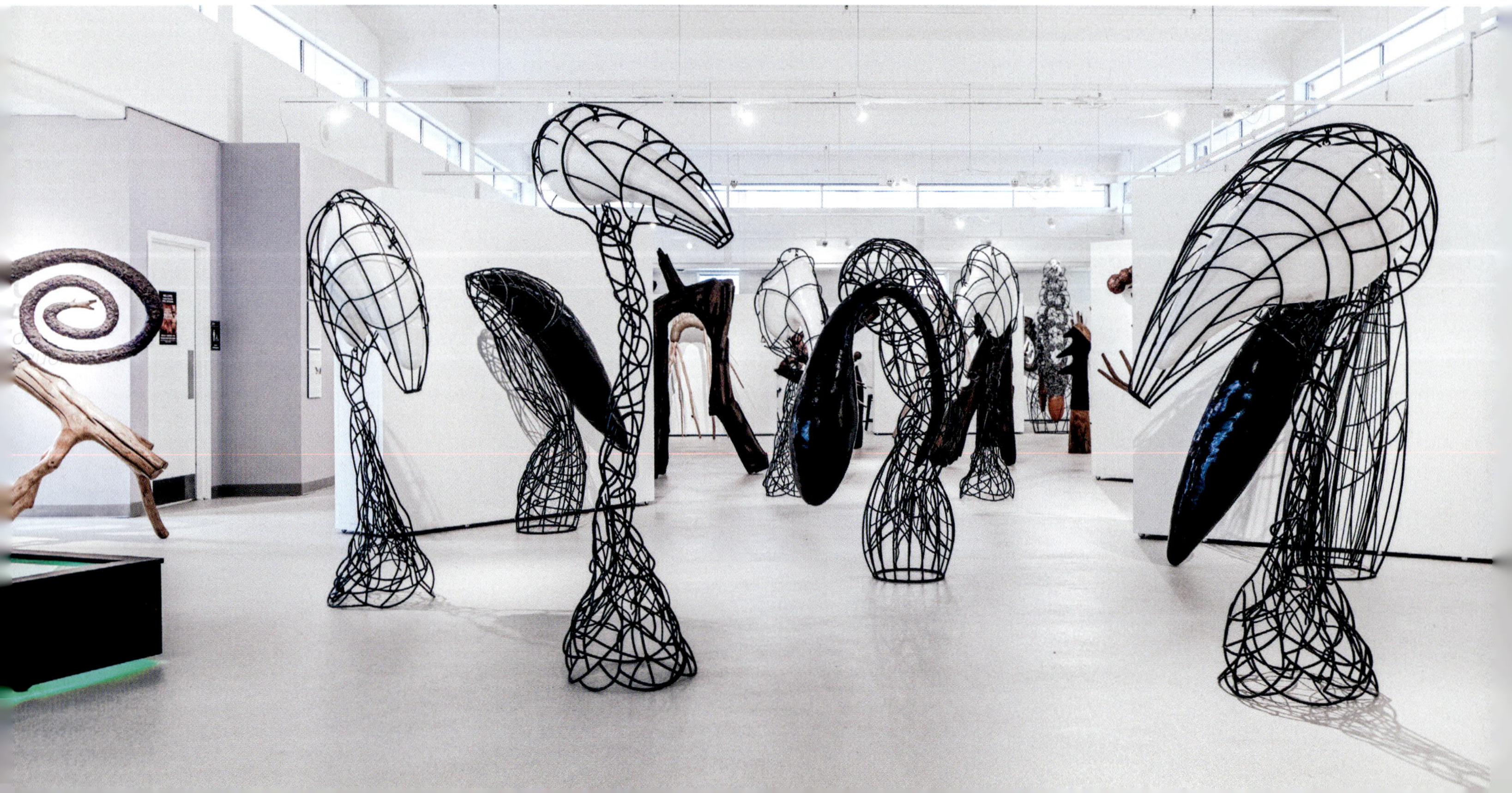

into the room to explode outdated thinking, and the fine arts at Troy University have never been the same.

Nall's influence also reinforced a movement that was in full swing at Troy when he was appointed artist-in-residence in 2000—internationalization of the University. By the time he arrived at Troy University, Nall, operating from his studios in Vence, France, had established a glowing reputation throughout Europe.

Nall's philosophy provided the perfect complement to another artist who reshaped our campus. We began forming a relationship with the late Huo Bao Zhu of Xi'an, China, shortly after Nall joined our faculty. Dr. Huo's work, including the *Thinker* statue, four *Trojan Warrior* statues on our Alabama campuses, and the famed *Terracotta Warriors*, provides a global flavor that befits our standing as Alabama's International University. As mentioned elsewhere in this book, it was Huo Bao Zhu, inspired by Nall's magnificent *Wounded Peace Dove* statue, who coined the theme "East meets West" that has marked our Janice Hawkins Cultural Arts Park and the adjacent International Arts Center.

It bears repeating: Nall has had a permanent impact on the fine arts at Troy, and he has influenced our vision as we look to the future. For example, we are working to build on Nall's global reputation to help take our International Arts Center galleries to new levels of recognition and service. Indeed, we believe Troy University should be a destination for the world's premier artists and their works.

Nall's influence is also changing the way we prepare students majoring in the fine arts—graphic design, studio art, theater, and dance. Going forward, students majoring in these disciplines at Troy will take courses in management and marketing which will prepare them for the business side of the fine arts world. If they desire a career in the arts, we want them prepared at the highest level.

We at Troy believe budding artists must pay their dues, but the "starving artist" stereotype is a cliché that no longer applies in the twenty-first century. A degree in the arts should prepare one to make a living as well as make a life. It is the right direction for our fine arts programs, and for that— and much more—we have Nall Hollis to thank.

Jack Hawkins Jr. is the Chancellor of Troy University

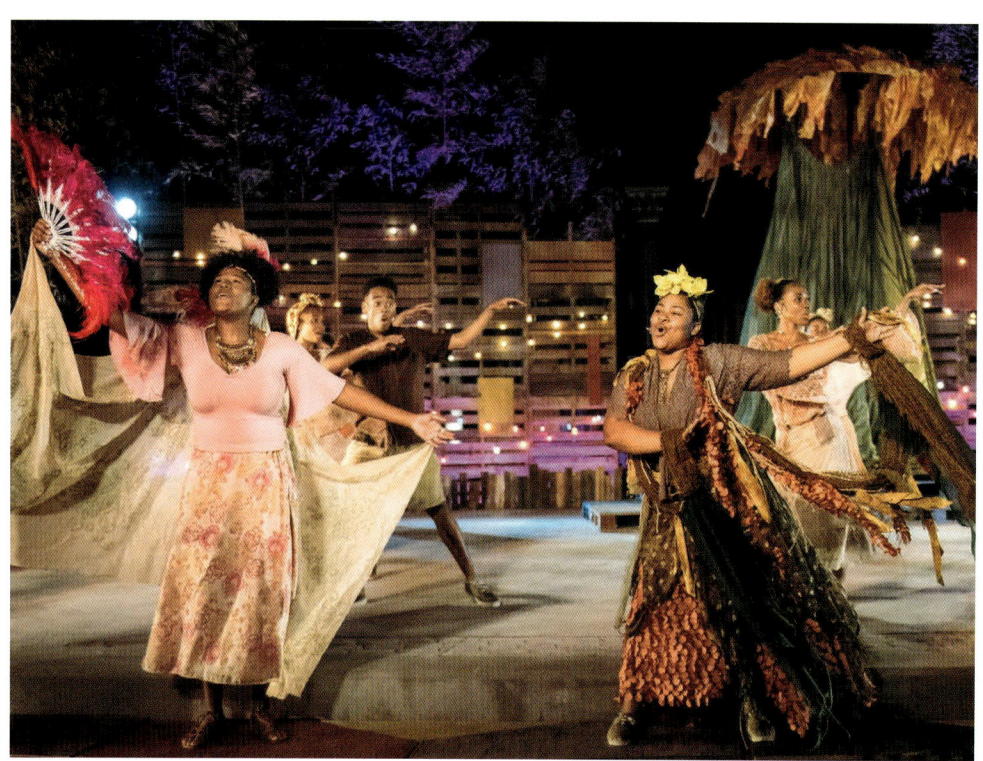

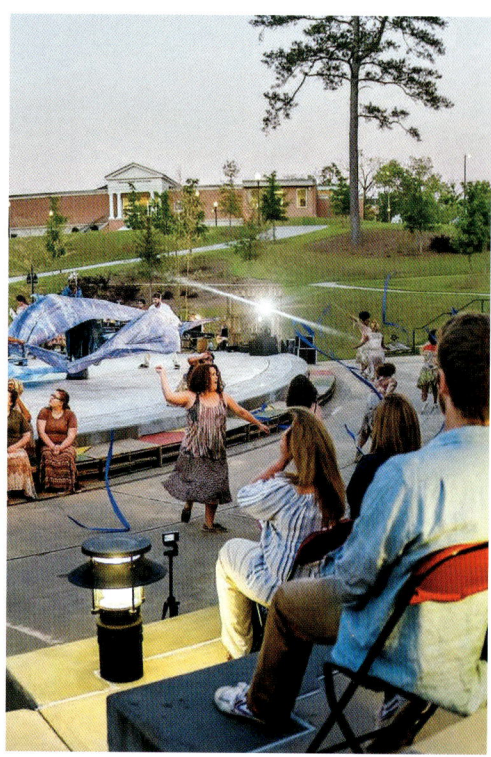

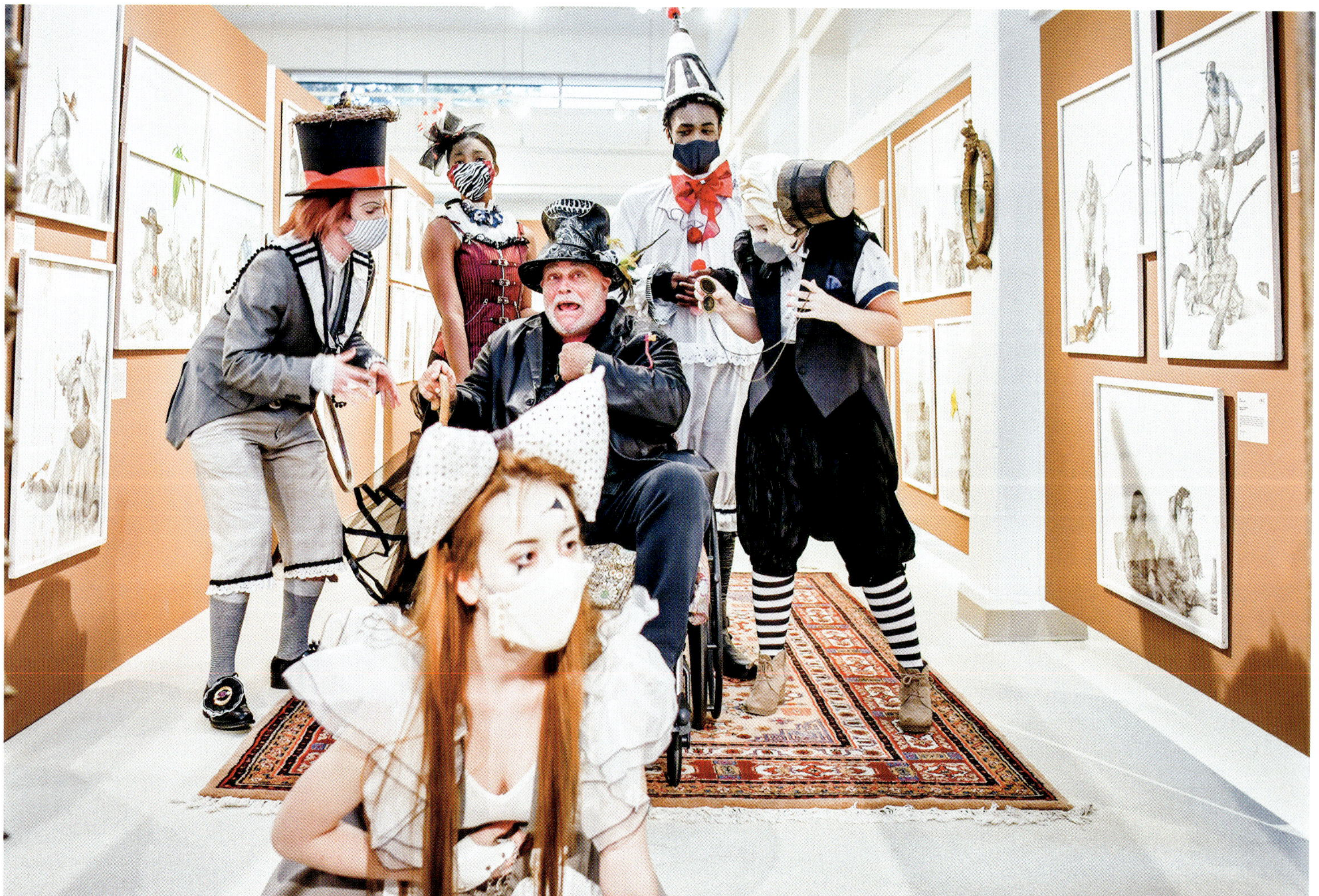

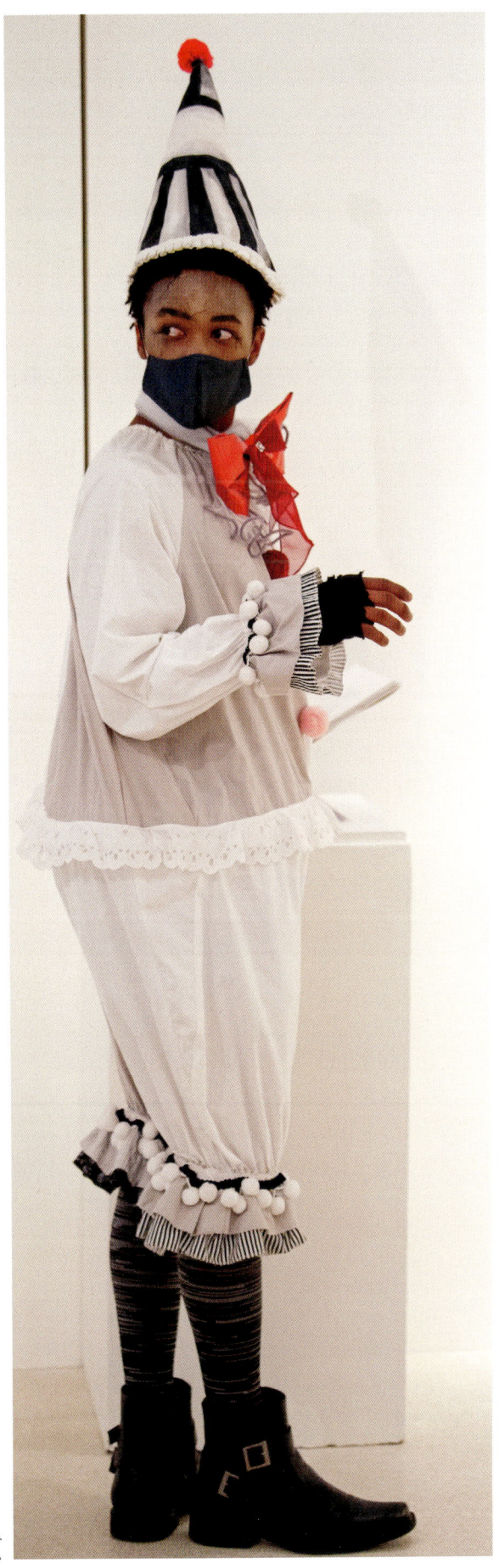

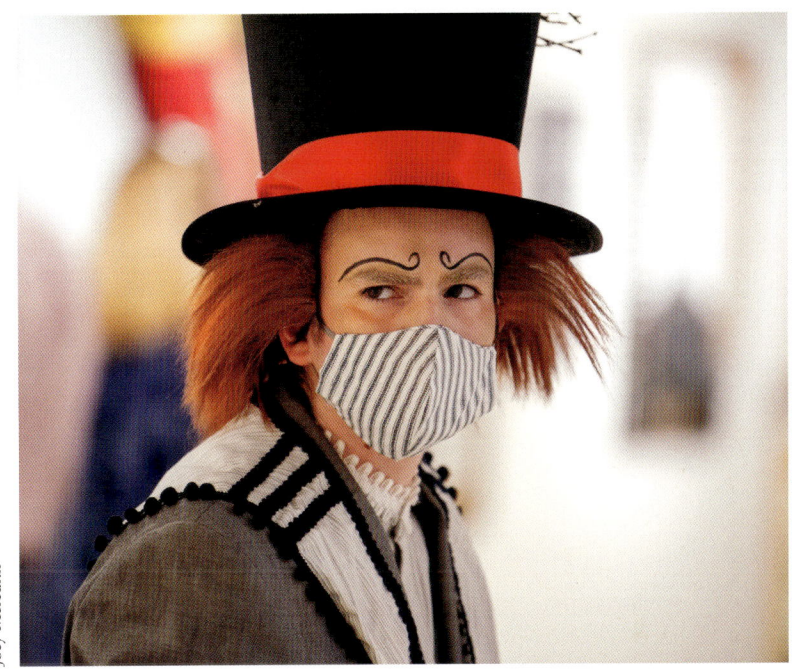

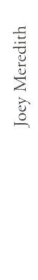

Joey Meredith

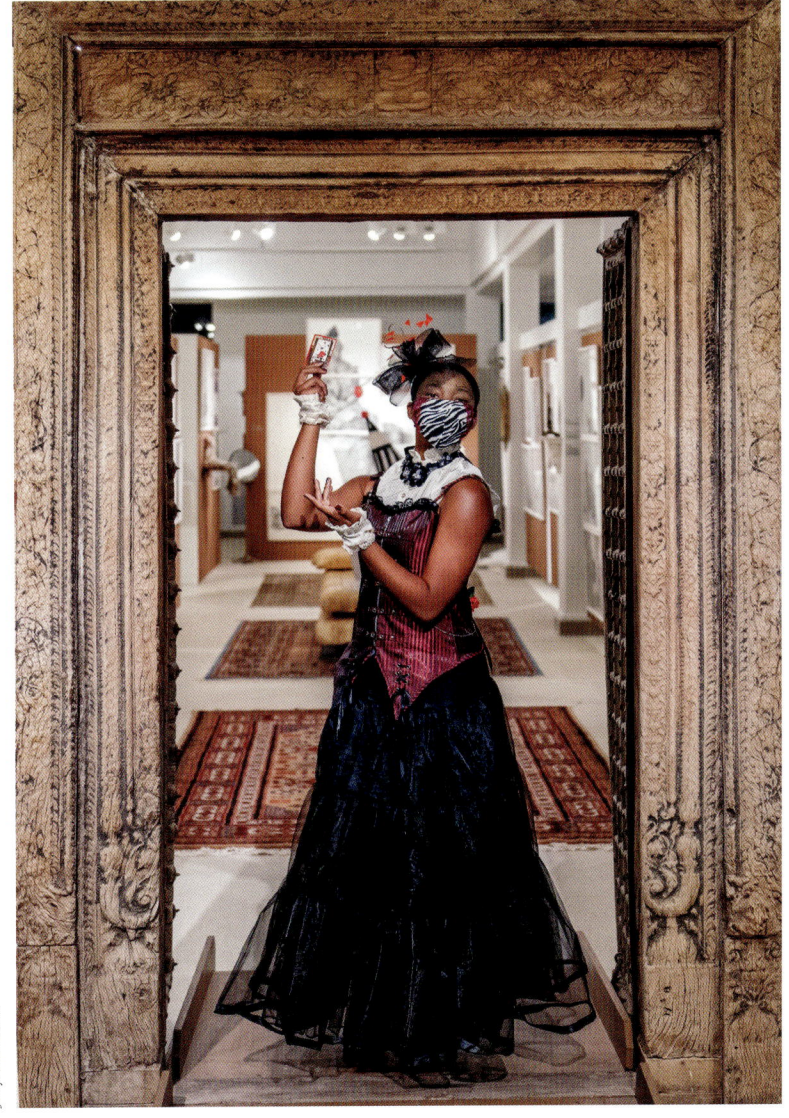

Joey Meredith

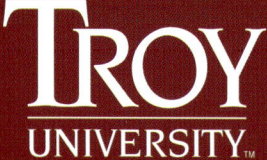

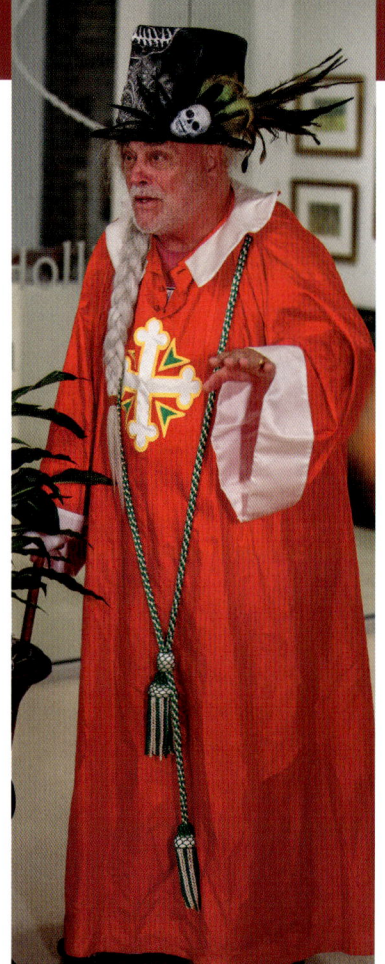

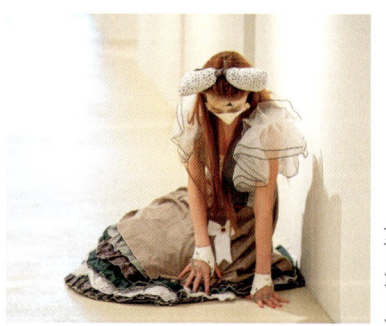

Joey Meredith

TROY UNIVERSITY THANKS the individuals and organizations who made this book possible.

First and foremost, Troy thanks Nall, the internationally acclaimed artist, who donated the artwork for this beautiful book. Troy appreciates Nall for the many ways he has supported the University, including his donation of magnificent art, his artistic talents he shares with our students, and most of all, the friendship he shows to all of us.

Thanks to the First Lady of Troy University, Mrs. Janice Hawkins, whose vision led to the creation of the International Arts Center. She has championed the arts since her arrival on the Troy campus in 1989, and her diligence, hard work, and friendship with Nall led to his generous donation to our permanent collection.

We thank Chancellor Jack Hawkins Jr., whose leadership has transformed Troy from a regional institution to an International University, creating a source of pride for all students, alumni, faculty, and friends of Troy. Further, we appreciate his devotion to the fine arts as a vital component of the university experience.

We thank Mr. Al Head, a longtime friend of Nall, Troy alumnus, and former executive director of the Alabama State Council on the Arts, whose writing is featured throughout this volume. Mr. Head's prose complements perfectly the works and artistic approach of Nall, and we are grateful to him for sharing his gift of writing.

We acknowledge Mrs. Alyson Jackson, cousin to Nall, who shared her knowledge of many of Nall's artworks and gave her time and energy freely.

We are grateful to Mr. Ed Noriega, professor and director of the Center for Design, Technology, and Industry at Troy University, for researching and designing the layout of this book to make sure it was both beautiful and representative of Nall's artistic genius.

We thank Mr. Mark Mosley of the marketing and communication staff for his beautiful photography. His artistry was crucial to the success of this project.

Thanks to Mrs. Carrie Jaxon, director of the International Arts Center, and Troy art and design students Jacob Boyce, Morgan Creech, Brandon Rice, and Paul Wolfe, who designed the Nall Studio and installed the Alice in Wonderland collection featured in this book. We are proud of these talented students.

Troy University staff who worked tirelessly on this project include Maj. Gen. Walter Givhan, Senior Vice Chancellor for Advancement and Economic Development, Ms. Becky Watson, Associate Vice Chancellor for Development, and Mr. Tom Davis, Executive Assistant to the Chancellor.

Last but not least, we acknowledge the Manuel and Mary Johnson Foundation and the Watson-Brown Foundation for their sponsorship of this publication. Their belief in the importance of this book was integral to the success of this project, as was their financial support.

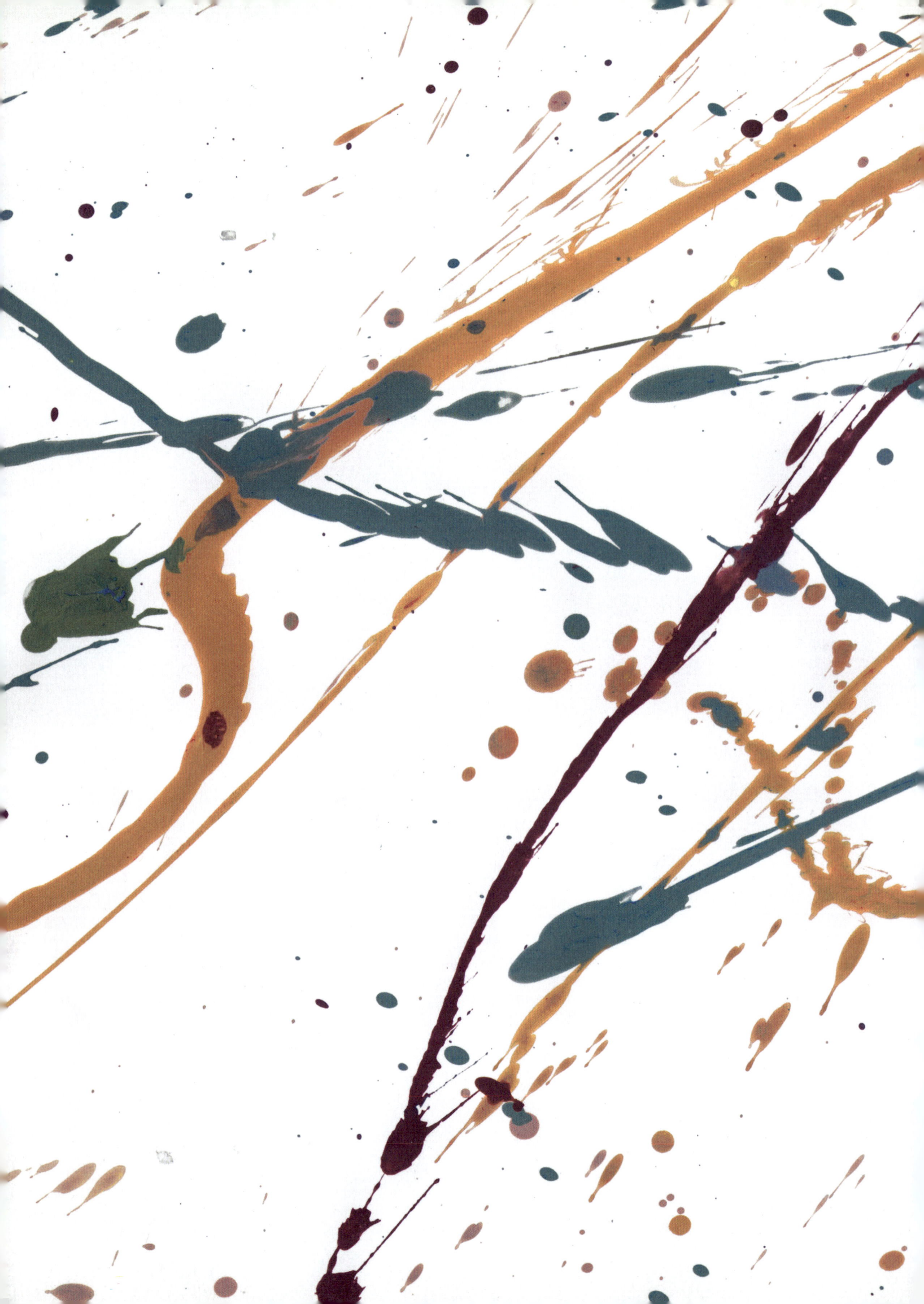